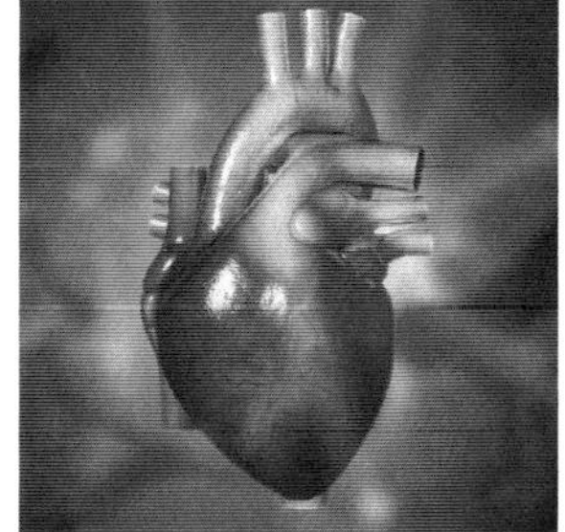

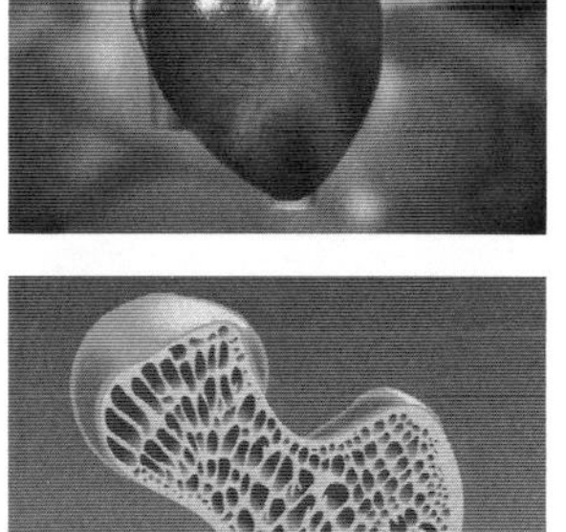

# 168-900R

# Anatomy & Physiology I

## Laboratory Manual For Online Students

Forsyth Tech Community College | Human Biology Department

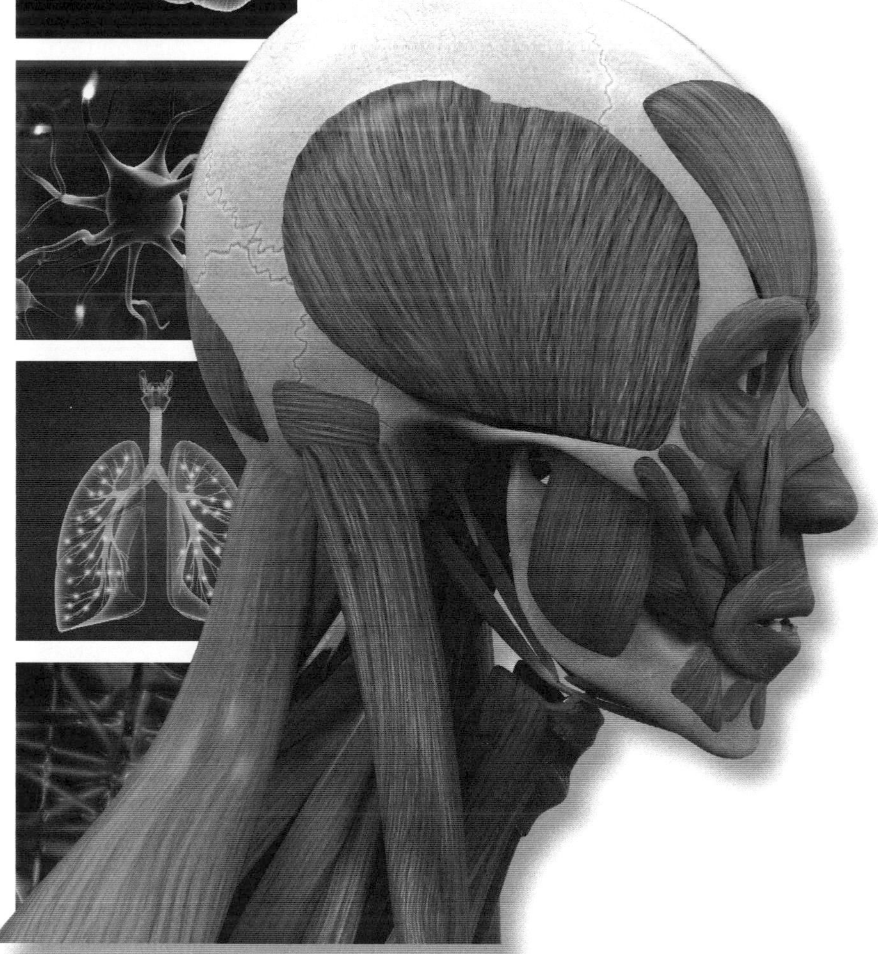

# Anatomy and Physiology I

BIO 168-900R Laboratory Manual For Online Students
Forsyth Tech Community College
Human Biology Department



Printed in the United States of America
10 9 8 7 6 5 4 3 2
ISBN: 978-1-61740-539-6

Van-Griner Publishing
Cincinnati, Ohio
www.van-griner.com

President: Dreis Van Landuyt
Project Manager: Maria Walterbusch
Customer Care Lead: Lauren Houseworth

Rudolph 539-6 F19
316404-319464

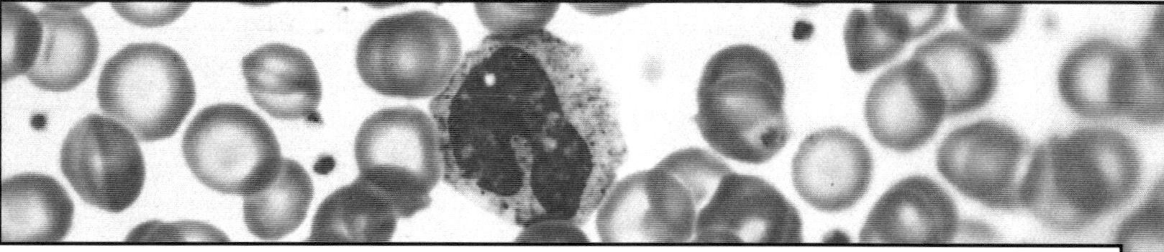

# TABLE OF CONTENTS

## LABORATORIES

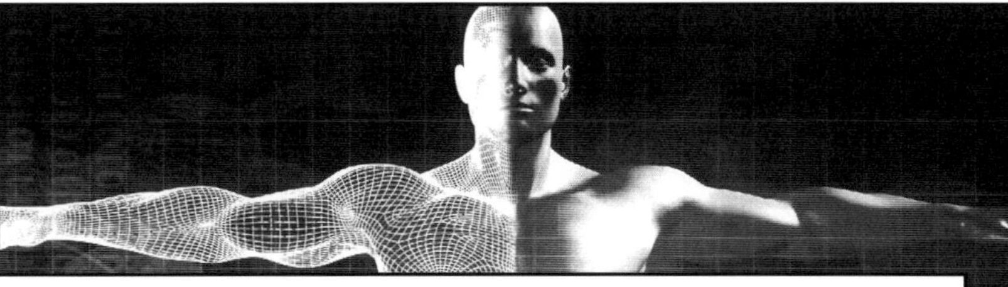

# THE BODY AS A UNIT—INTRODUCTION TO ANATOMICAL TERMINOLOGY
## PRE-LAB

Name: _______________________________  Section: _____________  Date: ____________

## LEARNING OBJECTIVES

- Describe anatomical position and directional terms.
- Use anatomical terms correctly.
- Define and label the body cavities, planes, regions, and quadrants.
- Describe the serous membrane structure and functions within the body.

## TERMINOLOGY

The purpose of anatomical terminology is not to confuse, but rather to increase precision and reduce medical errors. These terms derive from ancient Greek and Latin words, and we use them for bone names, muscles, blood vessels, etc. since their meanings will not change. To further increase the accuracy of naming the body, anatomists standardize the way in which they view the body. Just as maps are normally oriented with north at the top, the standard body "map," or **anatomical position,** is that of the body standing upright, with the feet at shoulder width and parallel, toes forward. The upper limbs are to each side, and the palms of the hands face forward. Using this standard position decreases confusion, so no matter how the body is positioned, we are always referring to the standard anatomical position. For example, a scar in the "anterior (front) carpal (wrist) region" would be present on the palm side of the wrist. We use the term "anterior" even if the hand were palm down on a table. *Learning these terms now will help you throughout the course!*

Other terminology that you will use includes those for body position. When a body is lying down, it is either prone or supine. **Prone** describes a facedown orientation, and **supine** describes a face up orientation. We use these terms when describing the position of the body during specific physical examinations or surgical procedures. *Remember, though, whenever using an anatomical term, you are always referring to anatomical position, whether viewing in the prone or supine position.*

Keep in mind that knowing prefixes and suffixes will be helpful to understand new terms you will encounter. **For example,** ante- means before, cubit- means elbow, cauda- means tail, and –al, -um, and –ic mean pertaining to. In addition, we will use the adjective ending of *–al* here for most of the terms and not the noun ending, which is *–um.*

You can see a large list of these at http://www.emory.edu/ANATOMY/AnatomyManual/Etymology.html

The body is compartmentalized into cavities, which are lined with membranes. Some cavities are open to the outside, so these are incomplete cavities and are lined with **mucous membranes** (including nasal cavity, anal cavity, etc.). **Serous** (serum = clear, watery liquid) **membranes** line the body cavities that are closed to the exterior of the body. These cavities are lined with two serous membrane layers: a visceral layer and a parietal layer. The **visceral** (viscera = organs) **layer** covers the organ itself, and the **parietal** (pariet = wall) **layer** attaches to and covers the ventral body wall. Serous fluid secreted by the cells of the thin squamous mesothelium lubricates the membrane and reduces abrasion and friction between organs. Serous membranes are identified according to locations.

# PRE-LAB ACTIVITY 1

**Anatomical Terms**—Study Figure 1.1 below and see how many anatomical terms you can remember before you go to lab this week. You will practice these with a partner in lab this week.

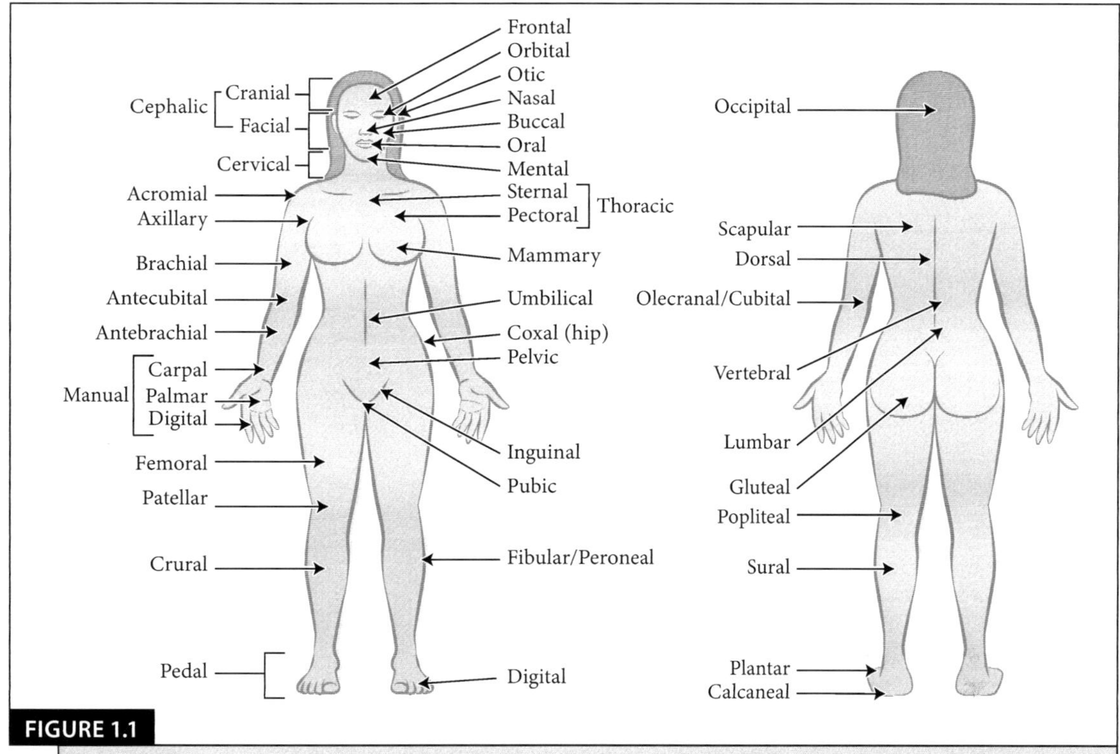


**FIGURE 1.1**

**Anatomical terms of the human body.** The human body is shown in anatomical position in an anterior view and a posterior view.

## PRE-LAB ACTIVITY 2

**Directional Terms**—Find these terms in Figure 1.2, add those not labeled, and define each below.

**1.** Superior—

**2.** Inferior—

**3.** Proximal—

**4.** Distal—

5. Lateral—

6. Medial—

7. Ipsilateral—

8. Contralateral (contra means opposite)—

9. Posterior—

10. Anterior—

11. Cranial—

12. Caudal—

13. Superficial—

14. Deep—

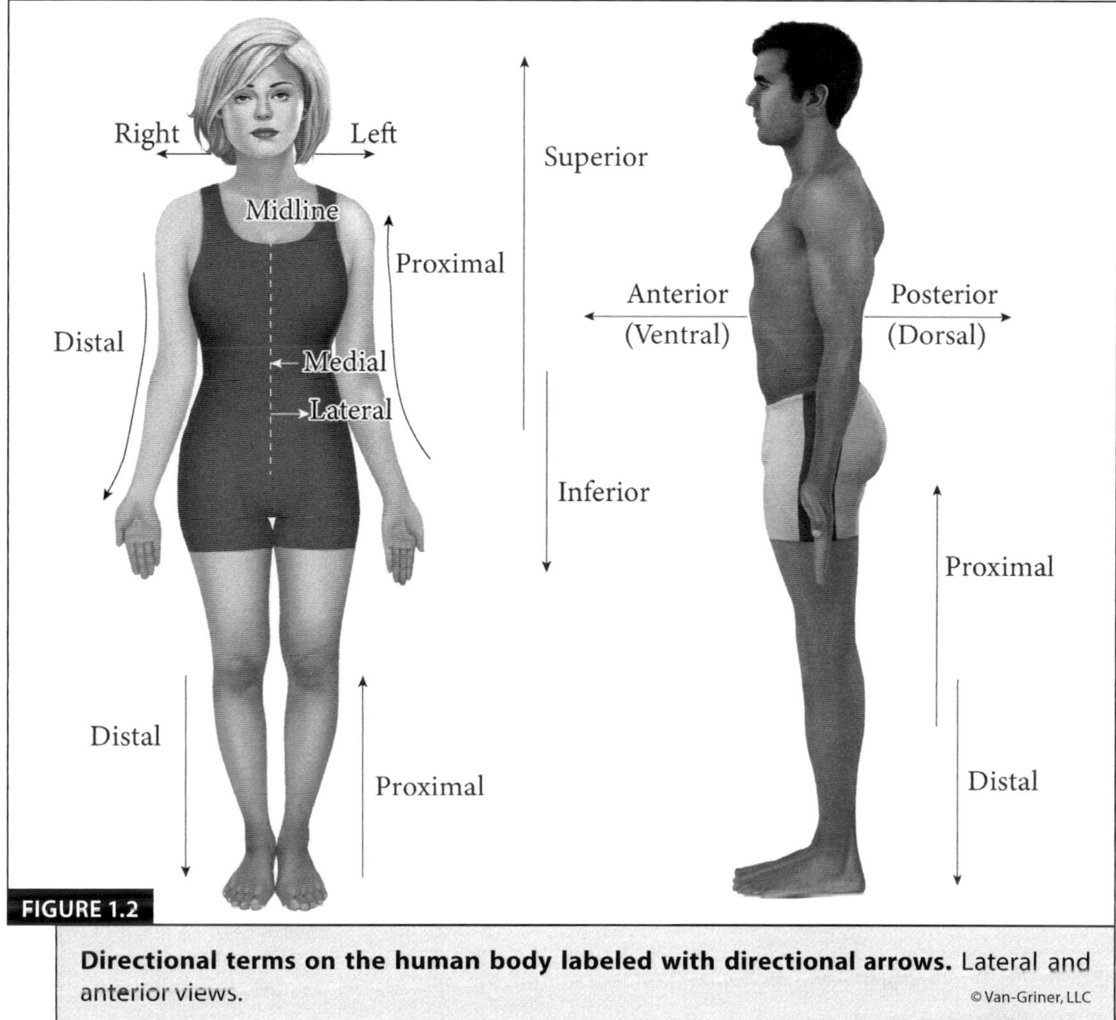


**FIGURE 1.2**

**Directional terms on the human body labeled with directional arrows.** Lateral and anterior views.

© Van-Griner, LLC

**15.** What is the difference between distal vs. inferior and proximal vs. superior?

**16.** If ipsi- means "self" or "same" and contra- means "opposite" then why use these terms and not just lateral?

**17.** What do the terms cross-section and longitudinal mean and when do we use these terms?

## REVIEW QUESTIONS

After you have reviewed the anatomical terms and the directional terms sufficiently, complete these sentences with the correct **directional term** or **body region.**

1. The metatarsals are _________________________________ to the patellar.

2. The carpal bones are to the upper limb as the _________________________________ bones are to the lower limb.

3. The antecubital region is to the upper limb as the _________________________________ is to the lower limb.

4. The brachial region is _________________________________ to the palmar region.

5. The sternum is _________________________________ to the umbilicus.

6. The blood vessels are _________________________________ to the skin.

7. The right peroneal/fibular region and the left femoral region are _________________ to each other.

## PRE-LAB ACTIVITY 3–5: BODY PLANES, CAVITIES, REGIONS, AND QUADRANTS

1. What are the 3 primary planes the body can be cut at for study?

2. What are the two cavities on the dorsal side of the body?

3. What are the three major cavities within the ventral cavity? (Be sure to notice that the mediastinum is not a cavity but a space in which the aorta, large veins, and the heart are housed.)

4. Into how many regions is the abdominopelvic cavity separated? _________________ How many quadrants are there? _________________

# PRE-LAB ACTIVITY 6: SEROUS MEMBRANES

Serous cavities are enclosed cavities lined by serous membrane (mesothelium). These are true cavities since they are enclosed, whereas open cavities include the mucous lined cavities of the digestive system. In the adult, serous cavities are the pericardial cavity, two pleural cavities, and the peritoneal cavity. In the adult, pericardial and pleural (pleura = rib) cavities, which surround the two lungs, are separated by the fibrous pericardium. In the adult, pleural cavities and the peritoneal cavity are separated by the diaphragm. The peritoneal cavity lines most of the abdominal organs except the kidneys, pancreas, bladder, and parts of the intestines. *You will find these cavities and organs on the models or dissections available in lab, so please review them well.*

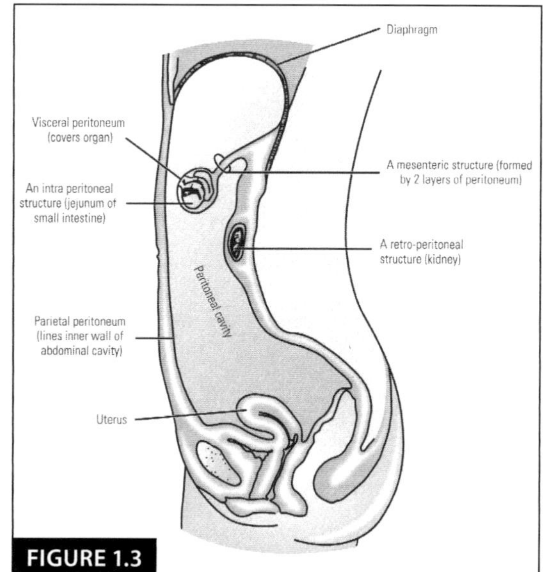


**FIGURE 1.3**

**Peritoneal cavity.** Midsagittal cut of the abdominopelvic cavity. The peritoneal cavity is surrounded by the peritoneal membrane. The peritoneal membrane are also called retroperitoneal organs. In addition, below the peritoneum would be the uterus and bladder outside the cavity. © Van-Griner, LLC

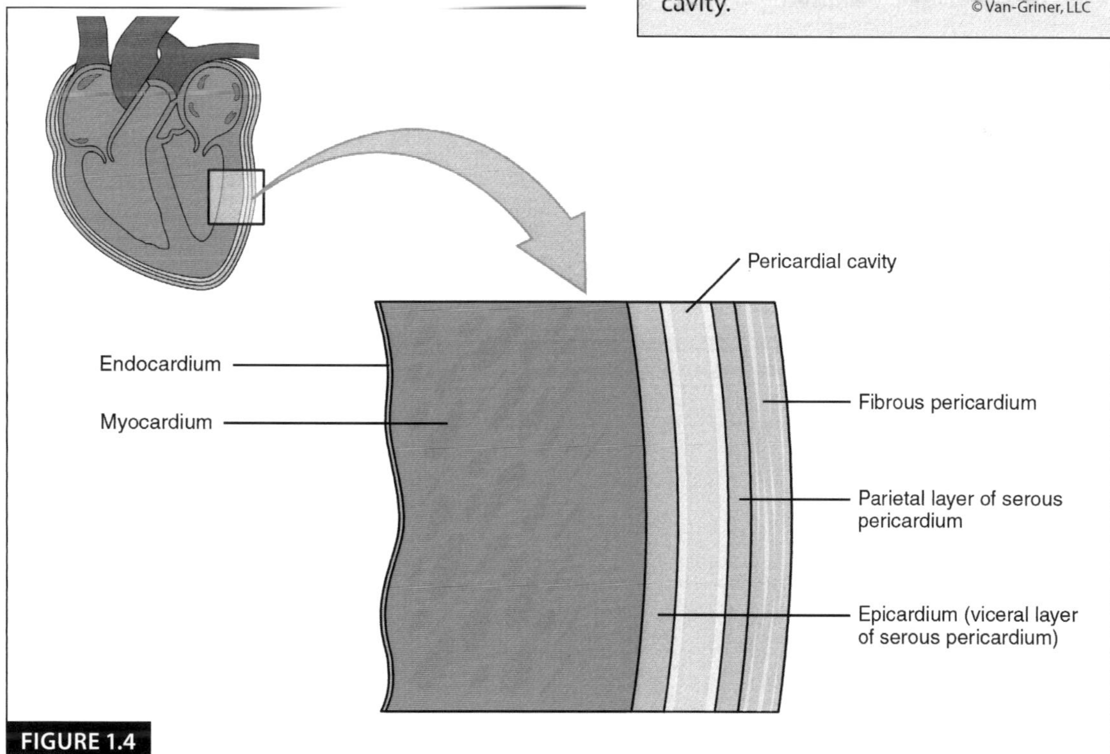


**FIGURE 1.4**

**Pericardial cavity.** Frontal cut of the heart and an enlarged picture of the pericardial layers and fibrous pericardium surrounding the heart. OpenStax College [CC BY 3.0 (https://creativecommons.org/licenses/by/3.0)]

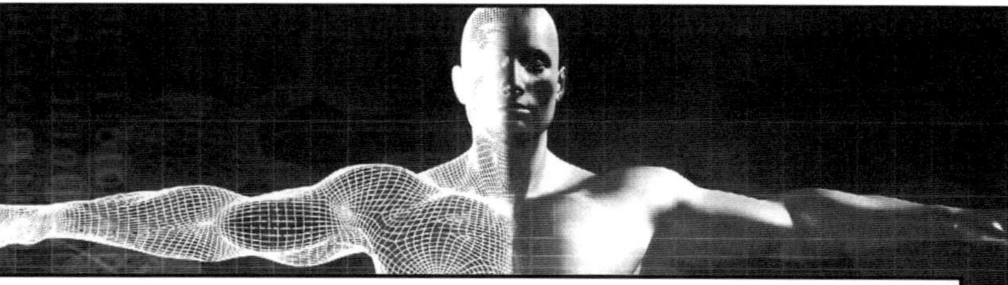

# THE BODY AS A UNIT—INTRODUCTION TO ANATOMICAL TERMINOLOGY
## IN-LAB ACTIVITIES

Name: _______________________  Section: __________  Date: __________

## LEARNING OBJECTIVES

- Describe anatomical position and its importance in health fields.
- Use anatomical and directional terms correctly.
- Identify planes of the body.
- Describe the structure, function, and locations for the serous membranes.
- Identify the regions and quadrants of the abdominopelvic cavity.

## PRE-LAB

Before going to lab, you must complete the following:

1. Read the online text for **Introduction to Human Anatomy.**
2. Read the **Pre-Lab** and answer all Pre-Lab questions.

*Note:* You will spend **2–2 hr and 30 min** in lab at Forsyth Tech to complete the following activities. This amount of time allows you and your lab partner to complete the activities by using the torso model and other models.

# THE FOLLOWING ACTIVITIES WILL BE COMPLETED DURING LAB

## ANATOMICAL POSITION AND ANATOMICAL TERMINOLOGY

When describing the human body, it is ***always identified*** as being in **anatomical position.** This is true even if a person is lying down on their back with their arms in the air! *You must remember this important concept.* Anatomical position refers to the body upright (or lying down face up), facing forward, feet shoulder width apart, and upper limbs out to the side with palms facing forward or anteriorly. See Figure 1.5 on the following page.

***Study Hint:*** For crural and sural, which are both part of the leg, crural is the leg itself and sural is the back—think "s" is further back in the alphabet so this term refers to the back (calf) of the leg. Remember that coxal is the hipbone, but this is not the same as coccyx, which is the tailbone.

## ACTIVITY 1

**Anatomical Terms**—With a lab partner review the following body regions.

1. Stand, facing one another. One partner will point to an area on his/her body. The other partner will then name the anatomical term being identified.

2. **Switch roles.** The opposite partner will now name the parts that the other partner is identifying.

3. Identify five parts each time before switching. (*If you study these in a mirror as well, it will help you to practice right and left sides on a patient sitting or standing opposite of you!)

Most of the following terms can be found on Figure 1.5:

1. Umbilical
2. Thoracic
3. Otic
4. Palmar
5. Acromial
6. Antecubital
7. Facial
8. Nasal
9. Cervical (neck)
10. Popliteal
11. Carpal
12. Antebrachial (forearm)
13. Dorsal
14. Axillary
15. Oral
16. Patellar
17. Sternal
18. Coxal (hip)
19. Fibular (peroneal) (lateral side of the leg)

20. Sural

21. Brachial (arm, but only the upper portion of the appendage)

22. Digital

23. Manual

24. Mammary

25. Buccal (BUCK–al )

26. Calcaneal

27. Plantar

28. Inguinal

29. Cephalic

30. Mental

31. Pedal

32. Orbital

33. Pubic

34. Femoral (thigh)

35. Cranial

36. Frontal

37. Vertebral

38. Occipital

39. Crural (leg, which only refers to the lower part of the appendage)

40. Lumbar

41. Pelvic

42. Scapular

43. Olecranal (cubital)

44. Pectoral

45. Gluteal

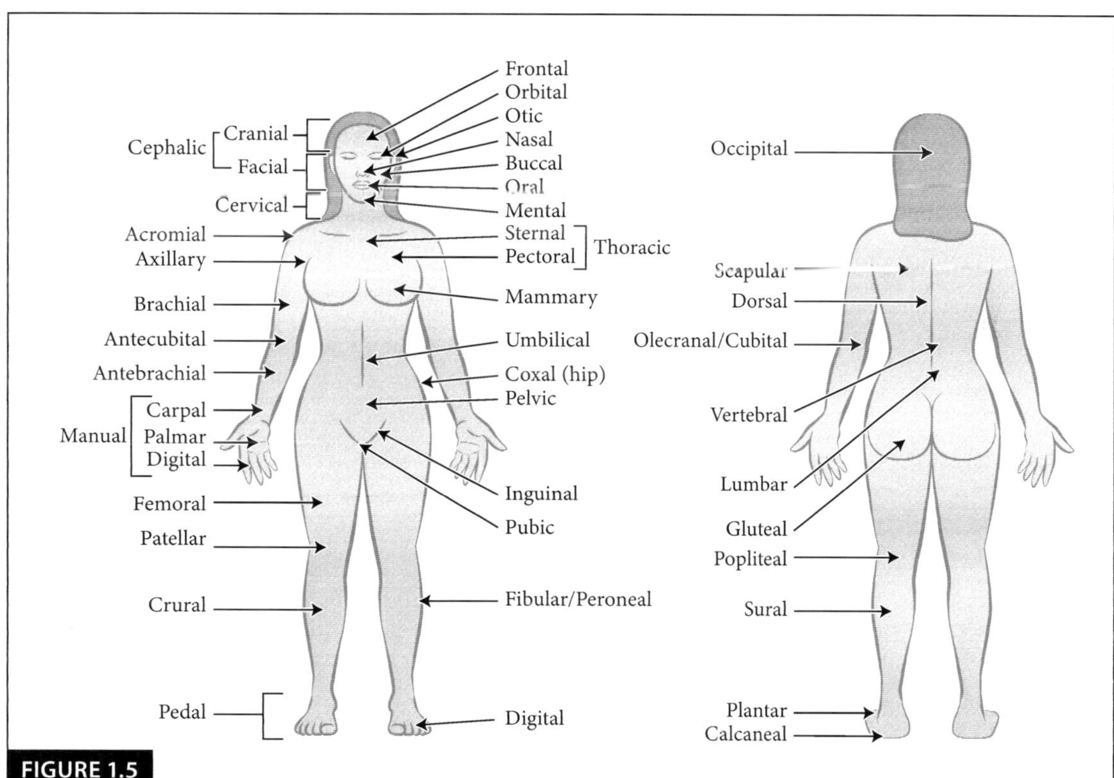


**FIGURE 1.5**

**Anatomical terms of the human body.** The human body is shown in anatomical position in an anterior view and a posterior view.

## ACTIVITY 2

**Directional Terms** are essential when describing the **relative locations** of different body structures. Figure 1.6 (below) shows the "anterior" (ventral), which refers to the direction towards the front of the body while "posterior" (dorsal) refers to the direction towards the back of the body. Each directional term has an opposing side or direction.

Using Figure 1.6 (below): Fill in the definition with the opposite directional term in the table below

| DIRECTIONAL TERM AND DEFINITION | OPPOSITE DIRECTIONAL TERM AND DEFINITION |
| --- | --- |
| Ventral | |
| Distal | |
| Caudal | |
| Contralateral | |

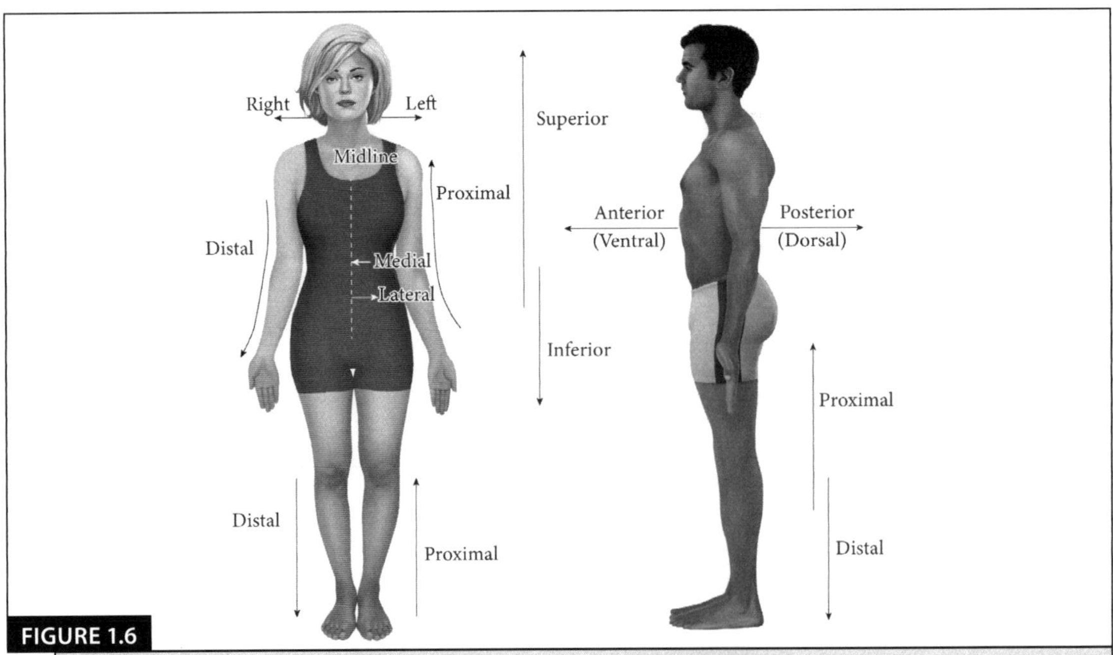


**FIGURE 1.6**

**Directional terms on the human body labeled with directional arrows.** Lateral and anterior views.

© Van-Griner, LLC

## ACTIVITY 3

**Body Planes:** A plane is an imaginary two-dimensional surface that passes through the body. There are three main planes dividing the body: however, in some situations other cuts can be made as well. These terms will be used throughout your career, so put them to memory now!

1. The **sagittal plane** divides the body or organ into equal right and left sides. **Define the two types below:** (think about the meaning of these prefixes realizing that *para* = beside)

   **a.** Midsagittal—

   **b.** Parasagittal—

2. The **frontal (or coronal) plane** divides the body or organ into anterior and posterior portions.

3. The **transverse plane** divides the body into superior and inferior portions.

Others cuts include the **oblique cut** (a diagonal cut), the **longitudinal cut** (lengthwise on the body or appendage, along the parasagittal plane), and the **cross sectional cut** (transversely on an appendage).

**Complete the following:**

4. Make all the cuts using a straw or tube in lab to show your understanding of the body planes. Indicate the cuts you have made in the tube picture to the right.

5. Label Figure 1.7. Once you have labeled Figure 1.7, identify the different sections using an apple or organ (the sheep brain on display), both of which are available in lab.

## BODY PLANES

Label the planes in Figure 1.7 and define the planes below.

1. Parasagittal (add to the diagram)—

2. Frontal (coronal)—

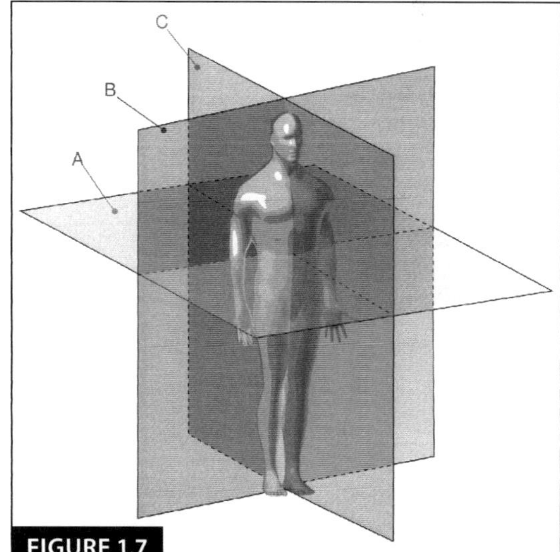



**FIGURE 1.7**

**Planes or cuts of the human body.** Three planes are displayed. Be sure to label them as well as draw and label the other two planes from the list above.

(Human_anatomy_planes.svg: GYassineMrabetTalk. This W3C-unspecified vector image was created with Inkscape. derivative work: Marek M [CC BY-SA 3.0])

**3.** Transverse—

**4.** Mid-sagittal—

**5.** Oblique (add to the diagram) —

# ACTIVITY 4

We **only** find **body cavities** in the head and trunk portions of the body. In Activity 4 you will do the following:

- **Observe** on the lab torsos the location and organization of the dorsal and ventral cavities.

- **Distinguish** between a major and minor cavity by location and tissue linings (see sagittal heads).

- **Find** the major organs located in each body cavity by removing and replacing torso organs.

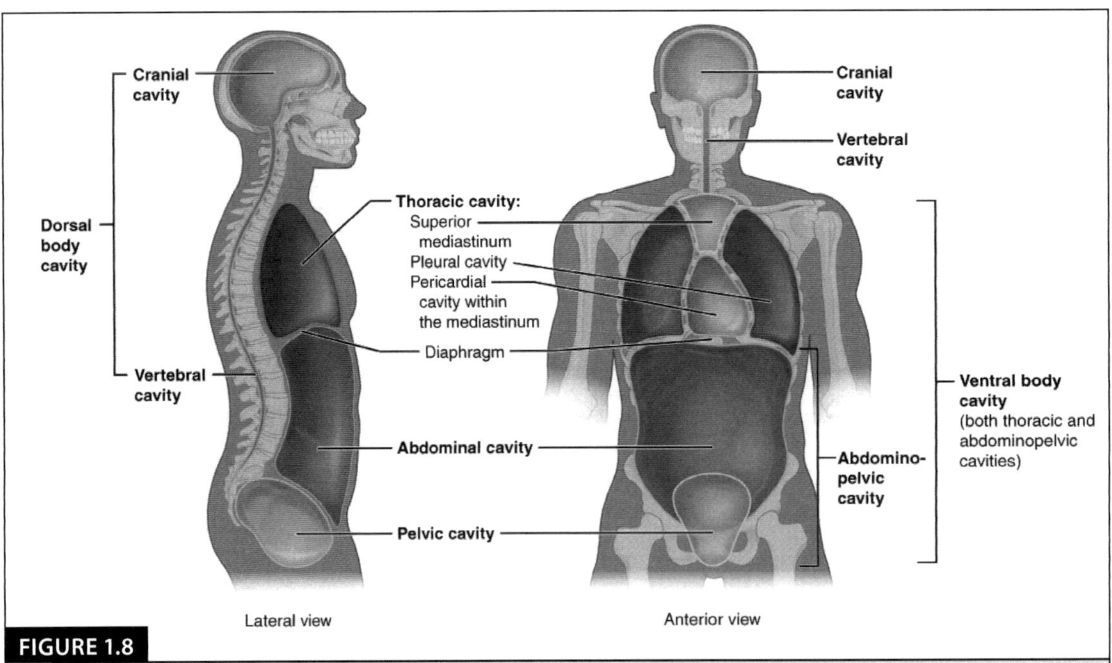


**FIGURE 1.8**

**The ventral cavity is composed of the thoracic and abdominopelvic cavities.** The diaphragm separates the thoracic and abdominal cavities. There is not a distinct separation between the abdominal and the pelvic cavity. The mediastinum is not a true cavity (not surrounded by serous membranes). https://commons.wikimedia.org/wiki/File:Dorsal_Ventral_Body_Cavities.jpg by Connexions [CC BY 3.0 (https://creativecommons.org/licenses/by/3.0)]

Body cavities are only found in the **axial portion** of the body. A **true cavity** is a space that is lined by two folds of **serous membranes** (visceral and parietal) and **does not** have an opening or direct connection to the outside of the body. There are several smaller minor cavities found in the head that are **not considered** to be true cavities since they are lined by **mucus membranes** and **do have openings** or channels to the outside of the body.

**Label** Figure 1.9 below with the appropriate *cavity name* in the boxes provided.

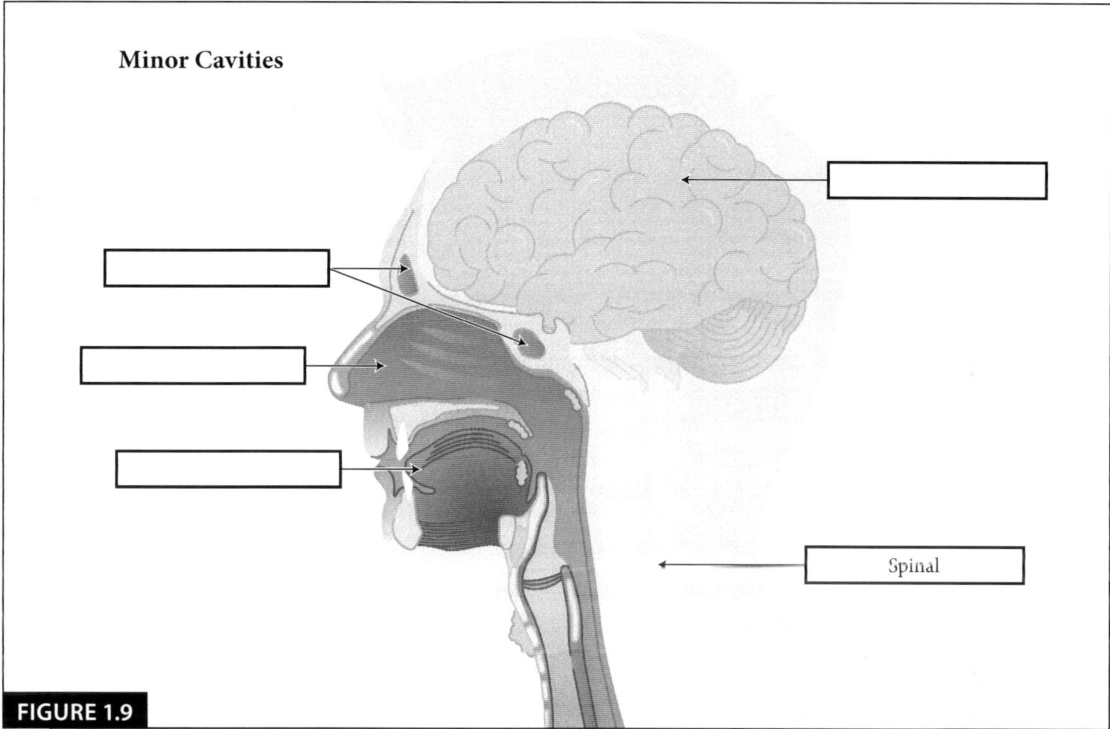


| **FIGURE 1.9** |
| :--- |

**The minor cavities are part of the ventral cavity.** The cranial and spinal cavity are both on the dorsal side. Label the minor cavities shown. Use the sagittal heads in lab or other models if available. (Terms: sinuses, cranial, oral, nasal cavity).

In lab, locate all the **major body cavities** on the **torso models** then using the models locate the organs within each cavity. Locate all of the **minor cavities** using the **sagittal head models.** Answer the following questions regarding specific body cavities. Lastly, you must be able to identify the location of the *major viscera* in each cavity.

## REVIEW QUESTIONS 1–6

1. The heart is located in the _________________________ cavity which is surrounded by serous membranes called parietal and visceral _________________________.

2. The lungs are located in the _________________________ cavity which is surrounded by serous membranes called parietal and visceral _________________________. These can be seen in the torso model. Notice the very thin space in between the two; it's only a slight space, enough for the thin serous fluid, which reduces _________________________.

3. The _________________________ is an area (not a cavity) located between the pleural cavities and contains the pericardial cavity. It contains the thymus gland, trachea, esophagus, and major blood vessels coming out of the heart.

4. The brain is located in the _________________________ cavity, while the spinal cord is located in the _________________________. They are both lined by serous membranes called _________________________.

5. The thoracic, pericardial, and abdominopelvic cavities are all part of the _________________________ cavity.

6. The two cavities that are part of the dorsal cavity are the _________________________ cavity and the _________________________ canal.

## ACTIVITY 5

**Body regions and quadrants:** When identifying the location of a patient's abdominal pain or a suspicious mass, health care providers promote clear communication by dividing up the cavity into either nine regions or four quadrants. Four quadrants being the Upper Right, Upper Left, Lower Right, and Lower Left.

A more detailed regional approach subdivides the cavity into **9 regions by the following:**

- One horizontal line directly inferior to the ribs
- One directly superior to the pelvis
- Two vertical lines drawn as if dropped from the midpoint of each clavicle (collarbone).

The **9 regions** are the following:

- Right inguinal (iliac)
- Hypogastric (gastric = stomach)
- Left inguinal (iliac)
- Left lumbar
- Umbilical

- Right lumbar
- Right hypochondriac
- Epigastric
- Left hypochondriac

*Note: Chondro-* refers to the cartilage areas where the ribs attach to the sternum (see skeleton model in lab). The simpler quadrants approach, which is more commonly used in medicine, subdivides the cavity with one horizontal and one vertical line that intersect at the patient's umbilicus (navel).

Complete the following:

1. Use the diagrams below to divide the abdominopelvic cavity into regions **and** quadrants. You may look back at the body landmarks if you need help identifying these regions. *Be sure to notice the organs that are found in each quadrant and region.

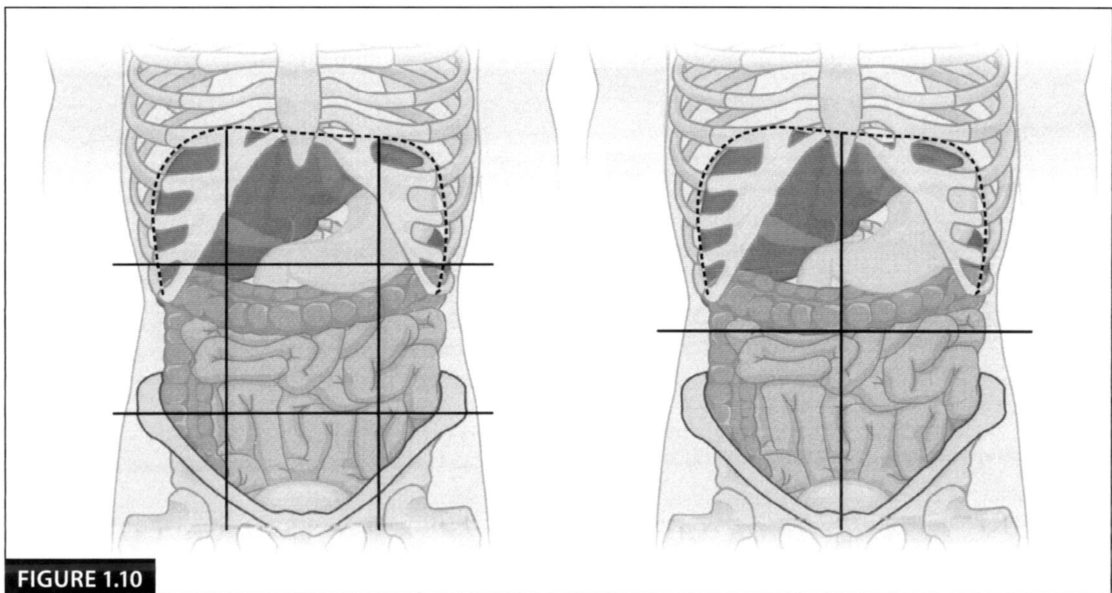

**FIGURE 1.10**

**Body regions and quadrants.** The left image shows the regions of the abdominopelvic cavity separated into 9 boxes like a tic-tac-toe board (numbered 1–9 from left to right along each row). The right-side image shows the quadrants of the abdominopelvic cavity with a few organs colored into the picture. These are not labeled in the image, but are named by the area they house—upper left quadrant, lower right quadrant, etc.
(https://commons.wikimedia.org/wiki/File:Abdominal_Quadrant_Regions_Cleaned.png by jmarchn, derived from figure by OpenStax. Download for free at http://cnx.org/contents/17e4eea8-a005-45af-b835-f756a014cd48@3. [CC BY 3.0 (https://creativecommons.org/licenses/by/3.0)]

2. **Identify** the abdominopelvic regions and quadrants on the torso models found **in the lab using** the **muscle women/men models** and some blue painter's tape to make the "tic-tac-toe" board **and** four square on the anterior side of the model. Be sure to identify where organs are located in each section. You will be using this model when answering the Review Questions at the end of lab. (Place regional lines just medial to the nipples from diaphragm to groin. Place horizontal lines near 9th rib and just inferior to iliac crest at the anterior superior iliac spine.)

## ACTIVITY 6

**Serous Membranes:** Serous cavities are enclosed cavities lined by serous membrane (mesothelium).

### IN THE ADULT

- Serous cavities are the pericardial cavity, two pleural cavities, and the peritoneal cavity.
- Pericardial and pleural cavities are separated by the fibrous pericardium.
- Peritoneal and pleural cavities are separated by the diaphragm.

*Find these on the models or dissections available in lab.*

### HOW TO MAKE A REPLICA OF THE SEROUS MEMBRANES FOR CLEAR UNDERSTANDING

1. Use a new or fairly new **1-gallon Ziploc (plastic zippered) bag.**
2. Release any air that is located in the bag and zip it tightly (no air in bag).
3. Have a lab partner make a fist and place it on one side of the bag (like an organ/beating heart).
4. Wrap the bag around their fist (organ) so that the bag surrounds it entirely.
5. Notice how two membranes surround the fist (organ) now.
   a. What do the two sides of the bag represent now?


   b. How difficult or easy can your fist 'pump' or move within the air-filled bag?


6. Next, open the bag and add about 50 mL of water.
7. Push out the extra air and re-zip it.
8. Have your lab partner make a fist again and wrap it with the water-filled bag.
   a. Was the hand movement easier or more difficult to do than with the air-filled bag?

## DISCUSSION QUESTIONS

1.  In the gallon bag, which serous membrane does the layer next to the fist/organ represent?

2.  In the gallon bag, which serous membrane does the outer layer of the bag simulate?

3.  What does the water represent?

4.  If you were to pump the fist (like a heart pumping) while surrounded by the bag, does the presence of the watery fluid make it easier for organs within to move or not? Explain.

5.  What do you think would change in the lungs or breathing as a result of an excess fluid in the pleural cavity called a pleural effusion (seen in Figure 1.11)?

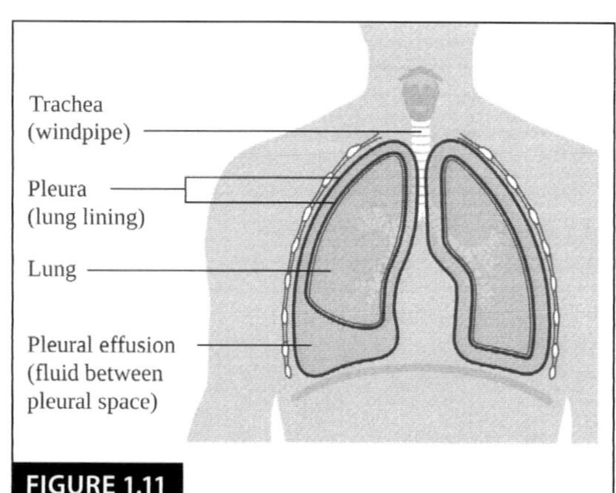


**FIGURE 1.11**

**The lungs are surrounded by two pleural cavities (right and left sides).** The cavity is surrounded by two membranes (visceral and parietal, not labeled here). The pathology shown is a pleural effusion or fluid in the pleural space.  Cancer Research UK [CC BY-SA 4.0 (https://creativecommons.org/licenses/by-sa/4.0)]

## REVIEW QUESTIONS

For questions **1–14** identify the body system to which the structures belong:

1. Sebaceous glands _______________
2. Esophagus _______________
3. Joints_______________
4. Pituitary gland _______________
5. Blood vessels _______________
6. Ovaries _______________
7. Liver _______________

8. Thyroid gland _______________
9. Trachea _______________
10. Spleen _______________
11. Ureters _______________
12. Diaphragm _______________
13. Hair and nails _______________
14. Tonsils _______________

For the following **directional terms,** give the **antonym** (opposite directional term).

15. Inferior _______________
16. Superficial _______________
17. Anterior _______________
18. Ipsilateral _______________
19. Distal _______________
20. Lateral _______________

Use the appropriate **directional term** to complete the following statements:

21. The elbow is _______________ to the shoulder.
22. The knee is _______________ to the ankle.
23. The nose is _______________ to the right and left eyes.
24. The stomach is _______________ to the abdominal muscles.
25. Your eyebrows are _______________ to your eyes.
26. Your fingers are _______________ to your wrist.
27. Your big toe is _______________ to your little toe.
28. Your left lung and your spleen are _______________.
29. The left lung is _______________ to the right lung.
30. The small intestine is more _______________ than the uterus.
31. The heart is _______________ to the left lung.

Identify the **medical/anatomical term** for the following body areas:

32. Neck _______________
33. Thigh _______________

34. Sole of the foot _______________
35. Arm _______________

**36.** Forehead _______________________

**37.** Cheek _______________________

**38.** Head _______________________

**39.** Wrist _______________________

**40.** Heel _______________________

**41.** Breastbone _______________________

**42.** Armpit _______________________

**43.** Fingers and toes _______________________

**44.** Back of the head _______________________

**45.** Front of elbow _______________________

**46.** Chin _______________________

**47.** Forearm _______________________

Identify in which **body cavity** the following structures are located:

**48.** The lungs are in the _______________________ cavity.

**49.** The urinary bladder is located in the _______________________ cavity.

**50.** The liver is located in the _______________________ cavity.

**51.** The pituitary gland is located in the _______________________ cavity.

**52.** The stomach is located in the _______________________ cavity.

**53.** The _______________________ separates the thoracic and abdominal cavities.

Identify in which **abdominopelvic quadrant** and **region** the following structures are located:

**54.** Urinary bladder (quadrant) _______________ (region) _______________________

**55.** Liver (quadrant) _______________ (region) _______________________

**56.** Appendix (quadrant) _______________ (region) _______________________

**57.** Spleen (quadrant) _______________ (region) _______________________

**58.** Stomach (quadrant) _______________ (region) _______________________

*Note:* Be sure to get your completed work checked off by a member of the lab staff and then keep this handout for your review.

# 2

# THE CELL AND MICROSCOPE
## PRE-LAB

Name: _______________________    Section: __________    Date: __________

## LEARNING OBJECTIVES

- Identify the parts of the compound microscope and explain their functions.
- Determine the total magnification of an object viewed under a microscope.
- Understand the advantages of parafocality and the relations between magnification and working distance, brightness/size of the field of view, and size of the image.
- Locate and focus on any specimen using the scanning, low, and high power objective.
- Understand the principle of staining biological material for microscopy.
- Identify organelles in cheek cells.

## PRE-LAB ACTIVITY 1: THE MICROSCOPE

- View the following video of the parts of the microscope. https://www.youtube.com/watch?feature=player_detailpage&v=Txhj2dRefAI
- Watch the tutorial on the microscope under the LABS section of the course website. https://www.youtube.com/watch?v=2GC7NX2A7ds&feature=youtu.be

## PRE-LAB ACTIVITY 2

Answer the following questions and label Figure 2.1.

### QUESTIONS

1. What is a **compound light microscope?**

2. If the ocular lens is 10× and the objective lens is 20×, what is the **total magnification?** _______________________________________________

3. What is the microscopic **field of view?** _______________________________________

4. You should **always** begin looking at a microscope slide with which objective lens? You should **always** store the microscope with which objective lens pointed downward? (**Hint:** same lens)

5. The glass slide is placed on the _________________________________ **between** the _________________________________ and **NOT** under them.

6. The only time you should use the **coarse** focus adjustment is while viewing with the lowest magnification called the _________________________________ objective.

7. You use the _________________________________ to move the slide around on the stage.

8. The objectives are attached to the _________________________________.

### LABEL THE PARTS OF THE MICROSCOPE. BE SURE TO STUDY THE MICROSCOPE IN YOUR LAB

- Eyepiece (ocular lens)
- Head
- Nosepiece
- Objective lens
- Stage
- Stage clips
- Mechanical stage knobs
- Substage light
- Base
- Iris diaphragm lever
- Arm
- Coarse and fine adjustment knobs

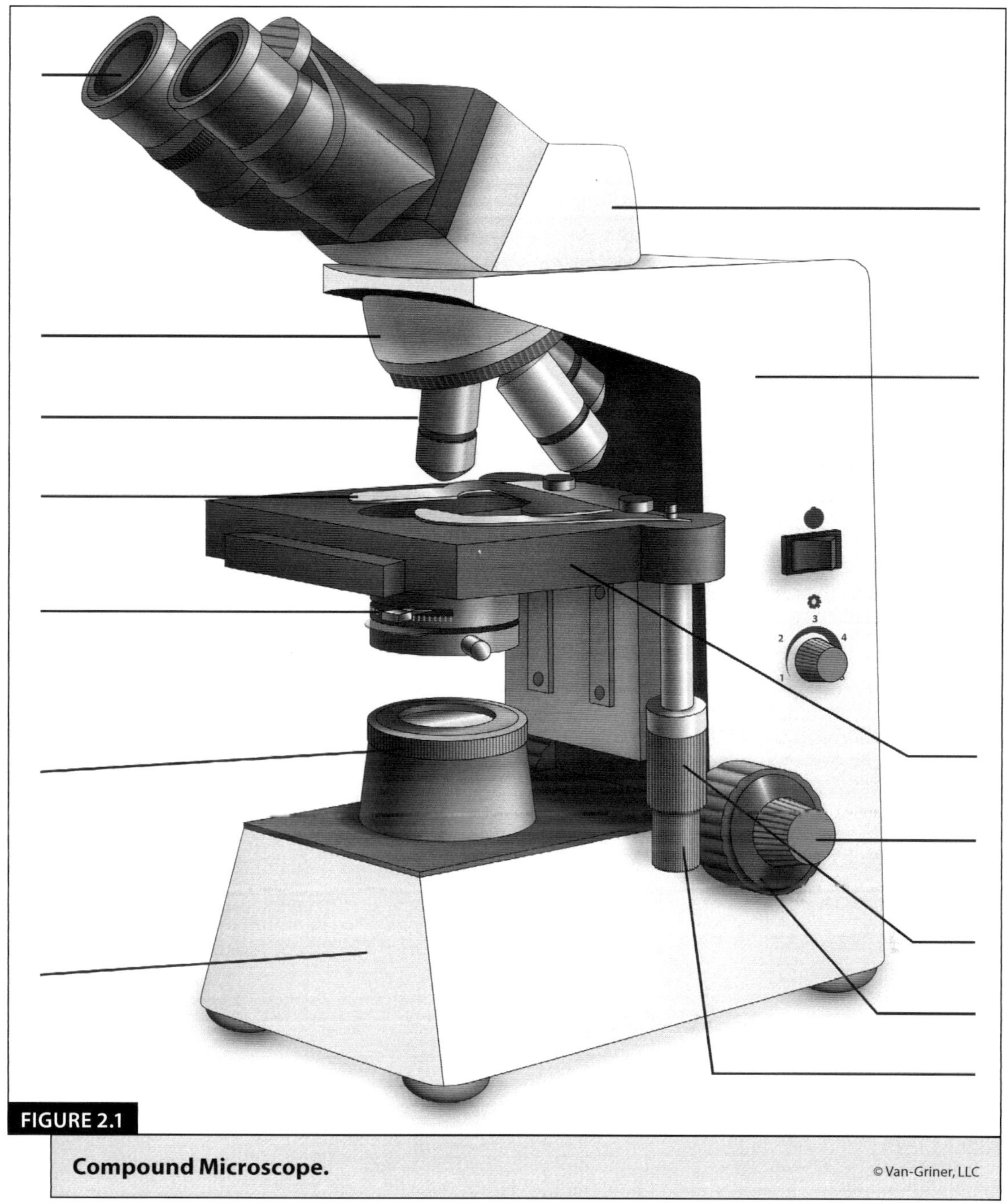

**FIGURE 2.1**

**Compound Microscope.**

# 2

# THE CELL AND MICROSCOPE
## IN-LAB ACTIVITIES

Name: _______________________________  Section: ___________  Date: _________

## LEARNING OBJECTIVES

- Identify the parts of the compound microscope and explain their functions.
- Determine the total magnification of an object viewed under a microscope.
- Understand the advantages of parafocality and the relations between magnification and working distance, brightness/size of the field of view, and size of the image.
- Locate and focus on any specimen using the scanning, low, and high power objective.
- Understand the principle of staining biological material for microscopy.
- Identify organelles in cheek cells.

## PRE-LAB

Before going to lab, you must complete the following:

1. Read the **Pre-Lab** and answer all pre-lab questions.

*Note:* You will spend **2 hr and 30 min** in lab at Forsyth Tech to complete the following activities. This amount of time allows you and your lab partner to complete the activities using the microscope.

## ACTIVITY 1

While in lab, review Pre-Lab: **All Parts of the Microscope.** You must know the microscope for the lab test! If you did not view the video beforehand, then you may do so during lab today (link below).

- https://www.youtube.com/watch?feature=player_detailpage&v=Txhj2dRefAI

## ACTIVITY 2

**Information:** Microscopes provide windows into the world of the cell. One type of microscope is the **Light Microscope** which is used for many general purposes. However, the light microscope's *resolving power* is limited. **Resolution** is the ability to distinguish between two separate objects that are close together. For example, the resolution of the unaided human eye is about 0.1 mm. The resolving power of an **electron microscope** is about 100,000 times the resolving power of the best microscope. Often times a **micrometer** (one millionth of a meter) is used to measure the length of microscopic objects.

Read the sections in the text book (or online text) about **electron microscopes.**

**Rules for Microscope Use and Care:** The microscope is a useful, precision instrument. If not treated properly, a microscope's performance can be reduced. Follow this list of rules at all times when working with microscopes:

1. The microscope must always be carried with two hands, one hand on the arm and the other hand on the base.

2. The microscope must always be placed away from the edge of the table or sink. This greatly reduces the chances of the microscope being knocked off the table, onto the floor, or into the sink.

3. The microscope's electrical cord should be placed in a position that will reduce the chance of the microscope being pulled off the table by the microscope cord.

4. The microscope's glass lenses should be cleaned with **lens paper only.** Use of other materials may damage the lens. (**DO NOT** use kimwipes.)

5. The high power objective can actually hit and crack the microscope slide being observed. Therefore, only use the **fine adjustment when the high power objective** is in place.

6. The microscope should be stored with the scanning power objective in place and the nosepiece on the body tube (head) all the way down.

By following these steps, microscopes can last for many years without problems.

**Total Magnification:** The microscopes used in lab are **compound microscopes**. What this means is that compound microscopes use two lenses to magnify a specimen. The objective lens and the ocular lens of a compound microscope magnify the image. The oculars we will be using have a magnification of **10×**. The **scanning objective** magnifies the image **4×**, **low power objective** magnifies the image **10×**, and the **high power objective** magnifies the image **40×** or **43×**. Take a moment to familiarize yourself with the scope and the magnifications.

**To determine the total magnification, multiply the magnification of the ocular/eyepiece by the magnification of the objective lens.** For example, the total magnification with the scanning objective in place is 40×.

For each of the following, **calculate the total magnification** of the specimen.

- Scanning objective lens _______________________________________________
- Low power objective lens _______________________________________________
- High dry objective lens _______________________________________________
- Oil immersion lens (***Do not use***—only for use with oil to see bacteria) ___________

# ACTIVITY 3

**Focusing the Microscope:** Our microscopes are *parfocal.* This means that once the image is in focus on one objective, the image will remain in reasonable focus as we switch to other objectives.

Complete the following:

1. To begin, you must locate the specimen. The easiest way to get the specimen in focus is by using the **scanning objective.**

   The reason for this is that the *field of view* is much larger with the scanning objective in place. The *field of view* is the circle of light you see when looking through the microscope. Because the field of view is much larger with the scanning objective in place, it is much easier to locate the specimen.

2. Take a letter "e" slide. View the letter "e" slide by itself **before** putting it on the stage.

   Draw it here:

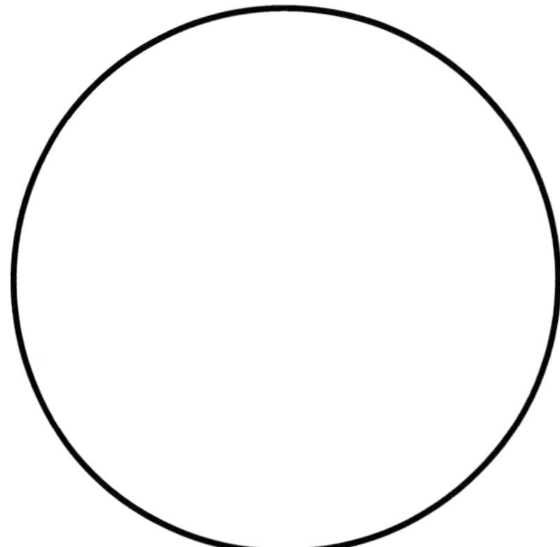

3. Once the specimen is in place on the stage (between the stage clips) under the scanning objective lens, you can move the stage all the way up by using the **coarse adjustment knob.**

4. Find the "e" image and focus it with the coarse and fine adjustment knobs.

5. Rotate the **nosepiece** up to *Low Power objective.*

6. Fine tune the focus using the **fine adjustment knob.**

   You will **not** have to move the stage again between objective lenses since it is ***parfocal.***

   a. How does the "e" look now under the microscope?


   b. Draw it here:

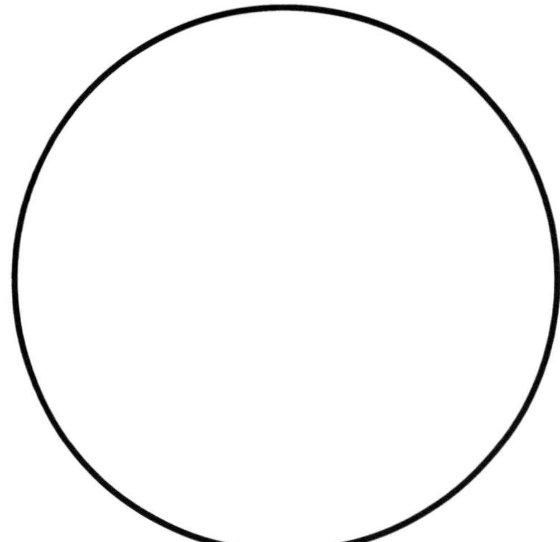

**c.** Is it upside down or backwards or both from how it is mounted on the slide?

**7.** Repeat the process but this time rotate the **nosepiece** up to *High Power objective* and fine tune the focus using the **fine adjustment knob.**

Can you see any part of the "e" now? (If not, you may be viewing the middle of the "e" that is white paper and not black ink.)

**8.** Adjust the stage adjustment knobs as needed until you can see the letter again.
   **a.** If you move the slide to the right on the stage, which way does it move when looking through the ocular lenses? _______________________ (left or right?)
   **b.** How much can you find? (May just be a black line)

   **c.** Draw it here:

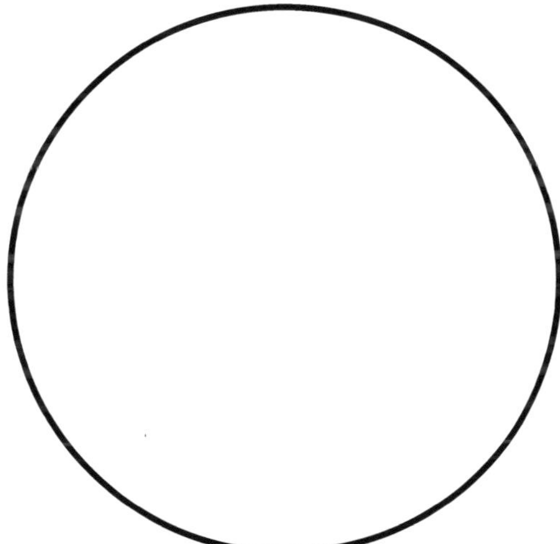

**9.** ***Do not*** use the oil immersion (100) lens since it is not necessary for our purposes.

**10.** Put the letter "e" slide away.

**Field of View:** The brightness of the field of view is an important component to understand. As the magnification increases, the brightness of the field of view decreases. This is not easy to see on computer images, but it will be noticeable when you use the microscope first hand. On high power, it is often necessary to adjust the **iris diaphragm** level to allow more light to illuminate the specimen.

**Observing slides with the microscope:** Cells come in many shapes and sizes. The largest human cell is an egg cell. A human egg cell is barely visible to the unaided eye (of course, you are never going to see one under normal circumstances). Human red blood cells are very small. There are 4–6 million red blood cells in 1 cubic millimeter of blood. A cubic millimeter of blood is a very small drop of blood.

- **Draw** a square with 1 mm dimensions in the space provided.
- As you can see, red blood cells are very tiny!

Specimens are placed on microscope slides for observation. A variety of microscope slides are available for your use today. You also have the opportunity to make your own slides from your inner cheek cells.

Find the **trachea slide.** Note the different stained areas, especially lining the middle open area of the tube, which has cilia (hair-like structures) on the cells called epithelial cells. You should also observe an area that looks like it has many eyeballs (or 'cat eyes'). This is cartilage that lines your trachea on the outside firmly so that it does not collapse.

Find the **blood slide.** Try to view the little pink dots under the scanning objective. The little pink dots are red blood cells. Focus under scanning first. Move the nosepiece over to the low power objective lens and refocus with the fine focus knob. You may be able to view little purple cells now, which are the white blood cells needed for immune responses. Move the nosepiece to high power and refocus with *only* the fine adjustment knob. Can you see the WBC and the RBC better now?

**Observe other slides that are available in the lab.**

Answer the following questions:

1. Images viewed under the microscope are _____________________ (upside down and backwards) in their position compared to the mount on the slide.

2. What happens to the field of view as the magnification increases? Why?

   Circle one     Increases     or     Decreases     or     stays the same?

   Why?


Once you have completed Activity 3, you may continue to Activity 4 (wet mount and draw cells).

## ACTIVITY 4: WET MOUNT AND DRAW CELLS

1. Obtain a clean microscope slide, and make sure it is free of fingerprints.

2. With a toothpick, gently scrape the inner side of the cheek. Carefully smear the content in the center of the microscope plate of about 1–1.5 cm area.

3. Let the slide air dry completely so the cells become fixed to the slide before you proceed.

4. Once the smear is dry, place the slide on the **staining tray** and cover the smear with a drop of methylene blue stain.

5. Leave the stain on the slide for 3 minutes.

6. After 3 minutes, hold the slide from the marked end at a 45° angle, and pour a stream of the distilled water near the end you are holding but ***not directly*** on the smear (see the arrow, which represents the water stream). If the stream is directly sprayed on the smear, it will rinse the cells off. *Proper rinsing involves allowing sufficient water to gently flow over the smear to remove the stain.

7. When done, gently blot the excess water off the slide with a kimwipe.

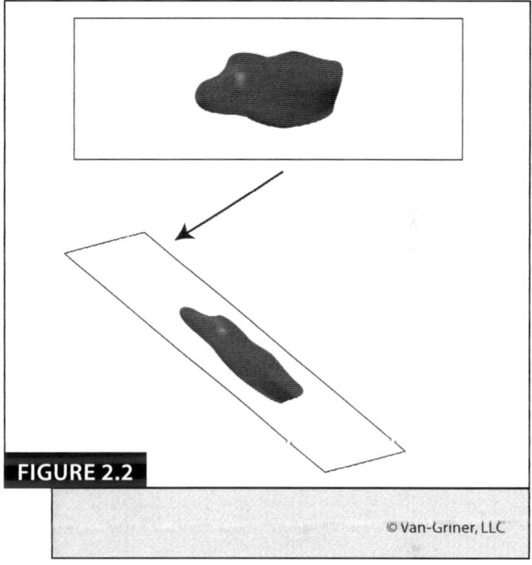

**FIGURE 2.2**

© Van-Griner, LLC

8. **Place the coverslip over the smear** and then gently tap on the cover slip with a pencil eraser to remove any air bubbles.

9. Observe it under the microscope.

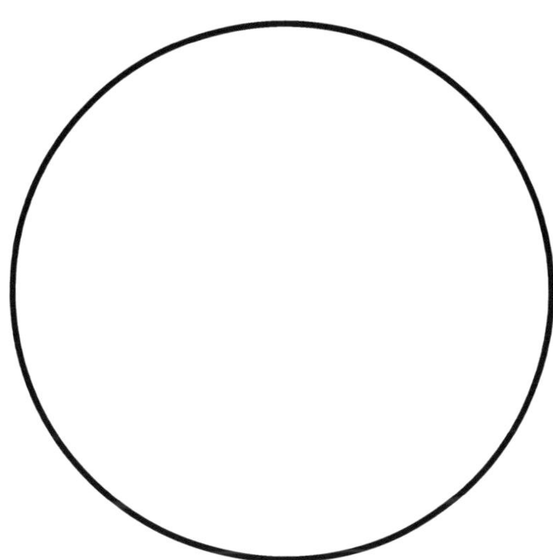

**10.** When finished making observations, wash your slide with 10% bleach, rinse thoroughly, and place on the dry rack.

**11.** Cover slip can be thrown away.

## QUESTIONS

1.  Why was stain used on the slide of your cheek cells?

2.  Which cell structures can you see under the scope?

## ACTIVITY 5

Refer to your Pre-Lab and/or textbook as needed to complete Activities 5–6.

1.  The nucleus of a cell contains one or more of these structures that are the site of production of ribosomes. Which organelle below forms ribosomes?

    **a.** Pore

    **b.** Histones

    **c.** Nucleolus

    **d.** Chromatin

    **e.** Centrosome

**Review** the cell model in lab and in Figure 2.3. (Legends for the cell model are available in lab.) Match the labels from Figure 2.3 with the following organelle name or description:

2.  Site of repackaging of proteins, lipids, and vesicle formation. _______________

3.  Secretes fatty acids and steroids, stores and releases calcium ions in muscle, removes toxins. _______________

4.  Nuclear membrane. _______________

5.  Forms the mitotic spindle and moves the chromosomes to opposite sides of the cell during cell division. _______________

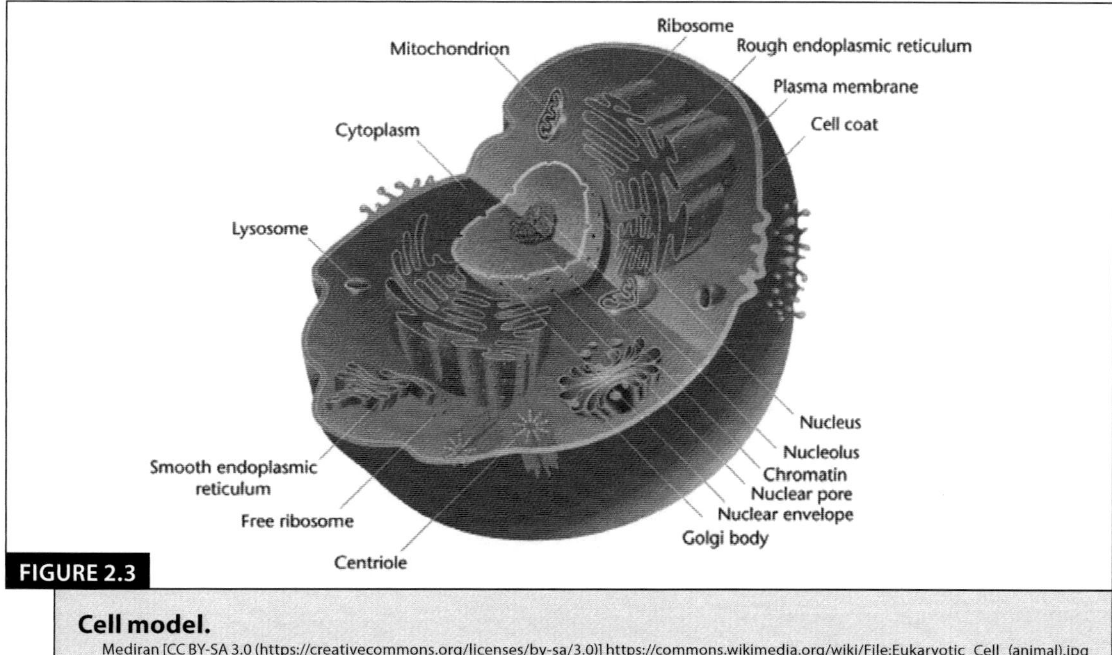


**FIGURE 2.3**

**Cell model.**
Mediran [CC BY-SA 3.0 (https://creativecommons.org/licenses/by-sa/3.0)] https://commons.wikimedia.org/wiki/File:Eukaryotic_Cell_(animal).jpg

# ACTIVITY 6

1. In somatic cell division, a cell undergoes a nuclear division called _______________ and a division of its cytoplasm called _______________.

   a. The cell cycle / cytokinesis

   b. Meiosis / mitosis

   c. Mitosis / cytokinesis

   d. Prophase / cytokinesis

   e. Mitosis / telophase

2.  Observe the **mitotic phases** under the microscope (**use the onion root tip or the whitefish slide**). Draw and label the metaphase and telophase cell phases, showing the distinct differences between the two.

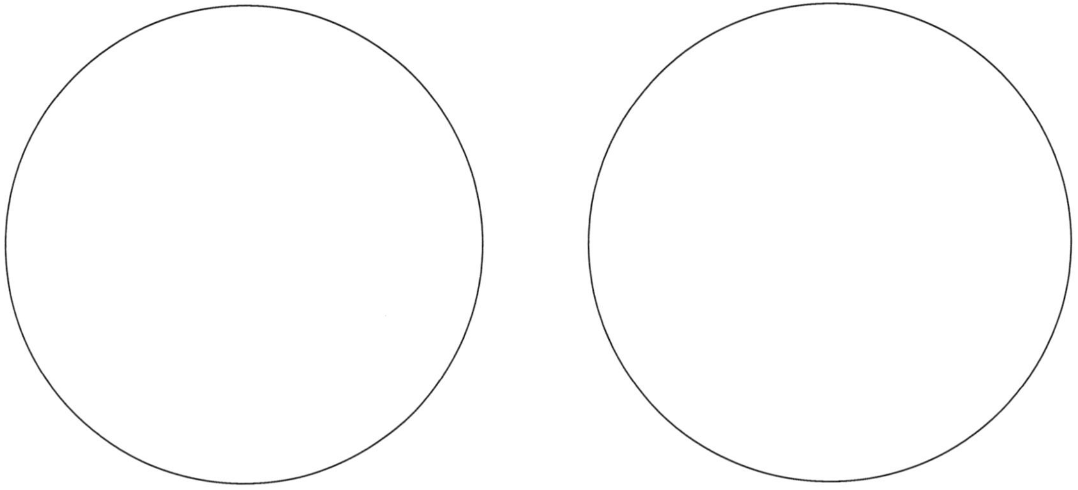

Metaphase      Telophase (w/ cytokinesis)

Review organelles and the phases of the cell cycle by **answering the following questions:**

3.  Fill in the table below using **your own words.** Find different ways these organelles are used by the body's cells that are not mentioned in the online text.

| CELLULAR STRUCTURE | FUNCTION | SPECIALIZATION |
| --- | --- | --- |
|  | Controls movement of substances into and out of the cell | Cilia microvilli |
| Ribosomes |  | Not membrane-bound |
|  |  | Only seen in male sperm cells |
|  | Detoxify ingested substances, etc. into | Found abundantly in liver cells |
| Lysosomes |  |  |

4. Observe the following cellular slides under the microscope. In your own words fill out the table below describing the specializations observed on each slide.

| CELLULAR SLIDE VIEWED | DESCRIBE THE SPECIALIZATION(S) OBSERVED |
|---|---|
| ——————————Draw cells here. | When mature, does not contain a nucleus, is doughnut-like in shape because it is biconcave and contains mostly pigments that carry oxygen. |
| Sperm—Draw cells here. | |
| Trachea (Pseudostratified ciliated columnar epithelium and Hyaline cartilage)—Draw cells with cilia and goblet cells here. | Observe the cilia on the inner lining of the lumen (white middle area)—cilia allows particles, small cells, etc. to move along the surface of the cells (Where else is cilia found in the body?)<br><br>Observe goblet cells—what do they secrete? |

## QUESTIONS

*Note:* Be sure to get your completed work checked off by a member of the lab staff and then keep this handout for your review.

1. What is the function of the iris diaphragm?

2. What is the total magnification under the low power objective?

3. When you look at a specimen under the microscope, how does it appear compared to the specimen on the slide itself?

4. What objective magnification should you always begin and end with when looking at a slide?

5. How does the size of the field of view change as you go up in magnification?

6. How does the lighting of the field of view change as you go up in magnification?

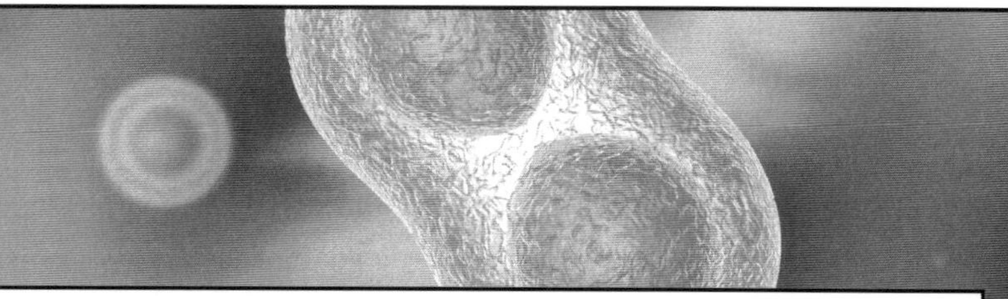

# TRANSPORT ACROSS THE PLASMA MEMBRANE— DIFFUSION AND OSMOSIS
## PRE-LAB

Name: ___________________________  Section: ____________  Date: __________

## OBJECTIVES

- Define diffusion; describe the effects of temperature on diffusion rate.
- Define osmosis; measure effect of solute concentration on rate of osmosis.
- Explain the tonicity of solutions; compare and contrast hypertonic and hypotonic solutions.
- Describe the processes of diffusion and osmosis.
- Describe the various types of transport across the cell membrane.

## INTRODUCTION

Our body cells are surrounded by a cell membrane called the *plasma membrane* (what are other names?). As you saw in the previous lab, this cell membrane is made from many different molecules and compounds including phospholipids, cholesterol, and protein channels. The cell membrane is a rather flexible structure composed primarily of back-to-back phospholipids (a "bilayer"). This bilayer of molecules allows very small, non-polar substances through the membrane, but not larger or polar items. Thus, the membrane is called *semi-permeable* because some molecules or ions can get through but others cannot. It's like a screen door where air and dust can get through but the flies and bugs cannot. Some **examples** of these are other lipids, oxygen and carbon dioxide gases, and alcohol. However, water-soluble materials—like glucose, amino acids, and electrolytes—need some assistance to cross the membrane because they are repelled by the hydrophobic tails of the phospholipid bilayer. When there are times the cell needs the larger compounds, like glucose that is used to make energy (or ATP), the protein channels help or facilitate their transport.

**This lab will explore when a semi-permeable membrane acts like a screen and allows some molecules to passively diffuse through it.**

Two types of passive transports across the plasma membranes of the cell include diffusion and osmosis. **Diffusion** is the movement of particles from an area of higher concentration to an area of lower concentration, which is a 'grade' from high to low (like going downhill). A *concentration gradient* is the difference in concentration of a substance across a space. Molecules (or ions) will spread/diffuse from where they are more concentrated to where they are less concentrated until they are equally distributed in that space. (When molecules move in this way, they are said to move *down* their concentration gradient.) An **example** of diffusion is a spoonful of sugar placed in a cup of tea. Eventually the sugar will diffuse throughout the tea until no concentration gradient remains (when diffusion ends, however, particles can still move about randomly, though equally now). In both cases, if the room is warmer or the tea hotter, diffusion occurs even faster as the molecules are bumping into each other and spreading out faster than at cooler temperatures. Having an internal body temperature around 98.6°F thus aids in diffusion of particles within the body.

**Osmosis** is the *diffusion of water* through a semipermeable membrane down its concentration gradient from the side with more water concentration to the side of lower water. If a membrane is permeable to water, though not to a solute, water will equalize its own concentration by diffusing to the side of lower water concentration (with higher solutes). Osmosis occurs when there is an imbalance of solutes outside of a cell versus inside the cell (or vice versa). A solution that has a *higher* concentration of *solutes* than another solution is said to be **hypertonic,** and water molecules tend to diffuse into a hypertonic solution. Cells in a hypertonic solution will shrivel as water leaves the cell via osmosis. In contrast, a solution that has a *lower* concentration of solutes than another solution is said to be **hypotonic,** and water molecules tend to diffuse out of a hypotonic solution. Cells in a hypotonic solution will take on too much water and swell, with the risk of eventually bursting. Two solutions that have the same concentration of solutes are said to be **isotonic** (equal tension). A critical aspect of homeostasis in living things is to create an internal environment in which all of the body's cells are in an isotonic solution. Various organ systems, particularly the kidneys, work to maintain this homeostasis.

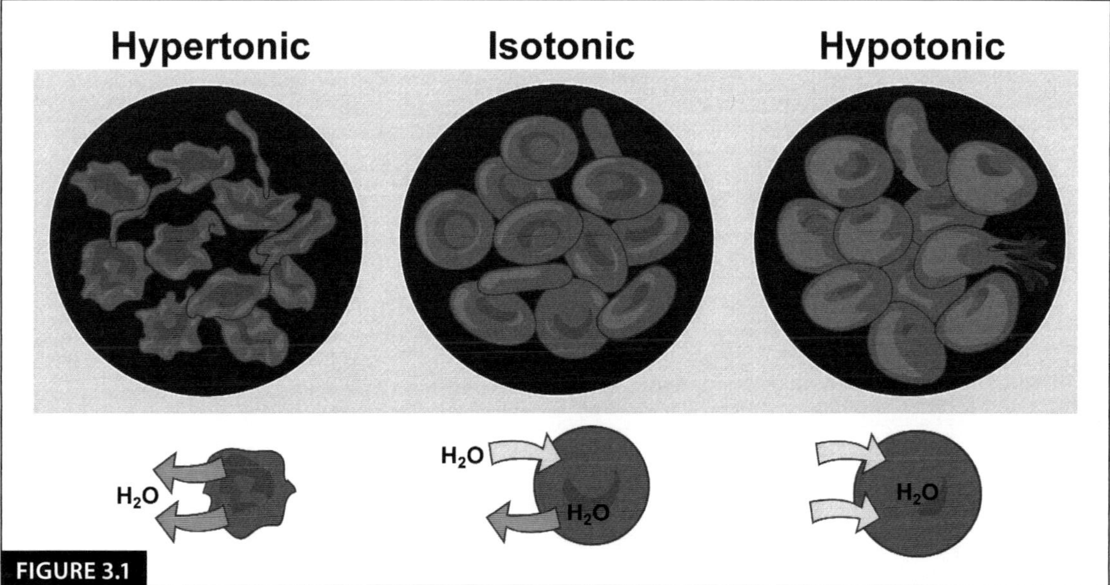


**FIGURE 3.1**

**A hypertonic solution has a solute concentration *higher* than another solution.** An isotonic solution has a solute concentration *equal* to another solution. A hypotonic solution has a solute concentration *lower* than another solution. http://sjcabiology.wikispaces.com/Hypotonic,+Isotonic,+Hypertonic+Solutions

LadyofHats [Public domain]

After reading further in your text source about the plasma membrane and transport mechanisms, answer the following questions.

1. The cell membrane is also called the _________________________ or plasma membrane.

2. What is passive transport?

3. What is the difference between diffusion and osmosis?

4. What is active transport?

5. Explain what the purpose of a channel protein might be for cellular transport.

6. The diffusion of substances within a solution tends to move those substances _________________________ (choose up or down) their _________________________ _ (choose concentration or electrical) gradient.

7. Recall what hydrophobic and hydrophilic mean. Explain these in your own words.

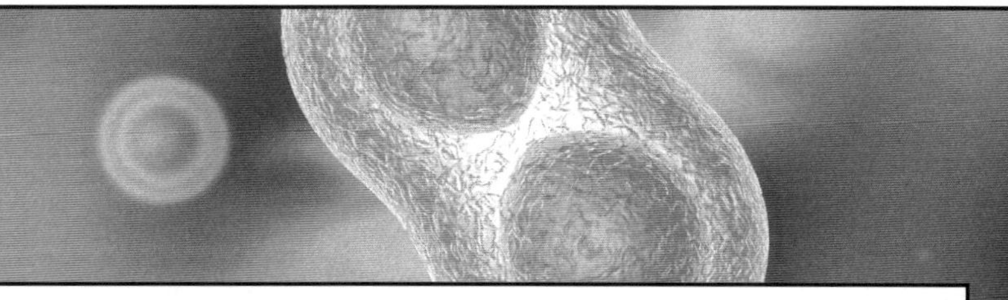

# 3

# TRANSPORT ACROSS THE PLASMA MEMBRANE— DIFFUSION AND OSMOSIS
## IN-LAB ACTIVITIES

Name: _______________________________  Section: ___________  Date: __________

## OBJECTIVES

- Define diffusion; describe the effects of temperature on diffusion rate.
- Define osmosis; measure effect of solute concentration on rate of osmosis.
- Explain the tonicity of solutions; compare and contrast hypertonic and hypotonic solutions.

## PRE-LAB

Before going to lab, you must complete the following:

1. Read the **Pre-Lab** and answer all Pre-Lab questions.
2. View the video directions about **making a cell of dialysis tubing** before lab.

## INTRODUCTION

Cells must exchange substances such as nutrients, wastes, and gases with their surroundings/environment. The **plasma membrane** is sometimes referred to as the cell's *gatekeeper* since it controls the movement of substances into and out of the cell. The plasma membrane is able to act as a gatekeeper because of its **selective permeability.** *Selective permeability* means the membrane allows some substances to pass across, but it will prevent the movement of other substances. There are two basic types of movement across the membrane—**active transport** and **passive transport.**

**Active transport** mechanisms move substances from an area of lower concentration to an area of higher concentration. This type of movement is said to go *against* the concentration gradient (moving from low to high concentration). The process is *active* because it requires energy (ATP) expenditure by the cell. This is analogous to a car driving up a mountain; without gasoline the car could not make it up the mountain.

**Passive transport** is the movement of a substance from an area of high concentration to an area of lower concentration. This type of movement goes *with* the concentration gradient (moving from an area of high concentration to an area of low concentration). This process is *passive* because the cell does not have to spend energy (ATP) to make it happen. In fact, sometimes the cell may not even be able to control passive transport. Passive transport relies on the natural tendency that substances have to spread out. The analogy here would be driving a car down a mountain; if the car's engine were turned off, the car could still roll down the mountain.

In this laboratory exercise, you will examine both diffusion and osmosis. **Diffusion** is simply the movement of a substance from an area of higher concentration to an area of lower concentration. Simply put, substances have the tendency to spread out. **For example,** perfume spreads from an area of higher concentration on the skin to an area of lower concentration in the atmosphere. Substances can diffuse across membranes if the membrane is **permeable** to the substance.

**Osmosis** is a special type of diffusion. *Osmosis* is the **diffusion of water** across a semi-permeable membrane. Osmosis is very important for cells. Cells may shrivel (crenate) or burst (lyse) if they are placed in solutions that are more or less concentrated than the cell.

There are three types of solutions relative to the concentration of the cell. A solution may be more concentrated than the cell, less concentrated than the cell, or identical to the cell's concentration. Water constantly moves back and forth across the cell's plasma membrane.

However, if there is a **concentration gradient** present, there will be a *net* movement of water across the plasma membrane towards the area with the greatest solute concentration. **Remember, water will always move towards the area with the highest solute concentration (if the membrane is permeable to water).** Consider Figure 3.2.

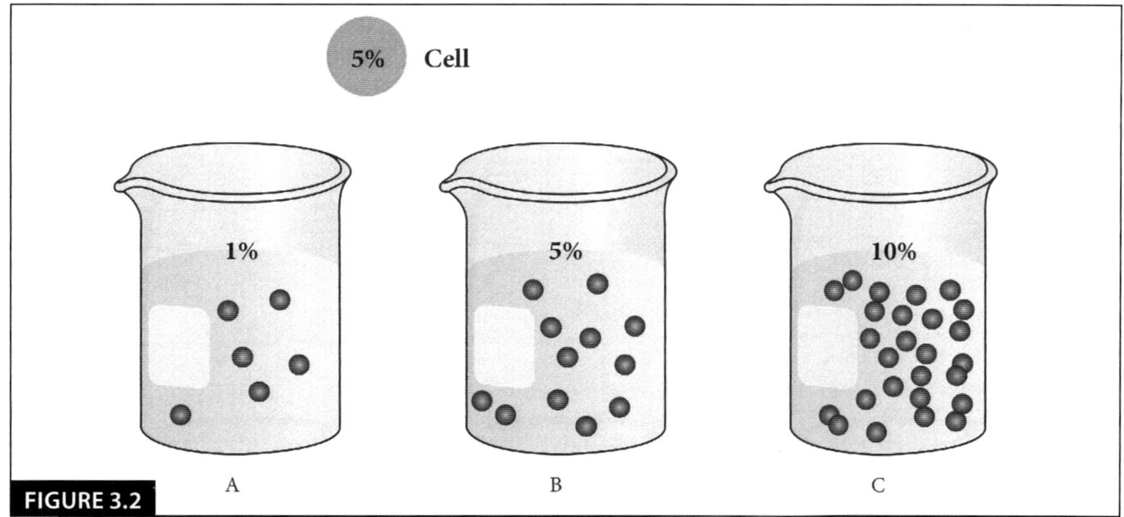


**FIGURE 3.2**

**The above cell has a 5% concentration.** Solution A is less concentrated than the cell (1% is less than 5%). Solution B has the same concentration as the cell (5% = 5%). Solution C is more concentrated than the cell (10% is greater than 5%). © Van-Griner, LLC

If the cell were placed into solution A, there would be a net movement of water *into* the cell because the cell is more concentrated than its extracellular solution. The cell would take on water and might lyse or burst as a result. A solution that is less concentrated than the cell is a ***hypotonic solution.***

If the cell were placed into solution C, there would be a net movement of water *out* of the cell because the extracellular solution is more concentrated than the cell. The cell would shrivel or **crenate** as it lost water. This solution is a ***hypertonic solution.***

Solution B is an **isotonic solution.** If the cell were placed into solution B, there would be *no net movement* of water across the plasma membrane.

What do the terms hypo-, hyper-, and iso- mean?

- Hypo- _______________________________________________
- Hype- _______________________________________________
- Iso- _______________________________________________

*Note:* You will spend **at least 2 hr** in Lab at Forsyth Tech to complete the following Activities (in Lab 3 and Lab 4). The activities below will help you gain a better understanding of diffusion, osmosis, and selectively permeable membranes. You should have read and studied these concepts **before** starting the laboratory exercises. **Read all exercises before beginning.**

# ACTIVITY 1: HYPERTONIC AND HYPOTONIC SOLUTIONS AND CELERY SLICE FLEXIBILITY

## OBJECTIVE

- Examine the effects of **hypertonic** and **hypotonic** solutions on cells.

## MATERIALS

- Fresh celery or potato
- Beakers or jars
- Knife
- Saturated salt solution

## PROCEDURE

1. Cut three identical slices of fresh celery (or potato) that are about 6 cm × 1 cm × 1 cm.

2. Place one slice into a beaker containing tap water for one hour.

3. Place the second slice into a beaker that contains a saturated salt water solution (add as much salt to the water while stirring as it will hold without precipitating out—in other words, completely dissolving) for one hour.

4. Bend the third slice back and forth, and note how firm or limber it is.

5. After one hour, remove the two potato slices from their solutions and bend them, noting any differences in their firmness or limberness compared to the third slice, which was not in any solution.

While you are waiting, use your knowledge of osmosis and cell structure to **write a hypothesis** about what will happen in the space below.

Based on your observations of the flexibility of the soaked slices, did you find that your hypothesis was correct? Why or why not? What do you think happened? Elaborate.

**Record** your thinking in the space below. In your description, be sure to include a way to measure the different outcomes of each potato slice.

## ACTIVITY 2: SOLUTE CONCENTRATION AND RATE OF OSMOSIS

*Note:* Once this lab experiment is set up and running, the Tissues or other lab activities in Lab 4 can be performed during the 15-minute intervals.

### OBJECTIVE

- Determine the effect of *solute concentration* on the *rate of osmosis.*
- In this exercise, you will use dialysis tubing that has small pores in its wall that will allow small molecules to pass but prevent other molecules from passing. Specifically, water molecules can fit through the pores but sugar molecules cannot because they are too large.
- You will create four different "cells" using the dialysis tubing.

### MATERIALS

- ¾ in dialysis tubing
- (3) 400 or 600-mL beakers
- Tap water
- Scissors
- Tubing clips or string
- Scales (digital or triple-beam, etc.)
- Timer

After reading the Procedure write a **Hypothesis.**

### PROCEDURE

1. Obtain three (3) medium beakers (400–600-mL) and fill each with 300 mL tap water.

2. Label the beakers 0%, 20%, and 40% respectively, using tape from the lab and permanent ink pens. (*If solutions are not already prepared for you in the lab, you learned how to make percent (%) solutions in the chemistry module of your text. The 0% solution is just water, though, as you know.*)

3. Use scissors to cut 3 pieces of dialysis tubing that are each 15 cm long.

4. One piece of dialysis tubing should be soaked in each beaker of water for approximately 10 minutes. This will make the tubing more flexible. It may have a "slimy" texture, but it is safe to handle.

5.  Make an overhand knot at one end of each piece of dialysis tubing (or fold the end over once and use a dialysis clip, if available). The knot should be tied as close to the end of each piece of tubing as possible. This will leave one end of each "cell" open.

6.  Fill each "cell" approximately three-fourths (¾) full with the sucrose solution (use sucrose or table sugar and three drops of red/blue food coloring per solution) corresponding to the label previously placed on the beaker. (**See a video about _Making a "cell" out of dialysis tubing_). Following the video directions, make sure you squeeze all air from the cell before tying off or clipping the other end. It is extremely important to make sure very little air is trapped in the cell before the other end is tied, no matter how much tubing is left at this end. (It should look like a deflated water balloon with space to add water.)**

7.  As you make each cell, place them on a labeled piece of paper towel until all cells are complete. _It is important that the "cells" are not mixed up; proper use of labels should prevent this from occurring._

8.  Once you have made all the cells, dry them off and weigh them using an electronic balance.

9.  After the 0% "cell" has been weighed and the mass recorded, the 20% "cell" should be immediately weighed and its mass recorded, followed immediately by the 40% "cell." Record the masses in the appropriate _"initial mass"_ cell in the data table at the end of this document.

10. After you weigh the cells, immediately place them in the corresponding beaker of water. It is important to put the cells into the beakers at approximately the same time because this will be the initial time.

11. Ten minutes after immersing the cells, weigh all three cells again. The measurements should start with the 0% "cell" and continue quickly in order until all cells have been weighed. Record the 10-minute mass in the appropriate cell in the data table found at the end of this document.

12. Return the cells to their appropriate solution once you have recorded their weight and mass.

13. Continue this process by recording the weight and mass of the cells in the data table at ten-minute intervals for 60 minutes. Record any color changes in the beaker water at each interval as well. (Perform other lab tasks/activities during this time.)

## DATA ANALYSIS

A lot of data is generated during this experiment. It is important to *analyze* this data appropriately and make logical *inferences* as a result.

## FURTHER EXPLANATION

Suppose someone told you about a baby who had a birth weight of one pound. Would you be concerned? Most people immediately answer, "Yes." What if the baby was a cocker spaniel puppy? That changes things, doesn't it? Alternatively, what if the baby was a great blue whale? The point is that the species of the baby is very important when considering its potential health relevant to its birth weight.

It is highly unlikely that the initial masses for each of your "cells" were identical. This would be hard to accomplish even if we were trying. Since the initial masses were probably not the same, it is important to treat the data in a way that will account for these different initial masses. In sport terms, we want to "level the playing field." It is logical to be concerned if a newborn's birth weight is 80% less than the average birth weight for that species.

Using the *percent difference* is a means of accounting for the different initial masses.

**Percent difference is calculated using this formula:**

$$\frac{new\ measurement - initial\ measurement}{initial\ measurement} \times 100$$

For this data, the new measurement will be the *mass of each "cell"* at **each ten minute interval,** and the *initial measurement* will be the *mass of each "cell"* **before** it was placed in **its respective solution.**

Calculate the percent difference at *each interval* for *each cell* and **graph** the data correctly. **Turn in the data table and graph with this lab report. As an alternative, your instructor may require you to submit a formal laboratory report.**

Make a **data table** that resembles the one shown here. (You may add a row for the color change.)

**Add your title here:** _______________________________.

| TABLE 3.1 | CELL SUGAR CONCENTRATION % | | |
|---|---|---|---|
| | **CELL 0%** | **CELL 20%** | **CELL 40%** |
| Initial Time 0 wt | g | g | g |
| 10 Min wt | | | |
| % Diff. | | | |
| 20 Min wt | | | |
| % Diff. | | | |
| 30 Min wt | | | |
| % Diff. | | | |
| 40 Min wt | | | |
| % Diff. | | | |
| 50 Min wt | | | |
| % Diff. | | | |
| 60 Min wt | | | |
| % Diff. | | | |

Make a **line graph** from your data collected in the data table above. Look at your data table to answer Questions 1–2.

1.  What was the total percent difference over time in each cell?

2.  How did the percent difference change over time with each cell? Did it go up or down or not change?

Look at your graphed data to answer Questions 3–5.

3. **Why** should you organize the data in a line graph rather than a bar graph or any other form?

4. **Why** did the 0% cell change or not change?

5. Which cell changed the fastest? **Explain** why it would have changed the fastest using the tonicity terms mentioned above in the Introduction.

6. How would our body cells (red blood cells specifically) react in these same situations? Hemolyze? Crenate? **Explain** your reasoning.

**Turn in this lab report according to the instructor's rubric.**

# POST-LAB REVIEW: LAB 3 OSMOSIS, DIFFUSION, AND TISSUES

1. In what direction did osmosis occur (into or out of the dialysis tubing "cell")? **Why?**

2. The solution that the dialysis tubing "cell" was placed in (the water) was hypotonic, isotonic, or hypertonic to the solution inside of the dialysis tubing "cell?"

3. Think about it! How would our RBCs react if they were in a similar watery environment in our blood vessels?

*Note:* Be sure to get your completed work checked off by a member of the lab staff and then keep this handout for your review.

# 4

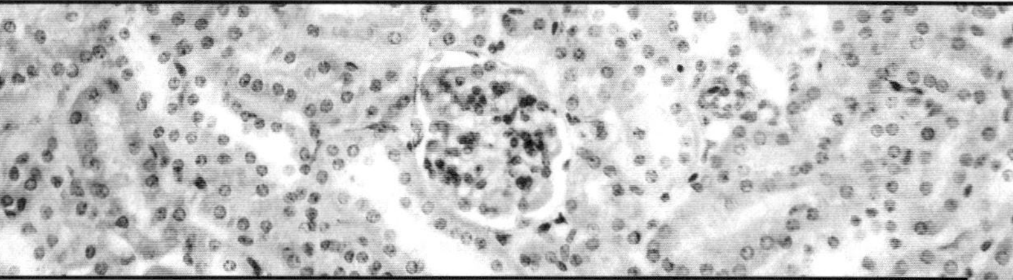

# HISTOLOGY—EPITHELIAL AND CONNECTIVE TISSUES
## PRE-LAB

Name: _________________________   Section: __________   Date: ________

## LEARNING OBJECTIVE

- Identify epithelial and connective tissues under the microscope.

## PRE-LAB ACTIVITY 1

1. Log in to your online account.
2. *Complete the tutorial* on epithelial and connective tissues, which is located under the **Course Documents** section of the course website.
3. Watch videos available in this handout and/or on your course website.
4. Answer the following questions and label the diagrams.

## QUESTIONS

1. Define the term "tissue."


2. List the primary tissues that make up the body.


3. List the **primary** types of epithelial tissue.

4. Define the following terms as they relate to epithelial tissue:

   **a.** Simple

   **b.** Stratified

   **c.** Pseudostratified

5. All epithelial tissue is attached to a ________________________ membrane, which is secreted by the deepest layer of epithelial cells.

6. Differentiate between the following terms as they relate to epithelial tissue:

   **a.** Apical surface

   **b.** Basal surface

7. To identify stratified epithelial tissue, you should look at the ________________ layer of cells to determine their shape.

8. The type of epithelial tissue that covers the inside of the urinary bladder is called ________________________________ epithelium.

9. Describe the characteristics of connective tissue.

10. What determines the "stiffness" of connective tissue?

11. The most common type of cartilage in the body is called ________________________ cartilage.

12. If cartilage is avascular (not penetrated by blood vessels), then how do the chondrocytes obtain oxygen and nutrients?

13. Cartilage cells are called ________________________ which are located in spaces within the matrix called ________________________.

14. Fibrocartilage is flexible because it contains ________________________ fibers.

15. Cells that produce the fibers found in connective tissue are called _________________ __________________.

16. Two types of fibers found in connective tissue are _________________________ and ____________________________.

17. The type of connective tissue that forms tendons and ligaments is called ____________________________.

18. The type of connective tissue that forms the dermis of the skin is called ____________________________.

19. The type of connective tissue that is used for insulation and storage of **lipids** is called _________________________. The cells that make up this tissue are called ____________________________.

20. Another term for **loose connective tissue** is ____________________________.

21. The type of connective tissue that holds the epithelial tissues together that form such organs as the liver and spleen is called ____________________________ tissue.

## PRE-LAB ACTIVITY 2

**Label the following diagrams.**

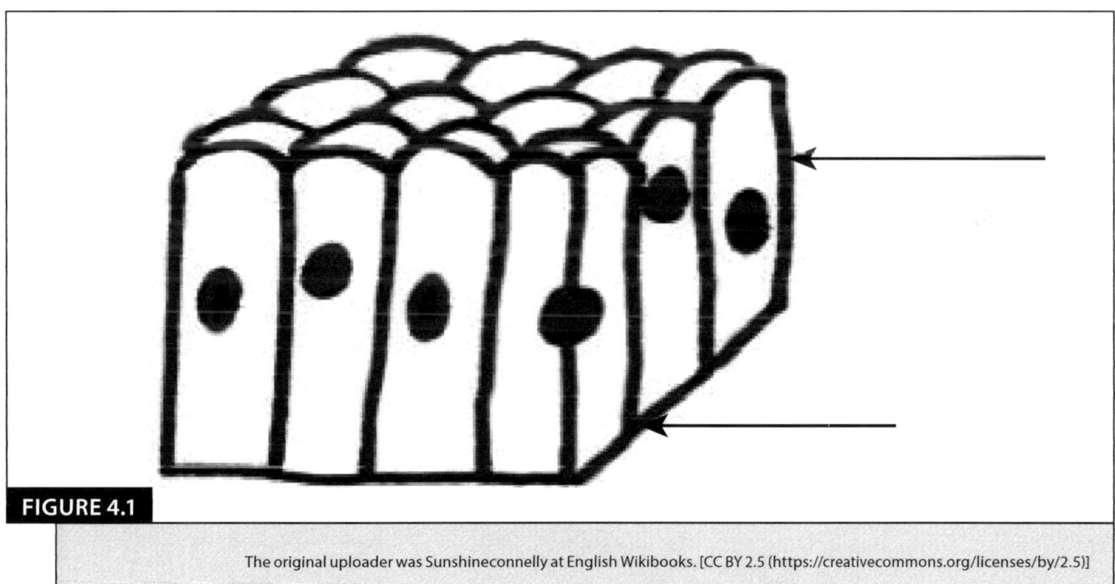

**FIGURE 4.1**

The original uploader was Sunshineconnelly at English Wikibooks. [CC BY 2.5 (https://creativecommons.org/licenses/by/2.5)]

**1.** Identify the following cell surfaces:

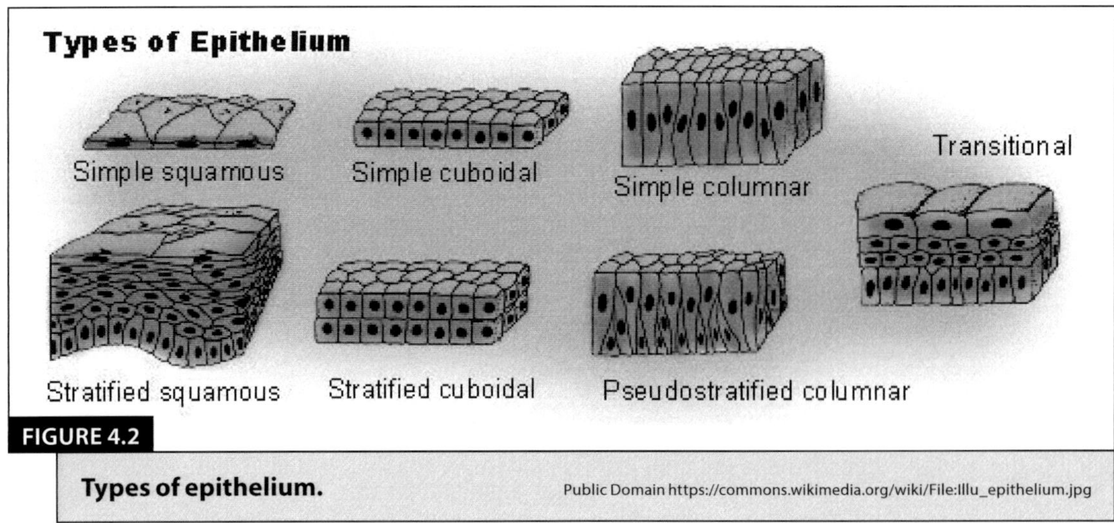



**FIGURE 4.2**

**Types of epithelium.**  Public Domain https://commons.wikimedia.org/wiki/File:Illu_epithelium.jpg

**2.** Identify the following types of epithelial tissues:

**3.** Identify the type of cartilage found in

   **a.** The ear—___________________________________________________

   **b.** The nose—__________________________________________________

# 4

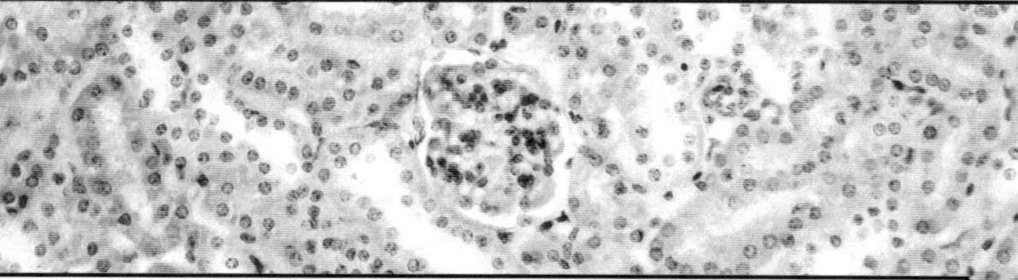

# HISTOLOGY—EPITHELIAL AND CONNECTIVE TISSUES
## IN-LAB ACTIVITIES

Name: _________________________  Section: __________  Date: _________

## LEARNING OBJECTIVE

- Identify epithelial and connective tissues under the microscope.

## PRE-LAB

Before going to lab, you must complete the following:

1. Read the **Pre-Lab** and answer all Pre-Lab questions.

*Note:* You will spend **1 hr and 30 min** in lab at Forsyth Tech to complete the following activities. This amount of time allows you to complete the activities using the microscope and models. Some tissue slides will be set on Microscopes for you—examples: simple cuboidal, transitional, pseudostratified columnar epithelium, adipose, and hyaline cartilage from connective and intercalated discs from the cardiac muscle.

## ACTIVITY 1

Observe the following slides under the microscope. Draw each tissue in the space provided.

### PART A: EPITHELIAL TISSUES

1.  Kidney, 400× = **simple cuboidal epithelium** (notice they are square/cube in shape).

    Draw your observation of the kidney under the microscope and describe how this tissue's cells look compared to the squamous or columnar cells in the spaces provided.

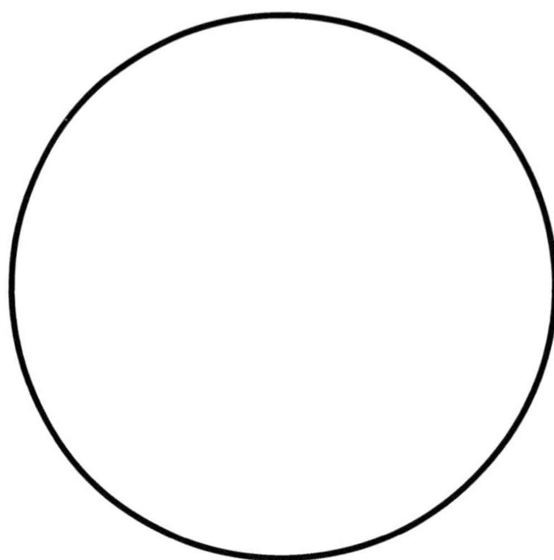

2.  Small Intestine (Goblet Cells), 100× and 400× = **simple columnar epithelium:** where this tissue is in the body and its function there (these are tall column-like cells with the nucleus in a line near the basement membrane).

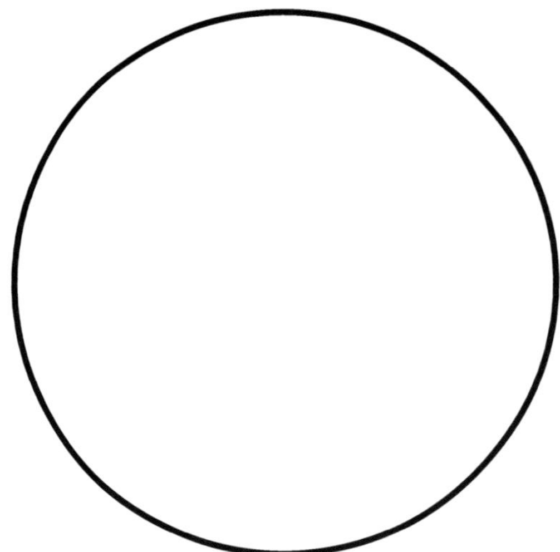

3.  Human Skin or Esophagus (thick skin or thin skin), 100× = **stratified squamous epithelium.**

    Why does our skin (or the esophagus) have to have stratified tissue?

    Always look at the apical surface of the tissue to name it. Notice how the cells change shape from the bottom at the basement membrane to the top layer at the lumen or skin surface. What makes this different from other tissues?

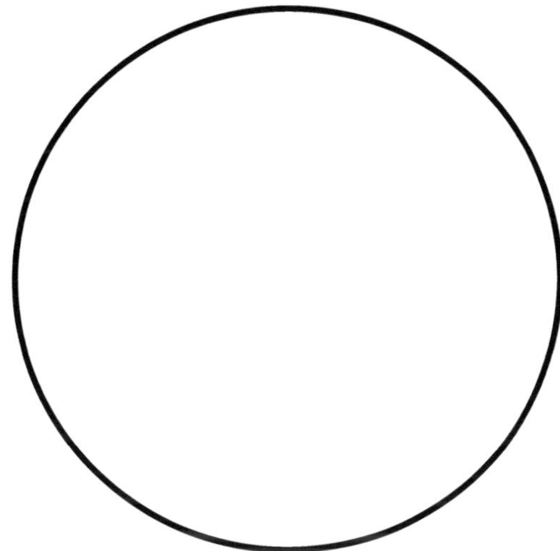

4.  Bladder, 100× or 400× = **transitional**

    Describe the difference between this tissue and human skin.

    Draw the transitional epithelial tissue as it is relaxed.

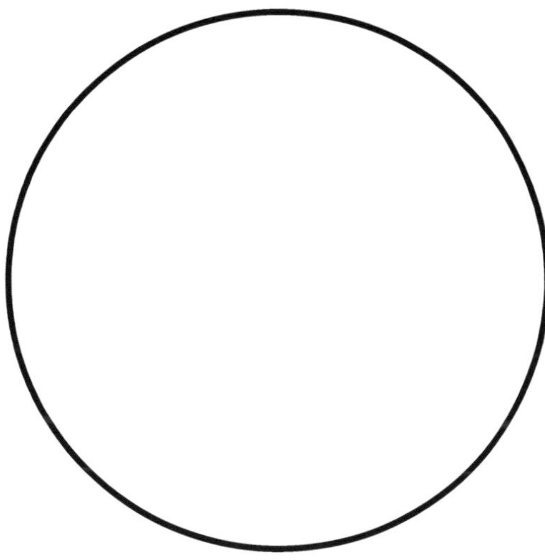

5.  Trachea, 400× = **pseudostratified columnar epithelium:** this has cilia; will be the *only slide/image on the lab test with cilia.*

Be sure to notice how the nuclei are not in a nice straight line, but this is not actually stratified either, so we call it falsely-layered or pseudostratified.

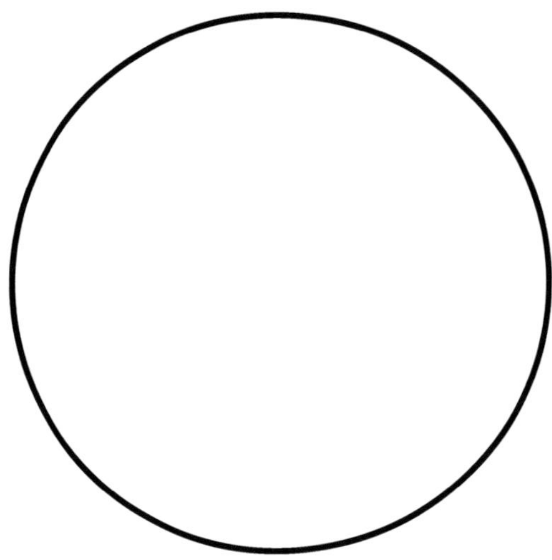

## PART B: CONNECTIVE TISSUES

1.  **Areolar,** 100× = Loose connective tissue/fibrous

Where is it found in the body?

**Draw** loose connective or areolar tissue to help you remember it.

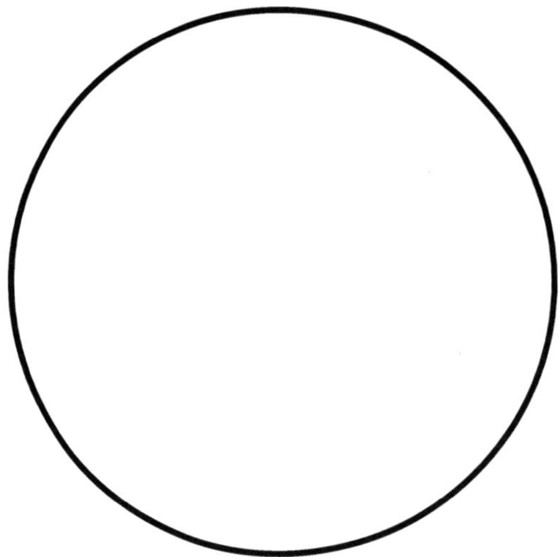

2.  **Adipose,** 100× = best seen in picture because it is hard to find on a slide; the stain is very faint.

    What is this tissue's function?

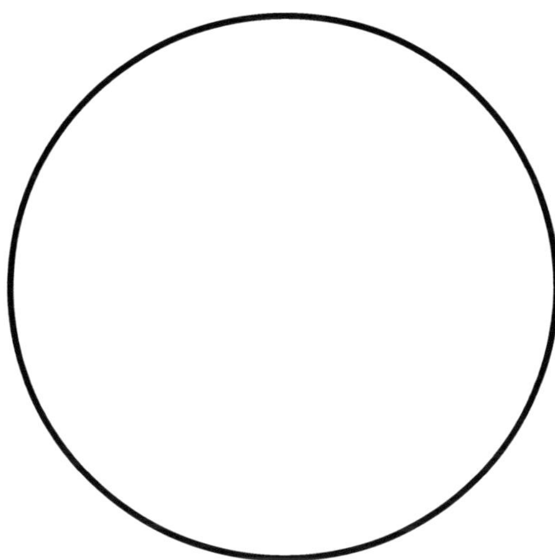

3.  Tendon, 100× or 400× = **dense regular connective tissue/fibrous.**

    Why is this called regular?

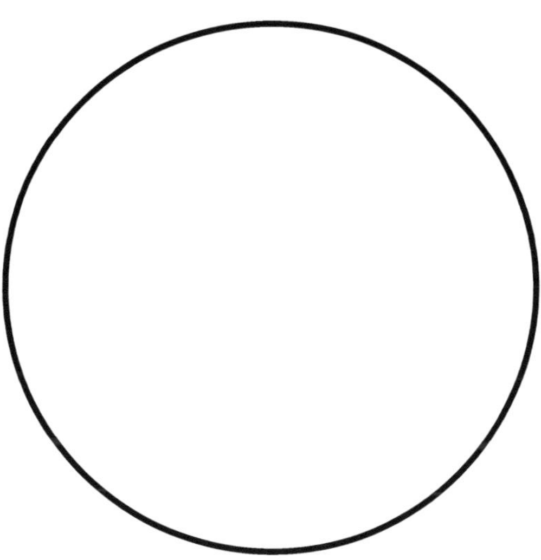

4. Dermis of Human Thick or Thin Skin slide, 100× = **dense irregular connective tissue.**

   Why is this called irregular?

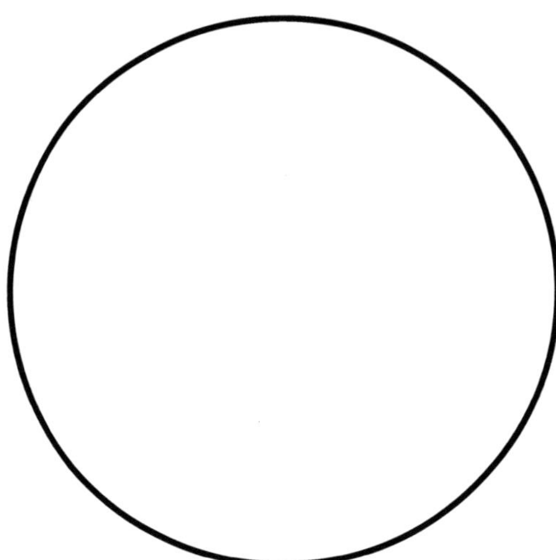

5. Trachea, 100 and 400× = **hyaline cartilage** (this is seen where the "eyeballs or cat eyes" are), and the matrix is in pale pink or purple stain.

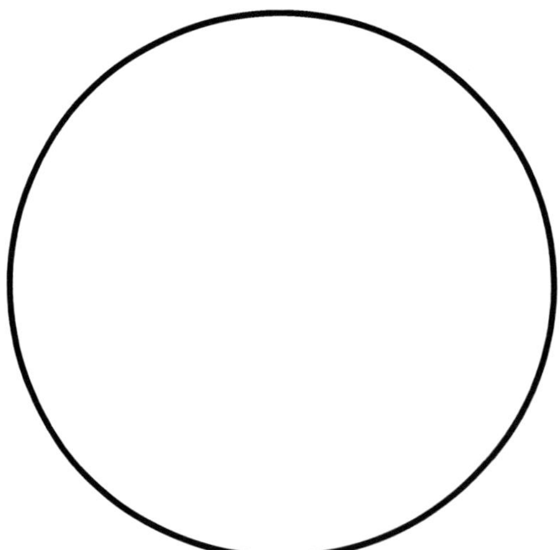

**6.** Blood smear, 400× = **human blood** connective tissue.

Why is human blood considered as connective tissue?

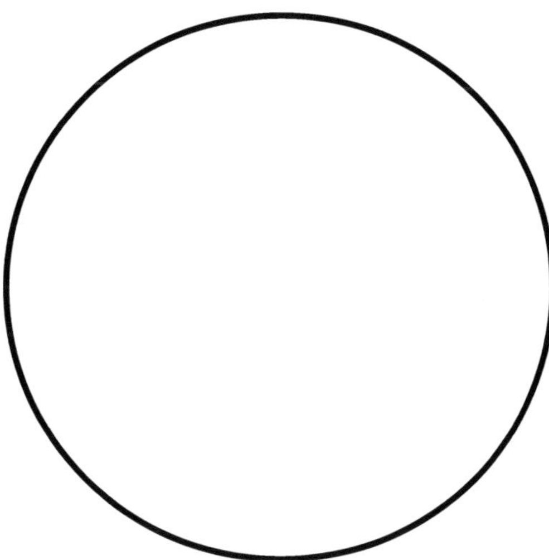

**7.** Observe **compact bone,** 100× and **cardiac (heart) intercalated disc** slide, 400× if they are available.

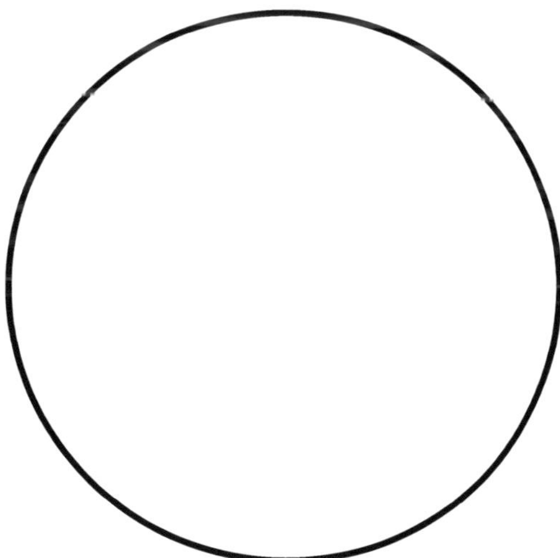

*We will cover muscle and nervous tissues later.*

## POST LAB REVIEW: TISSUES

1. Name the **primary tissue** type that is described (epithelial, connective, muscle, or nervous) for each.

   a. Tissue contains more extracellular matrix than cells.

   b. Cells contain processes that generate and receive electrical signals.

   c. Cells shorten and cause movement.

   d. Cells are close together and attached to a basement membrane.

2. Name the type of **epithelial tissue** for each.

   a. Protects underlying tissue subject to abrasion. Thickest of the epithelial tissue.

   b. Lines the bladder and ureter and is able to be stretched.

   c. Lines nasal passages and trachea.

3. Name the **connective tissue** for each.

   a. Found in the tendon and packed with parallel bundles of collagen.

   b. Contains lipid storing cells.

   c. Found in the skin and packed with bundles of collagen fibers running in many different directions.

*Note:* Be sure to get your completed work checked off by a member of the lab staff and then keep this handout for your review.

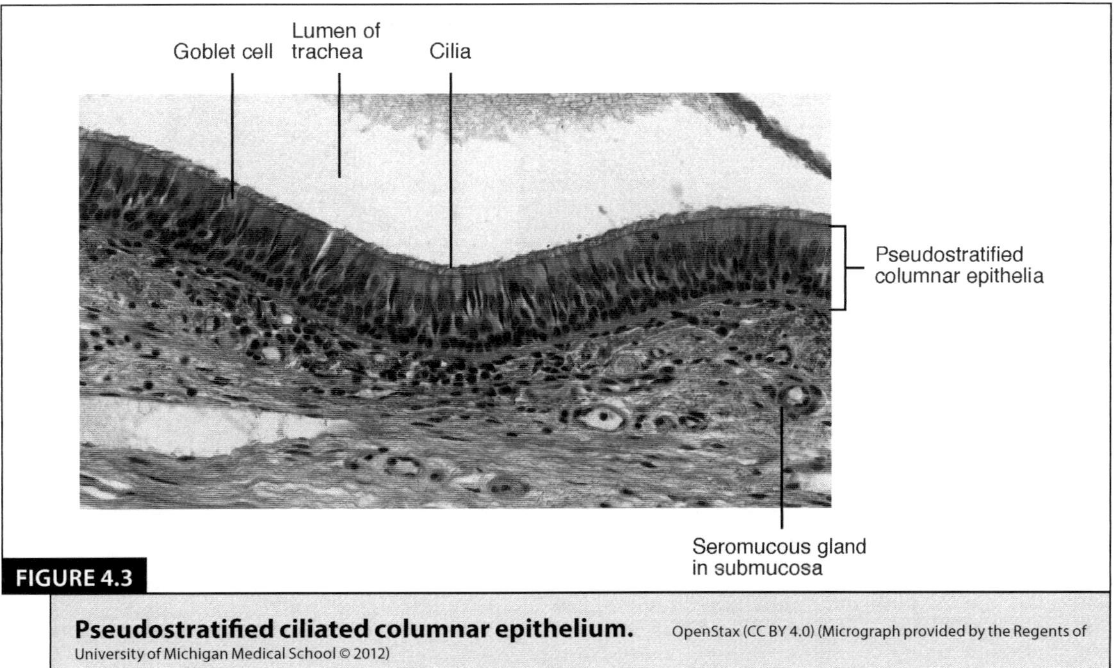


**FIGURE 4.3**

**Pseudostratified ciliated columnar epithelium.** OpenStax (CC BY 4.0) (Micrograph provided by the Regents of University of Michigan Medical School © 2012)

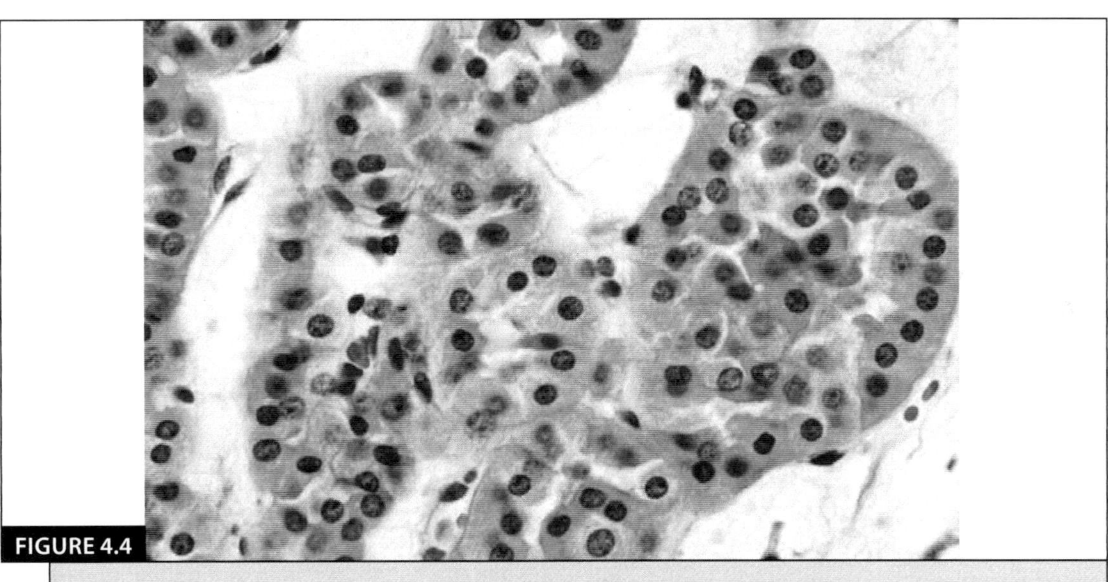

**FIGURE 4.4**

**Simple cuboidal epithelium of the kidney.**
No machine-readable author provided. KGH assumed (based on copyright claims). [CC BY-SA 3.0 (http://creativecommons.org/licenses/by-sa/3.0/)]

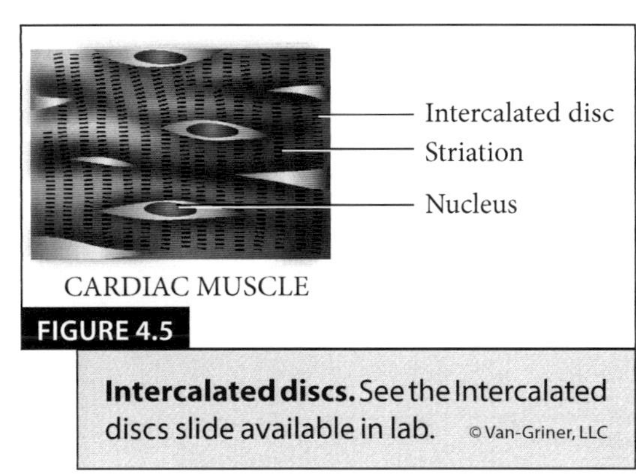


**FIGURE 4.5**

**Intercalated discs.** See the Intercalated discs slide available in lab. © Van-Griner, LLC

# 5

## INTEGUMENTARY SYSTEM
### PRE-LAB

Name: _______________________________   Section: ____________   Date: __________

## LEARNING OBJECTIVE

- Identify differences in thin and thick skin.

## INTRODUCTION

The integumentary system is the largest organ in the human body. Parts of the integumentary system include the skin, hair, nails, glands and nerve receptors. The integumentary system works to waterproof, cushion, and protect the body from infection, according to the **National Institutes of Health.** Sensory receptors, keratin, water, other proteins, lipids, and different minerals and chemicals are embedded in parts of the system. Several processes such as the immune system, skin coloration, and the excretion of sweat are correlated with parts of the integumentary system.

One of the steps in the first line of defense includes physical barriers that help the body combat infections. The *cutaneous layer* of the body (skin) is definitely one of the key parts. The skin tries to stop foreign invaders from entering the body. Many microorganisms try to enter the body daily. In this aspect, the integument is serving as the first line of defense for the immune system. In addition to preventing microbes from penetrating the skin , we sense touch, pressure, and vibration through nerve endings and receptors in the dermis and epidermis. By using receptors such as *mechanoreceptors,* the skin sends messages to the brain to respond to the change in environment.

A person's skin tone (color) is determined by the interaction of pigments. Along with UV radiation, *melanin* and *hemoglobin* are pigments that are shown in the skin and give humans the appearance of different and unique hues (eumelanin-rich pigmentation). UV radiation stimulates photo protective pigmentation rendering darker coloration. **The pigmentation actually protects the body.**

The integumentary system contains *melanocytes,* which are cells that produce melanin. The more melanin the darker the skin. Lighter complexions are due to hemoglobin circulation through connective tissue under skin that produces less melanin. It is important to mention that the types of cells that you have in your body are genetic. The ability to have functional melanocytes is dictated by your genetic make-up, which is passed down from generation to generation. An **example** is the condition known as *albinism,* which is an inherited genetic condition that reduces the amount of melanin pigment formed in the body. The condition leaves a person with decreased coloration in the skin, hair, and eyes.

Another task of the integumentary system is excretions. *Excretions* usually are byproducts of cellular metabolism that is unwanted or toxic to the body. The integumentary system houses glands called *exocrine glands* that aid in excretion. **Sweat glands including oil secreting glands and mucus glands are examples of glands in the integumentary system that release excretion.**

The skin is made up of two primary layers: the *epidermis* and the *dermis.* The underlying hypodermis (or subcutaneous layer) is an insulating, energy storage layer of adipose tissue. Epidermal layers include the Stratum Corneum, Stratum Lucidum (only in thick skin), Stratum Granulosum, Stratum Spinosum, and Stratum Basale (ba-sal-ee). The epidermis protects the underlying blood vessels, receptors, glands, etc. from damage and pathogens. The dermis has the superior papillary layer and the deeper reticular layer containing most of the functional parts of the skin.

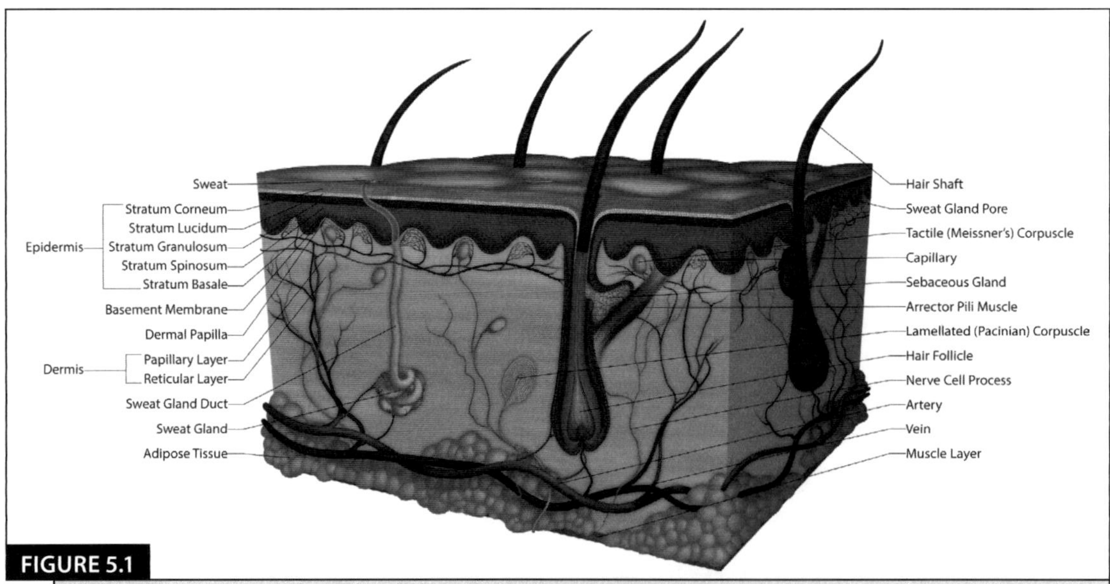


**FIGURE 5.1**

**Parts of the epidermis and the dermis: epidermal layers are the stratum corneum, stratum lucidum (only in thick skin), stratum granulosum, stratum spinosum, and stratum basale (ba-sal-ee).** The epidermis protects the underlying blood vessels, receptors, glands, etc. from damage and pathogens. The dermis has the superior papillary layer and the deeper reticular layer containing most of the functional parts of the skin. Adipose is under these two layers of the skin, and muscle is seen under that. (CC BY Brittany Crews created by c3bc via Forsyth Tech)

# PRE-LAB ACTIVITY 1

**Review and label** the skin model diagram in Figure 5.2.

Add lines to Figure 5.3 below and label the following parts: epidermis, the two layers of the dermis—papillary and reticular, hypodermis, Stratum Corneum, Stratum Lucidum (lighter layer seen here, but only in thick skin of palms and souls of feet), Stratum Granulosum, Stratum Spinosum, Stratum Basale (ba-sal-ee), and adipose tissue.

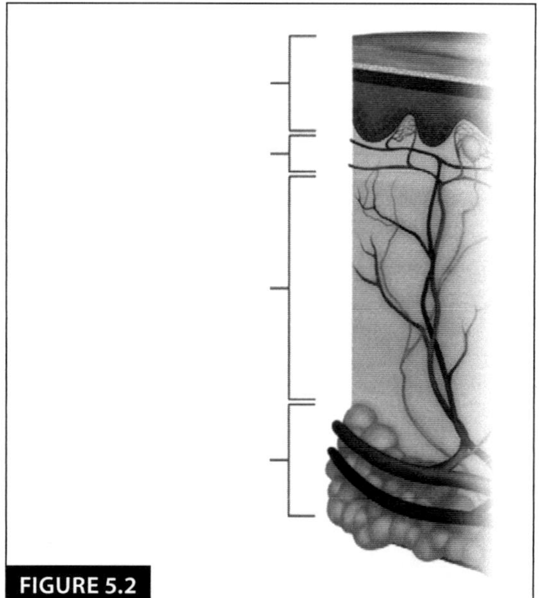

**FIGURE 5.2**

**Cross-section illustrating skin layers: a smaller cross-section with the layers of skin (epidermis, the two layers of the dermis- papillary and reticular, and hypodermis.** Label these on the diagram. (CC BY Brittany Crews created by c3bc via Forsyth Tech)

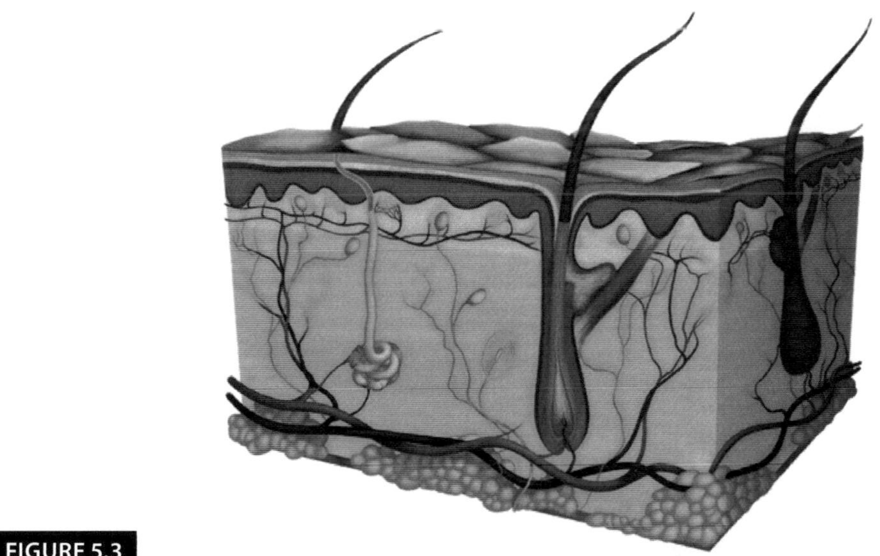

**FIGURE 5.3**

**Cross-sections illustrating skin layers: a cross-section of skin and many of its internal structures.** In this diagram you can tell that the epidermis is thin (shown in the darker colored layers at the top and only about 0.1 mm deep!), and the dermis contains most of the skin's functional parts. The hypodermis is shown beneath the dermis and is made of adipose tissue resembling groups of balls. (CC BY Brittany Crews created by c3bc via Forsyth Tech)

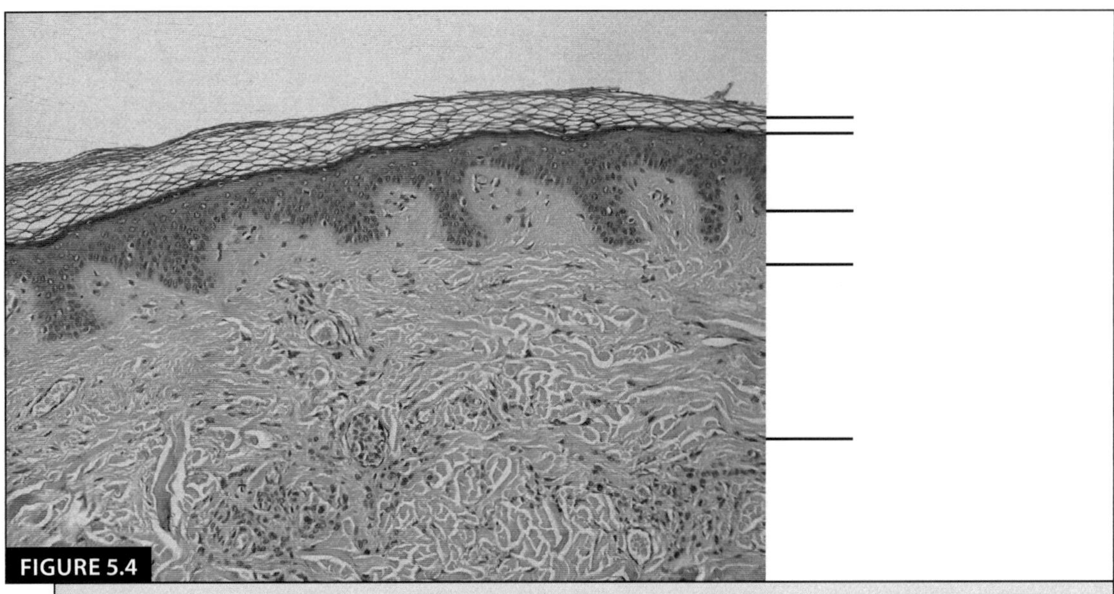

**FIGURE 5.4**

**Cross-sections of epidermal layers and dermal layers under light microscope.** From the diagrams above, can you label the parts of the skin micrograph here? This is thin skin, so the Stratum Lucidum is missing.                                                Kilbad [Public domain]

# PRE-LAB QUESTIONS—ANSWER THE FOLLOWING

1. What two layers make up the cutaneous layer?

    a. ______________________________________________________________

    b. ______________________________________________________________

2. When a person gets sunburned, what skin layer is destroyed? ____________________

3. Is sunburn a 1st degree, 2nd degree, or 3rd degree burn? ____________________

4. What are the effects of UV on the skin?




5. What layer of the epidermis has melanocytes embedded? ____________________

6. What layer of the epidermis goes through rapid mitosis? ____________________

7. What is another name for the hypodermis? ____________________

8. What are macrophages? ____________________

9. What glands in the skin are responsible for producing oil? ____________________

10. What glands release sweat? ____________________

# 5

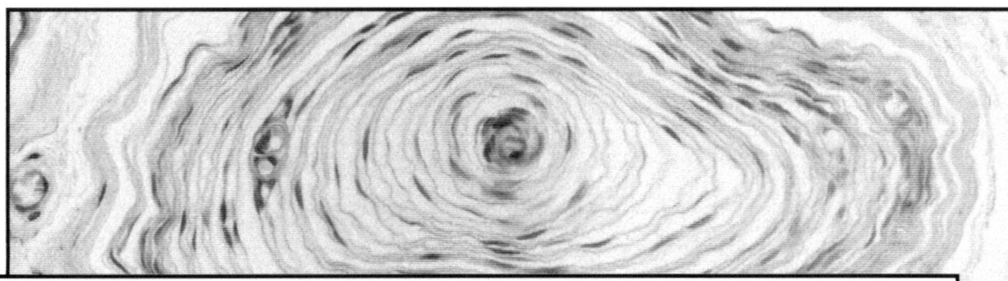

# INTEGUMENTARY SYSTEM
## IN-LAB ACTIVITIES

Name: _______________________     Section: __________     Date: _________

## PRE-LAB

Before going to lab, you must complete the following:

1. Read the **Pre-Lab** and answer all Pre-Lab questions.

*Note:* You will spend **1–2 hr or so** in lab at Forsyth Tech to complete the following activities. This amount of time allows you to complete the activities as well as work with a lab partner.

## ACTIVITY 1: HUMAN SKIN

### OBJECTIVE

- Identify differences in thin and thick skin.

### MATERIALS

- Magnifying glass
- Colored pencils

### PROCEDURE

1. Examine palm and back of your hand.

## OBSERVATIONS

1.  In the space provided, draw a diagram of a small area (3 cm × 3 cm) of the palm of your hand.

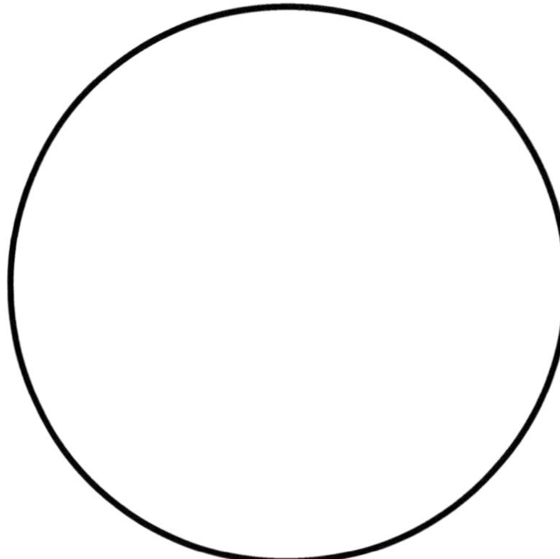

2.  In the space provided, draw a diagram of a small area (3 cm × 3 cm) of the back of your hand.

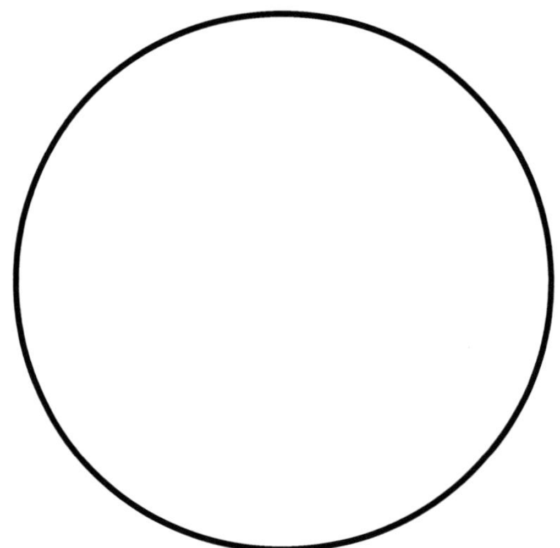

**3.** What is different in the patterns on the palm and on the back of the hand? What is different between the thicknesses of both sides of the hand? Compare and contrast in the table below.

| ANTERIOR HAND (PALM) | POSTERIOR HAND |
|---|---|
| | |
| | |
| | |
| | |

# ACTIVITY 2: SKIN NERVE RECEPTORS (ACCESSORY ORGANS OF THE SKIN)

## OBJECTIVE

- Examine three types of skin sensory receptors.

## MATERIALS

- Feather
- Tuning fork
- Skin models in lab

## PROCEDURE

The skin has several sensory structures that are called *sensory receptors.* These receptors respond to stimuli (changes in the environment) and send information about the change to the brain. **Skin receptors detect touch, pressure, vibration, temperature, and pain.**

- Receptors in hair follicles sense when a hair changes position.
- Tactile corpuscles (Meissner's corpuscles) are a type of mechanoreceptor in the skin responsible for sensitivity to light touch.
- Lamellar corpuscles (Pacinian corpuscles) are a type mechanoreceptor cell in the skin responsible for sensitivity to vibration and pressure.

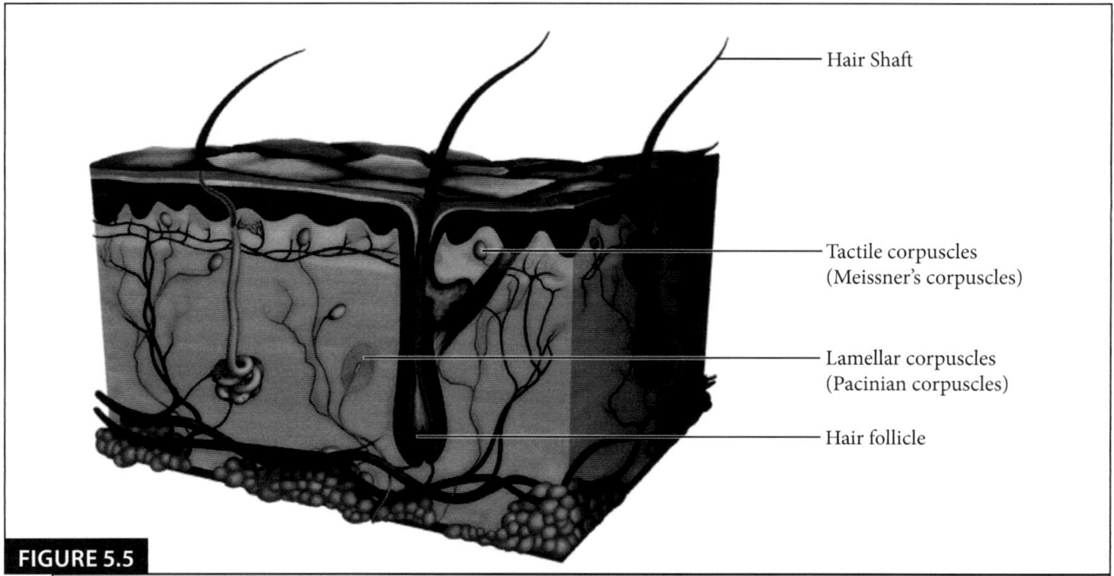


**FIGURE 5.5**

**Cross section of skin.** Labels include the hair shaft, tactile corpuscles, lamellar corpuscles, and the hair follicle.  CC BY Brittany Crews created by c3bc via Forsyth Tech

1. **Hair and Hair root**

   *Note:* **Use the skin models in lab to find these structures. These models are used on our lab tests. See the master list of anatomical terms for the integumentary system at the end of this lab.**

   Draw a diagram of **your hair (hair root still attached)** as seen under the microscope in the drawing box below. (Yes, pull out a piece of your own hair with the hair root.) **If available in lab, observe the Human Scalp or Human Hair slide.**

<br><br>

Diagram of hair root seen under microscope in lab.

2.  If slide is available in lab, **observe the *Lamellar corpuscles*** (Pacinian Corpuscles), which will appear as a group of concentric circles ("layers" – lamella in the corpuscle).

    Observe the layers. Notice the location of these sensory receptors. What is the function of the corpuscle?

3.  **Sensory 1**
    a.  Blow in the palm of your hand using a clockwise circular motion for 3 seconds.
    b.  Repeat the procedure using the posterior portion of your hand this time.
    c.  Finally compare and contrast the two in the table below.

| ANTERIOR HAND (PALM) | POSTERIOR HAND |
|---|---|
|  |  |
|  |  |

4.  **Sensory 2**
    a.  Using a feather this time, stroke a 3-inch line down the center of the palm.
    b.  Repeat the same process on the posterior side of your hand.
    c.  Compare and contrast these in the table below:

| ANTERIOR HAND (PALM) | POSTERIOR HAND |
|---|---|
|  |  |
|  |  |

5. **Sensory 3**

   a. Using a tuning fork, strike the fork causing it to vibrate.

   b. Place the base of the fork in the center of the palm.

   c. Repeat procedure on the posterior side of the hand.

   d. Compare and contrast your observations in the table below:

| ANTERIOR HAND (PALM) | POSTERIOR HAND |
|---|---|
|  |  |
|  |  |

# DISCUSSION

With a lab partner discuss the following questions and respond here in your own words.

1. On your hand, where does the skin appear to be the thickest?

2. Why does the skin vary in thickness?

3. What two main skin receptors are activated when you blow on your hand?

4. Which side of the hand is more sensitive to the wind created by blowing?

5. Why is one side of the hand more sensitive to the wind created by blowing?

6. What main skin receptor is activated when the tuning fork is placed on your hand?

7. Which side of the hand is more sensitive to the tuning fork?

8. Why is one side of the hand more sensitive to the tuning fork?

## PROTECTION FROM UV

Ultraviolet radiation is part of the electromagnetic (light) spectrum from the sun. There are short wavelengths and long wavelengths. These wavelengths are classified as UVA, UVB, or UVC. At 320–400 nanometers, UVA is the longest. UVB and UVC are shorter. The majority of UVC is absorbed by the ozone layer and does not reach the earth, leaving humans to deal with UVA and UVB. Both types of waves can damage the skin. Premature skin aging, eye damage (including cataracts), and skin cancers are some of the ways the sun damages the body. In addition, an increased amount of radiation can suppress the immune system making it harder to fight off pathogens and other maladies. Melanin is a protective pigment in skin which blocks UV radiation. UV radiation targets the DNA of cells causing mutations. These mutations can lead to cancer.

## ANATOMY SKIN LIST

In addition to the above, while you are in lab, look at the skin models and slides and be able to identify the following. Model keys should be available for your use in the lab.

### SKIN

Identify the following structures on models, diagrams, and slides:

1. Epidermis
   a. Stratum corneum
   b. Stratum lucidum (only in thick skin)
   c. Stratum granulosum
   d. Stratum germinativum
      i. Stratum spinosum
      ii. Stratum basale (main germinal layer)

2. Dermis
   a. Papillary layer (contains dermal papillae and areolar tissue)
   b. Reticular layer

3. Hypodermis (subcutaneous layer) (superficial fascia)
   a. Adipose connective tissue

### SKIN ACCESSORY STRUCTURES

4. Hair
   a. Hair shaft
   b. Root of hair
   c. Hair follicle
   d. Hair papilla [with associated blood vessels and nerves]
   e. Arrector pili muscle

5. Exocrine glands
   a. Sudoriferous glands (sweat glands)
      i. Eccrine sudoriferous glands (white on the models)
      ii. Apocrine sudoriferous glands (larger and only found in axillary and inguinal areas)
   b. Sebaceous glands

6. Sensory nerve receptors (see more in senses)

   a. Pacinian corpuscles

   b. Free nerve endings

   c. Meissner's corpuscles

7. Melanocytes (use slide of pigmented skin)

*Note:* Be sure to get your completed work checked off by a member of the lab staff and then keep this handout for your review.

Label the other layers of the skin or cutaneous membrane. Is this thick or thin skin?

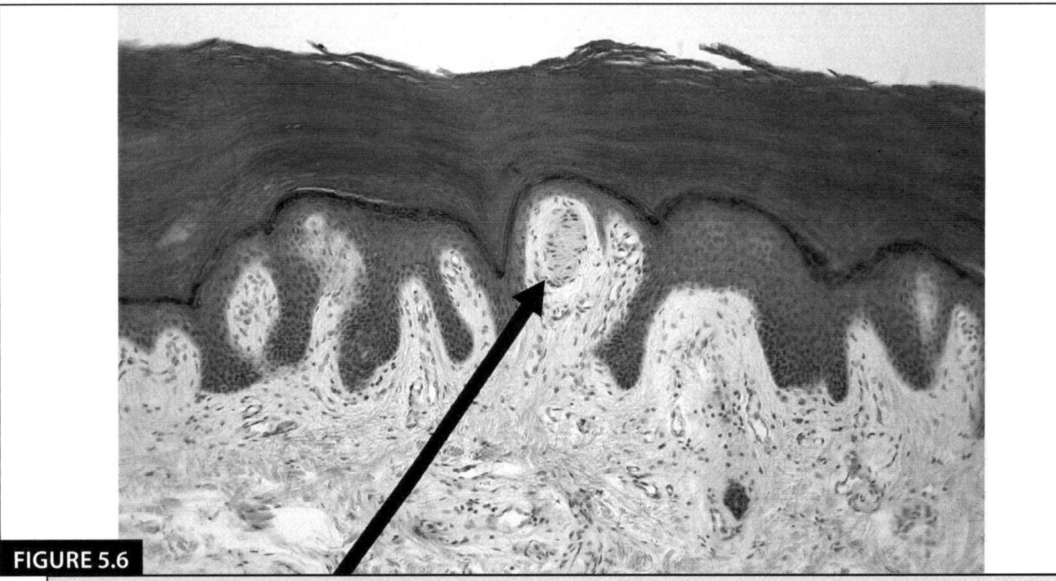

**FIGURE 5.6**

**Micrograph of human skin showing Meissner's corpuscle in the papillary layer of the dermis.** Wbensmith [CC BY 3.0 (https://creativecommons.org/licenses/by/3.0)]

# 6

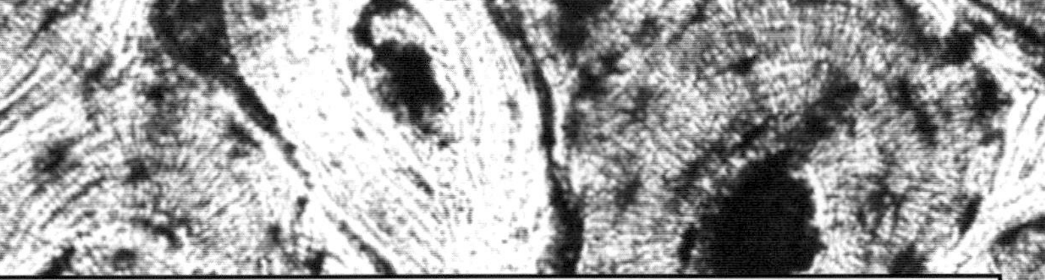

# THE SKELETAL SYSTEM—BONE TISSUE
## PRE-LAB

Name: _____________________ Section: _________ Date: _________

## LEARNING OBJECTIVES

- Be able to describe the structure, function, and common disorders affecting the skeletal system.
- Explain the anatomy of the bone and its functions.

## INTRODUCTION

Bones are living tissue with blood vessels and various other tissues that are constantly being remodeled. Bones are composed of several different tissues working together. Osseous tissue contains both compact and spongy bone, which are supported by dense fibrous connective tissue and epithelium. Cartilage, nervous, and adipose tissue make up the rest. The bone framework of fibers and minerals, their cartilages, and ligaments and tendons constitute the skeletal system.

Like other connective tissues, **bone,** or **osseous tissue** (OS-ē-us), contains specialized cells surrounded by an extracellular matrix that contains fibers and various mineral salts. These salt crystals form when calcium phosphate and calcium carbonate combine to create hydroxyapatite (hī-drok-sē-AP-a-tīt), which incorporates other inorganic salts like magnesium hydroxide, fluoride, and sulfate as it crystallizes, or calcifies, on the collagen fibers (so these fibers act as a scaffold for the crystals to build bone). The hydroxyapatite crystals give bones their hardness and strength, while the collagen fibers give them flexibility so that they are not brittle. Although bone cells compose a small amount of the bone volume, they are crucial to the function of bones. Four types of cells are found within bone tissue: osteoblasts, osteocytes, osteogenic cells, and osteoclasts.

The **osteoblast** is the bone cell responsible for building new bone and is found in the growing portions of bone, including the periosteum and endosteum. Osteoblasts, which do not divide through mitosis, synthesize collagen and secrete the matrix and calcium salts. As the secreted matrix surrounding the osteoblast calcifies, the osteoblast becomes trapped within it; as a result, it changes in structure and becomes an **osteocyte,** the primary cell of mature bone and the most common type of bone cell. Each osteocyte is located in a space called a **lacuna** and is surrounded by bone tissue (see these on the bone tissue model in lab and on the slides in lab). Osteocytes maintain the mineral concentration of the matrix via the secretion of enzymes. They can communicate with each other and receive nutrients via long cytoplasmic processes that extend through **canaliculi** (singular = canaliculus), little, canal-like channels within the bone matrix.

Osteoblasts and osteocytes are incapable of mitosis, so how are they replenished when old ones die? The answer lies in the properties of another category of bone cells—the **osteogenic cell.** These osteogenic cells are stem cells with high mitotic activity, and they are the only bone cells that divide. Immature osteogenic cells are found in the deep layers of the periosteum (find the periosteum on the model in lab) and the marrow. They differentiate and develop into osteoblasts.

The dynamic nature of bone means that new tissue is constantly formed, and old, injured, or unnecessary bone is dissolved for repair or for calcium release. The cell responsible for bone resorption (meaning the breakdown or cutting away of bone) is the **osteoclast.** They are found on bone surfaces, are multinucleated, and originate from monocytes and macrophages, two types of white blood cells, not from osteogenic cells. Osteoclasts are continually breaking down old bone while osteoblasts are continually forming new bone. The continuous balance between osteoblasts building up bone and osteoclasts cutting it away is responsible for the constant but subtle reshaping of bone so that over about 10 years you have a new skeleton.

*Study Tip:* Use the word "builder" to remember the function of Osteoblasts and "cutter" to remember that Osteoclasts cut away at the bone.

**Preview the textbook content in Odigia, Lumen, or another source for Bone Tissue using the images there to see the parts of compact and spongy bone before attending your lab this week.**

# KEY WORDS

- Long bone
- Diaphysis
- Epiphysis
- Bone marrow

- Osseous tissue
- Cartilage tissue
- Compact bone
- Spongy bone

1.  How is the skeleton like the framework of your house?

    **a.**

    **b.**

2.  What are the other functions of the skeletal system?

    **a.**

    **b.**

    **c.**

    **d.**

    **e.**

## PRE-LAB REVIEW QUESTIONS

1.  Bone tissue is made up of four types of bones cells: osteogenic (aka: osteoprogreni-tor) cells, osteoblasts, _______________________, and _______________________.

2.  Which of the bone cells cut away or remodel the bone? _______________________

3.  What is the primary structure or functional unit of compact bone?


4.  Bones can be classified by shape: long, short, irregular, sesamoid, or flat. Find examples of these in the lab.


5.  The skeleton has two main divisions: _______________________ and _______________________

6.  Of the skeleton, which part can you say has the most midline support?


7.  What major areas of the body does the Axial skeleton include?


8.  What major areas does the appendicular skeleton include?

# 6

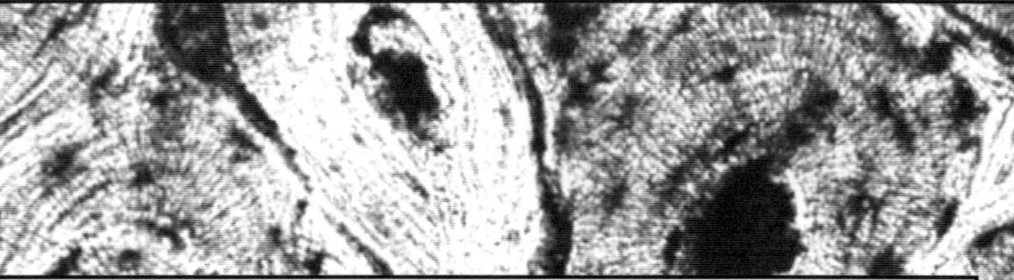

# THE SKELETAL SYSTEM—BONE TISSUE
## IN-LAB ACTIVITIES

Name: _________________________  Section: __________  Date: _________

## LEARNING OBJECTIVES

- Identify the shapes and anatomical features of a bone.
- Define and list examples of bone markings.
- Describe the histology of bone tissue.
- Compare and contrast compact and spongy bone.
- Identify the structures that compose compact and spongy bone.
- Identify the accessory parts of bone.

## PRE-LAB

Before going to lab, you must complete the following:

1. Read the **Pre-Lab** and answer all Pre-Lab questions.

*Note:* You will spend **1–1 hr and 30 min** or so in lab at Forsyth Tech to complete the following activities (along with beginning the Axial skeleton study today). This amount of time allows you to complete the activities by using the skeletal models, bones, and other models as well as working with a lab partner.

## ACTIVITY 1

**Bone Shapes:** The 206 bones that compose the adult skeleton are divided into five categories based on their shapes (see table below). Each categorical shape of bone has a distinct function based on that shape.

View the different bone shapes in lab, and fill out the following table:

| BONE CLASSIFICATION | EXAMPLES IN THE LAB |
|---|---|
| Long | |
| Short | |
| Flat | |
| Irregular | |
| Sesamoid/Round | |

## ACTIVITY 2: PARTS OF THE LONG BONE

If available in lab, observe the **longitudinal cut femur bone** (or beef bone). Observe the following parts of the long bone: diaphysis, epiphysis (proximal and distal), medullary (marrow) cavity, compact, and spongy bones *(note where these are located in the bone).*

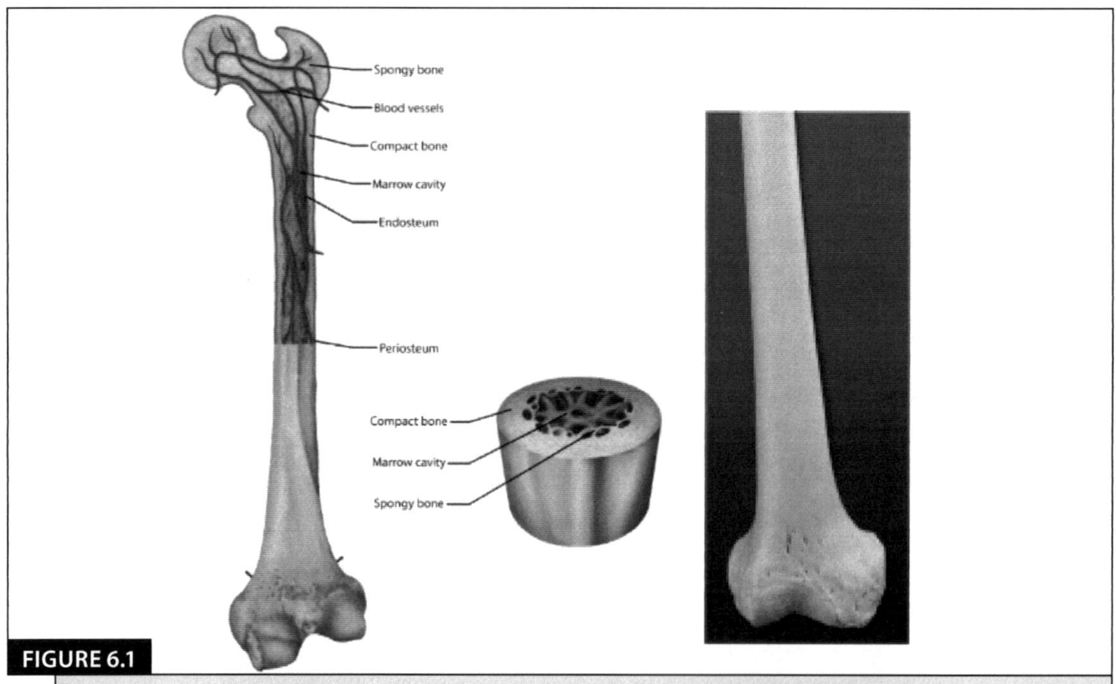


**FIGURE 6.1**

**Long bone (femur) cut longitudinally to show the marrow cavity.** Other labels include spongy bone, compact bone, and the periosteum membrane on the outside of bone. Also, a cross section cut of bone showing the marrow cavity lined with spongy (cancellous) bone and surrounded by compact bone. Left: CC BY Brittany Clark created by c3bc via Forsyth Tech Right: © Jeff Spencer

**Review** these with a lab partner and **quiz** yourselves until you are sure you understand the anatomy of the long bones and each part's function.

## ACTIVITY 3: BONE HISTOLOGY

1.  See the **Compact Bone Model** in your lab (it will look similar to Figure 6.2 located on the next page).

**Identify** the parts labeled in Figure 6.2 on the **model** in lab.

Let's look at the histology of the bone and cartilage involved in joints between bones.

2.  Use the **slides** in lab (if available) to **view under the microscope** the list below, and **DRAW** a basic sketch of each one in the space provided below its name.

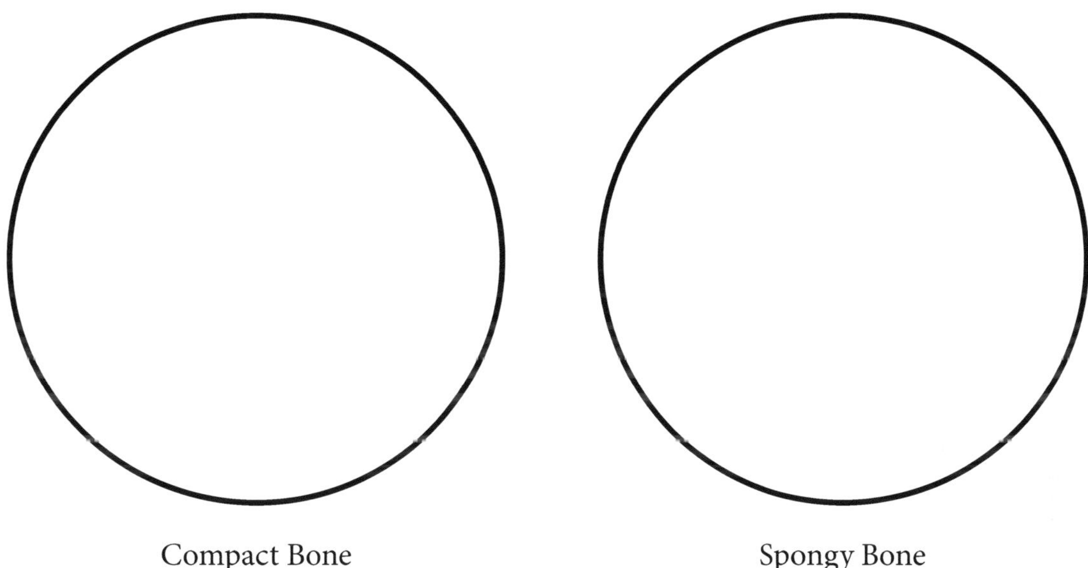

Compact Bone                    Spongy Bone

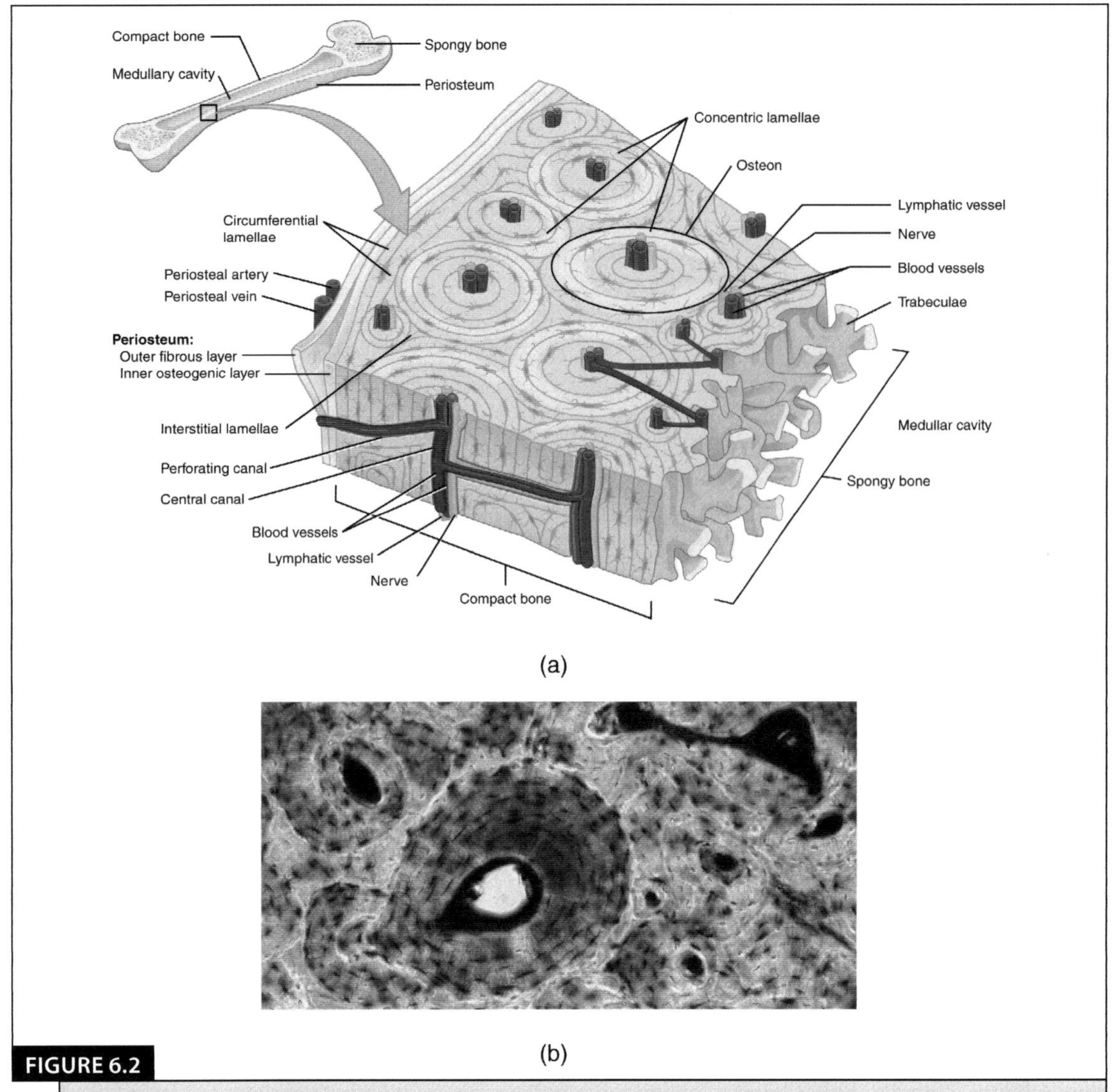


**FIGURE 6.2**

**In this micrograph and artist sketch of the osteon, you can clearly see the concentric lamellae and central canals.** Also, note the spongy bone of the sketch in (a). LM × 40

OpenStax College [CC BY 3.0 (https://creativecommons.org/licenses/by/3.0)]

**3.** Compare and contrast the similarities and differences between compact and spongy bone in the table below. How do they look? Is the matrix different? Does the spongy bone have osteons as seen in the compact bone? What other differences do you notice? List them below.

**Similarities and differences between compact and spongy bone observed under the microscope.**

TABLE 6.1

| COMPACT BONE | SPONGY (CANCELLOUS) BONE |
| --- | --- |
|  |  |
|  |  |
|  |  |
|  |  |
|  |  |
|  |  |
|  |  |

## ACCESSORY PARTS OF BONE: CARTILAGE— ELASTIC, FIBROCARTILAGE, HYALINE

Where do you find these tissues in the body? Notice how each tissue appears to have "eyeballs" that are the lacuna holding the chondrocytes of the tissues. Whenever you notice the "eyeballs," you know you have cartilage connective tissue.

- Use the slides in lab and find these under the microscope (Hyaline = trachea slide).
- **Sketch** and **label** them below in a way that will help you recall and ID them later.

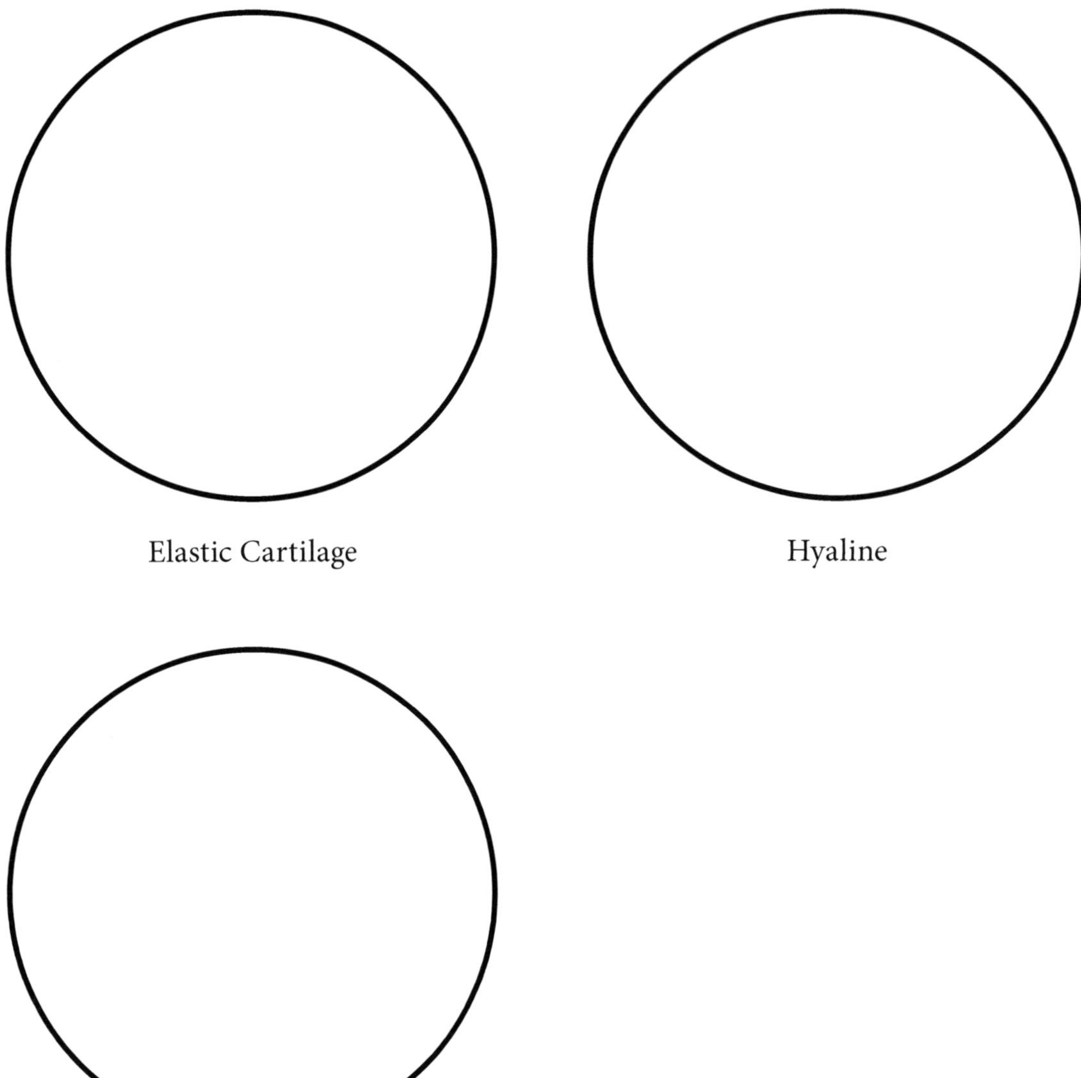

Elastic Cartilage                         Hyaline

Fibrocartilage

4. In a group of 2–3, use the large paper provided to **sketch** the basic skeletal system and **an example** of each area of cartilage (intervertebral discs, sutures, etc.). Label the major bones and list (in a legend format along the side) where you find these three cartilage tissues in the body.

5. Next, **compare** your sketches (your skeletal masterpiece) with others from the lab room groups for locations (not artistic ability!), or you can quiz your lab partners.

6. Label where you find these cartilages you saw earlier. Where is cartilage on the tibia bone? Where do you find fibrocartilage? Hyaline?

   a. Elastic cartilage—

      i. Nose

      ii. ?

   b. Hyaline cartilage—

      i. Trachea

      ii. ?

   c. Fibrocartilage—

      i.

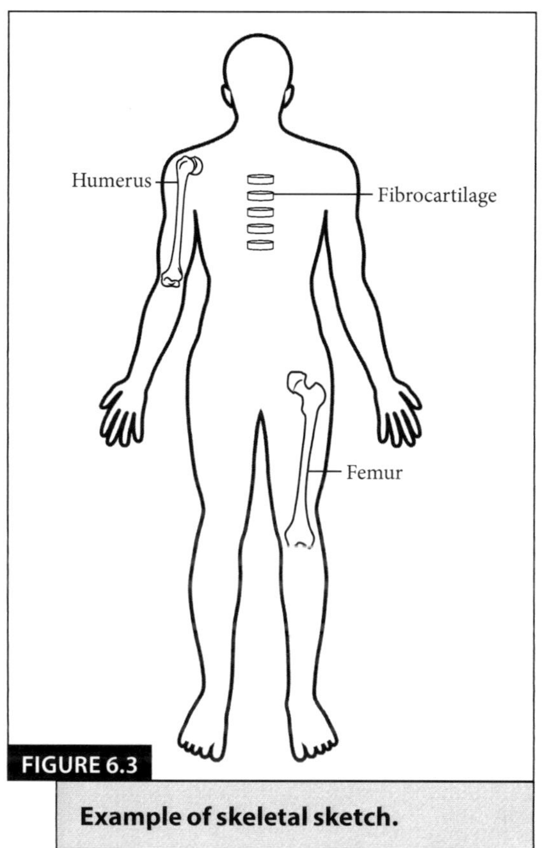


**FIGURE 6.3**

**Example of skeletal sketch.**

Alternatively, use the available box of bones to put together a full skeleton. Use sticky notes to ID where the cartilages are in the skeleton, and take a picture of your masterpiece to study! *Send the picture to your instructor for verification and extra lab points. List all the group members' names.

**Keep going until you are familiar with the locations of cartilages!**

*Note:* Be sure to get your completed work checked off by a member of the lab staff and then keep this handout for your review.

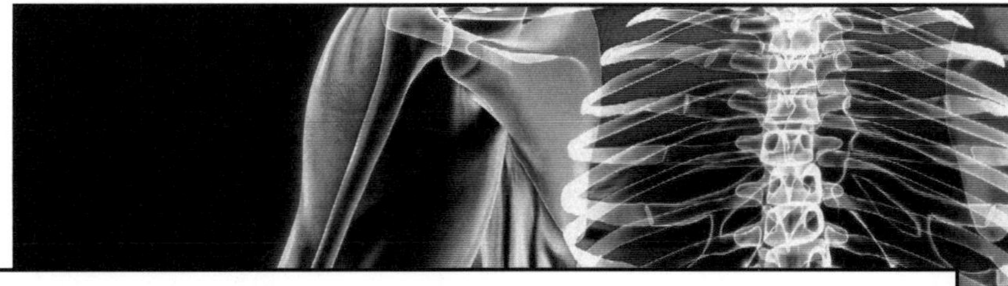

# THE SKELETAL
# SYSTEM—AXIAL SKELETON
## PRE-LAB

Name: _________________________     Section: __________     Date: _________

## LEARNING OBJECTIVES

- Be able to describe the structure and function of the skeletal system.
- Examine the axial and appendicular skeleton.

## PRE-LAB ACTIVITY

**View pictures and skeleton in lab.** See your lab's **skeletal list of bones and bone markings** that you are responsible for learning. You will review these during your lab time.

1. What specific parts of the body do the **axial** skeleton bones protect?

   a.

   b.

   c.

   d.

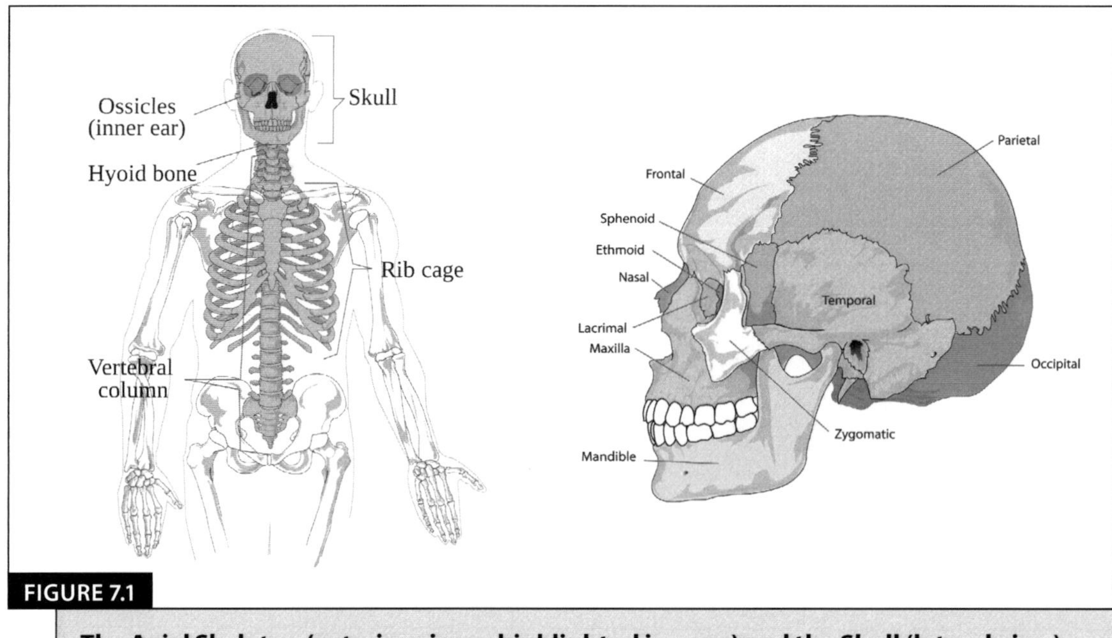


**FIGURE 7.1**

**The Axial Skeleton (anterior view—highlighted in gray ) and the Skull (lateral view).**
LadyofHats [Public domain]

2. The sternum is made of three parts:

_________________________________,

_________________________________,

and ______________________________.

3. In the table below fill in the type of vertebral bone that matches the description.

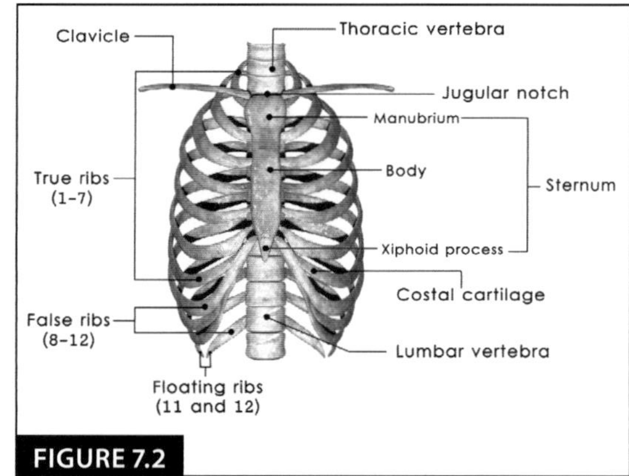


**FIGURE 7.2**

**View of the thoracic cage.** Labeled are the true ribs, false ribs, clavicle, and sternum. http://devindevon.wikispaces.com/sonny's+page

| DESCRIPTION OF VERTEBRA | TYPE OF VERTEBRA |
|---|---|
| Have foramina in the transverse processes | |
| Have a round-shaped vertebral foramen | |
| Has an odontoid process called the ________ | |
| Does not have a body or spinous process | |
| Three to five fused vertebrae | |

## CRANIUM

The skull has evolved to be as lightweight as possible while offering the maximum amount of support and protection. In order to be light, the skull is made of flat and irregular bones and has hollow spaces such as the *sinuses*. It offers protection to the brain, eyeballs, inner ears, and nasal passages.

The human skull is divided into two sections—the cranium and the face. In most people, the cranium has eight bones and the face has 14 bones. Often, the ossicles of the ear and the hyoid bone count as part of the skull, giving the normal human skull 29 bones. (Note that variations in bones are not necessarily abnormal.)

**Observe the skulls in lab, pictures, and these videos to learn and understand the functions of these bones and sutures.**

**4.** List 4 main sutures of the skull:

__________________________________________,

__________________________________________,

__________________________________________,

and __________________________________________

**Watch this Cranial Bones video before attending lab and while in the lab to find these bones and markings:**

- https://youtu.be/NRZvr8tUEbI

## BONES OF THE CRANIUM

The calvaria, or the top hemisphere of the cranium, includes flat bones: the superior part of the frontal bone, the parietal bones, and the superior part of the occipital bone.

The base of the cranium consists of the ethmoid, sphenoid, temporal, and occipital bones. There are three distinct regions in the base of the cranium, seen from above with the calvaria removed. These are called *fossae* and are named by their position with respect to the body:

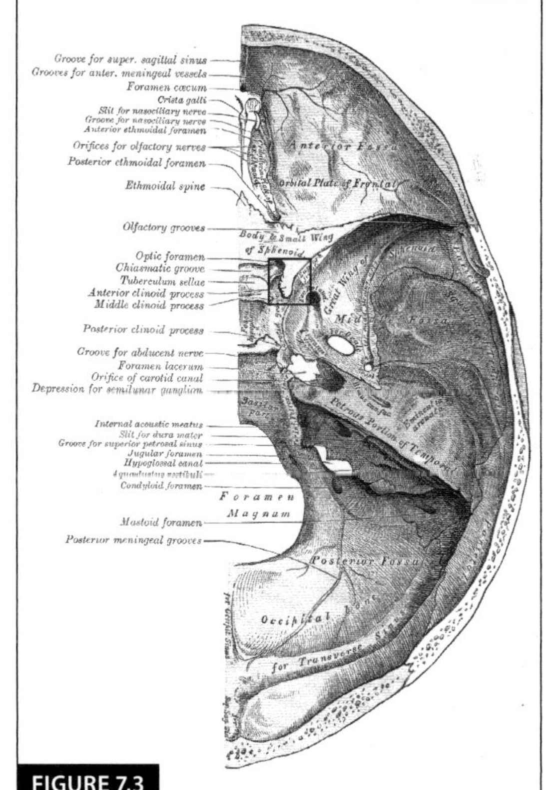

**FIGURE 7.3**

**Base of the skull.** Upper surface. (Anterior cranial fossa is the area above the middle cranial fossa. The posterior cranial fossa is shown below the middle cranial fossa.) Public Domain https://en.wikipedia.org/wiki/Anterior_clinoid_process

anterior, middle, and posterior fossae. The base of the cranium has several holes called *foramina* (singular, *foramen*) which allow blood vessels and nerves to enter and leave the cranium.

## FORAMEN AND CANALS

The largest, most obvious foramen is located at the base of the occipital bone and is called the *foramen magnum*. The spinal cord passes through this large opening and connects to the brain at the *medulla oblongata*. Other openings include the foramen ovale, the foramen rotunda, and the jugular foramen. You can see the carotid canals (foramen) just anterior to the jugular foramen on the inferior side of the skull models in lab. If you have a real skull, feed some fishing line through the opening to see how it forms a canal.

**Watch this Facial Bones video before going to your lab time.**

- https://youtu.be/Zu4XWkblsG0

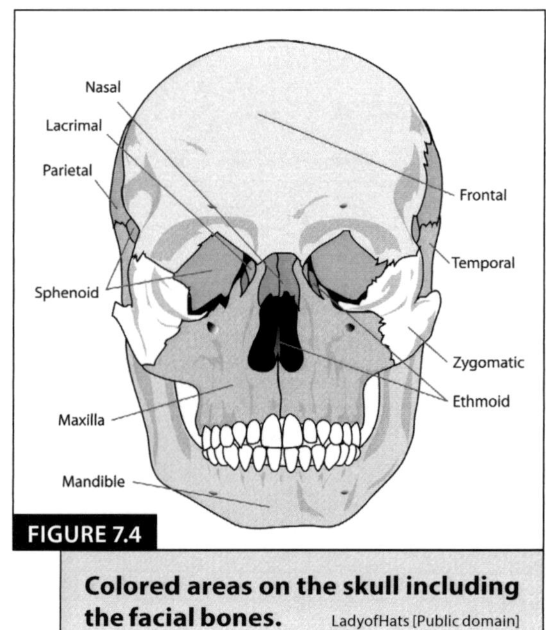


**FIGURE 7.4**

**Colored areas on the skull including the facial bones.** LadyofHats [Public domain]

In lab, you will review bone tissue and view slides of compact and spongy bone. In addition, you will use the skeletons and skulls in lab to observe and learn the bones of the axial skeleton.

## PRE-LAB REVIEW QUESTIONS

1. Classify the following bones based upon their shape:

   a. Maxillary bone _______________________________________________

   b. Parietal bone _______________________________________________

   c. Radius _______________________________________________

   d. Carpal bones _______________________________________________

2. The _______________________________ suture separates the frontal bone from the parietal bone.

3. The paranasal sinuses include _______________________, _______________________ air cells, _______________________, and the _______________________. Two of these can be found on the sagittal head model if available and the rest on a real skull.

4. What is the function of the sinuses?

5. List the bones that form the eye. There are actually seven (7), but list at least five. You will find these on the skulls in lab.

   a. _________________________________________________

   b. _________________________________________________

   c. _________________________________________________

   d. _________________________________________________

   e. _________________________________________________

   f. _________________________________________________

6. The functional unit of compact bone is the _________________________________________________.

**Take this to lab along with your bone list.**

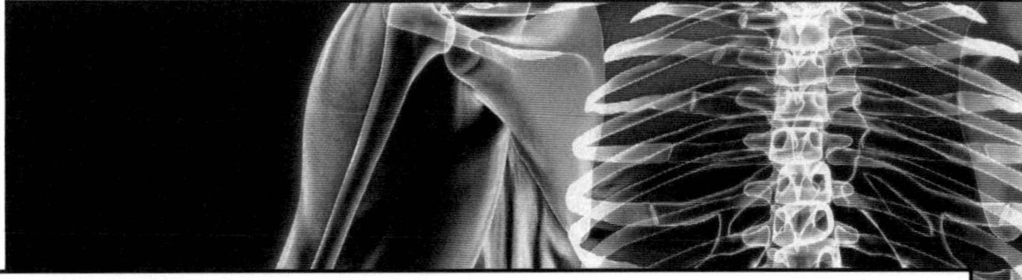

# THE SKELETAL SYSTEM—AXIAL SKELETON
## IN-LAB ACTIVITIES

Name: ___________________________   Section: ___________   Date: __________

## LEARNING OBJECTIVES

- Review the bone tissue model and bone shapes.
- Identify the parts of the long bone.
- Identify the required individual axial bones on the skull and thoracic cavity.

## PRE-LAB

Before going to lab, you must complete the following:

1. Read the **Pre-Lab** and answer all Pre-Lab questions.
2. Bring Pre-Lab with you to the lab time.

*Note:* You will spend **2–2 hr and 30 min** in lab at Forsyth Tech to complete the following activities (along with bone tissue). This amount of time allows you to complete the activities by using the skeletal models and bones and review other models while working with a lab partner. View the videos to help you with the names in the skull, etc. Then in lab find these structures on the skull and skeletal models.

## SKELETAL IDENTIFICATION

**Tissue, Shapes, and Skull/Axial—can be done with the Bone Tissue Lab; the rest of the Axial list can be done with the Appendicular Skeleton. Check off each as you master them, not just observe them, but master them!**

1.  Identify the following on the **compact osseous connective tissue model:**
    a.  Osteon (Haversian system)
    b.  Osteonic canal (Haversian canal) (central canal)
    c.  Lamellae
    d.  Canaliculi
    e.  Lacunae (may contain osteocytes)
    f.  Matrix
    g.  Volkmann's canals (perforating canals)
    h.  Periosteum
    i.  Sharpey's fibers (perforating fibers)

2.  Identify specific bones according to the following **shapes:**
    a.  Long
    b.  Short
    c.  Flat
    d.  Irregular
    e.  Round (sesamoid)

3.  Identify the following **structures on a long bone:**
    a.  Proximal and distal epiphyses
    b.  Diaphysis
    c.  Medullary cavity
    d.  Epiphyseal line
    e.  Cancellous osseous connective tissue (spongy bone)
    f.  Compact osseous connective tissue

4.  Identify the following **specific bones and bone markings.** View the teaching video on Blackboard/Odigia for help with these anatomical names and locations.

## AXIAL SKELETON

1. Cranium
   a. Frontal bone
   b. Parietal bone
   c. Temporal bone
      i. Mastoid process
      ii. External auditory (acoustic) meatus
      iii. Internal auditory (acoustic) meatus
      iv. Zygomatic process (component of zygomatic arch)
      v. Zygomatic arch (composed of zygomatic process and the temporal process of zygomatic bone)
      vi. Mandibular fossa
   d. Occipital bone
      i. Foramen magnum
      ii. Occipital condyles
   e. Sphenoid bone
      i. Greater wings
      ii. Sella turcica
      iii. Optic canals (optic foramina)
   f. Ethmoid bone
      i. Middle nasal conchae (turbinates)
      ii. Crista galli
      iii. Cribriform plates
         1. Olfactory foramina (cribriform foramina)
   g. Sutures
      i. Sagittal suture
      ii. Coronal suture
      iii. Lambdoid suture
      iv. Squamous suture

2. Facial bones
   a. Maxillae (maxillary bones)
   b. Palatine bones
   c. Zygomatic bones
      i. Temporal process (component of zygomatic arch)
   d. Lacrimal bones
   e. Nasal bones
   f. Vomer
   g. Inferior nasal conchae (turbinates)
   h. Mandible
      i. Body
      ii. Mental foramen
      iii. Mandibular ramus
      iv. Mandibular condyle
   i. Sinuses
      i. Frontal sinuses
      ii. Maxillary sinuses
      iii. Sphenoidal sinuses
      iv. Ethmoidal sinuses (ethmoidal air cells)

3. Hyoid bone

**SSL Staff and students: The list above can be completed during and after the Bone Tissue lab. The list below can be completed during the Appendicular Skeleton lab *if* more time is needed. See your lab schedule for these lab weeks.**

4. Vertebral column—be able to tell the difference between cervical, thoracic, lumbar, and sacral vertebral levels (easiest to count: 7 cervical, 12 thoracic, 5 lumbar, 1 sacrum of 5 fused vertebrae, 1 coccygeal bone/coccyx)

   a. Typical vertebra
      i. Body (vertebral body)
      ii. Transverse process
      iii. Vertebral foramen
      iv. Spinous process
   b. Cervical vertebrae
      i. Transverse foramen (in all 7 bones)
      ii. Atlas ( first cervical vertebra)
         1. NO spinous process or vertebral body
      iii. Axis ( second cervical vertebra )
         1. Dens (odontoid process)
   c. Thoracic vertebrae
      i. Intervertebral foramen
      ii. Round-shaped vertebral foramen
   d. Lumbar vertebrae
      i. Intervertebral foramen
      ii. Triangular-shaped vertebral foramen
      iii. Transverse processes are longer
   e. Sacrum
      i. Sacral body
      ii. Sacral foramina
   f. Coccyx
   g. Intervertebral disc

5. Thoracic cage

   a. Ribs (costal bones)
      i. Vertebrosternal ribs (rib #s 1–7) = true ribs
      ii. Vertebrochondral ribs (rib #s 8–10) = false ribs
      iii. Vertebral ribs (floating ribs #s 11–12) = false ribs
   b. Costal cartilage
   c. Sternum
      i. Manubrium
      ii. Body (gladiolus)
      iii. Xiphoid process

*Note:* Be sure to get your completed work checked off by a member of the lab staff and then keep this handout for your review.

Find each of the bones listed on the 3-D bones in the lab. This lab test will consist of these bones, especially the skull.

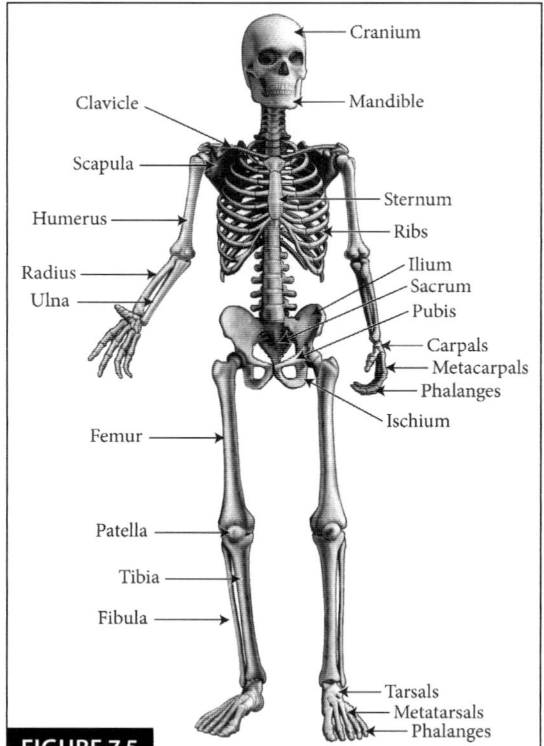
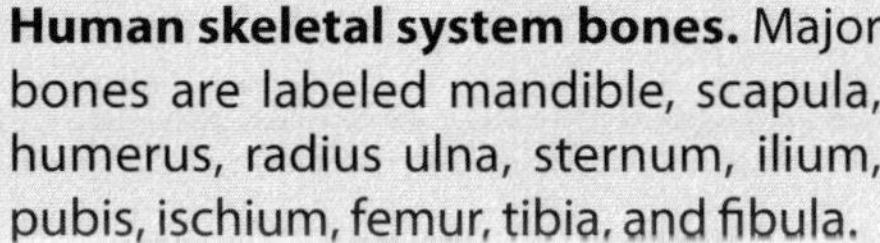


**FIGURE 7.5**

**Human skeletal system bones.** Major bones are labeled mandible, scapula, humerus, radius ulna, sternum, ilium, pubis, ischium, femur, tibia, and fibula.

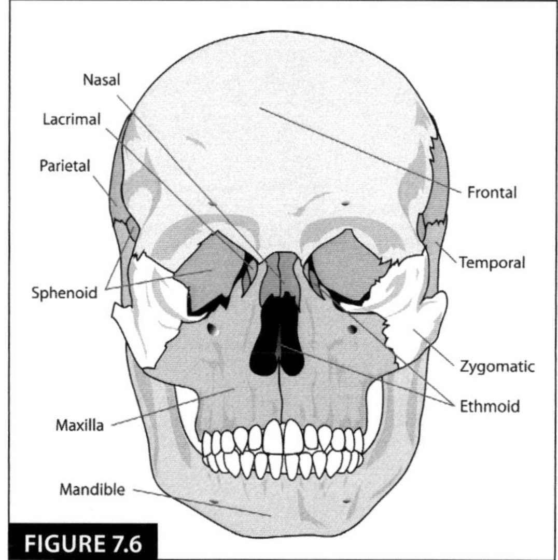


**FIGURE 7.6**

**Human skull, anterior view.** Major bones labeled: frontal, parietal, temporal, sphenoid, nasal, lacrimal, zygomatic, maxilla, mandible, as well as several bone markings.

LadyofHats [Public domain]

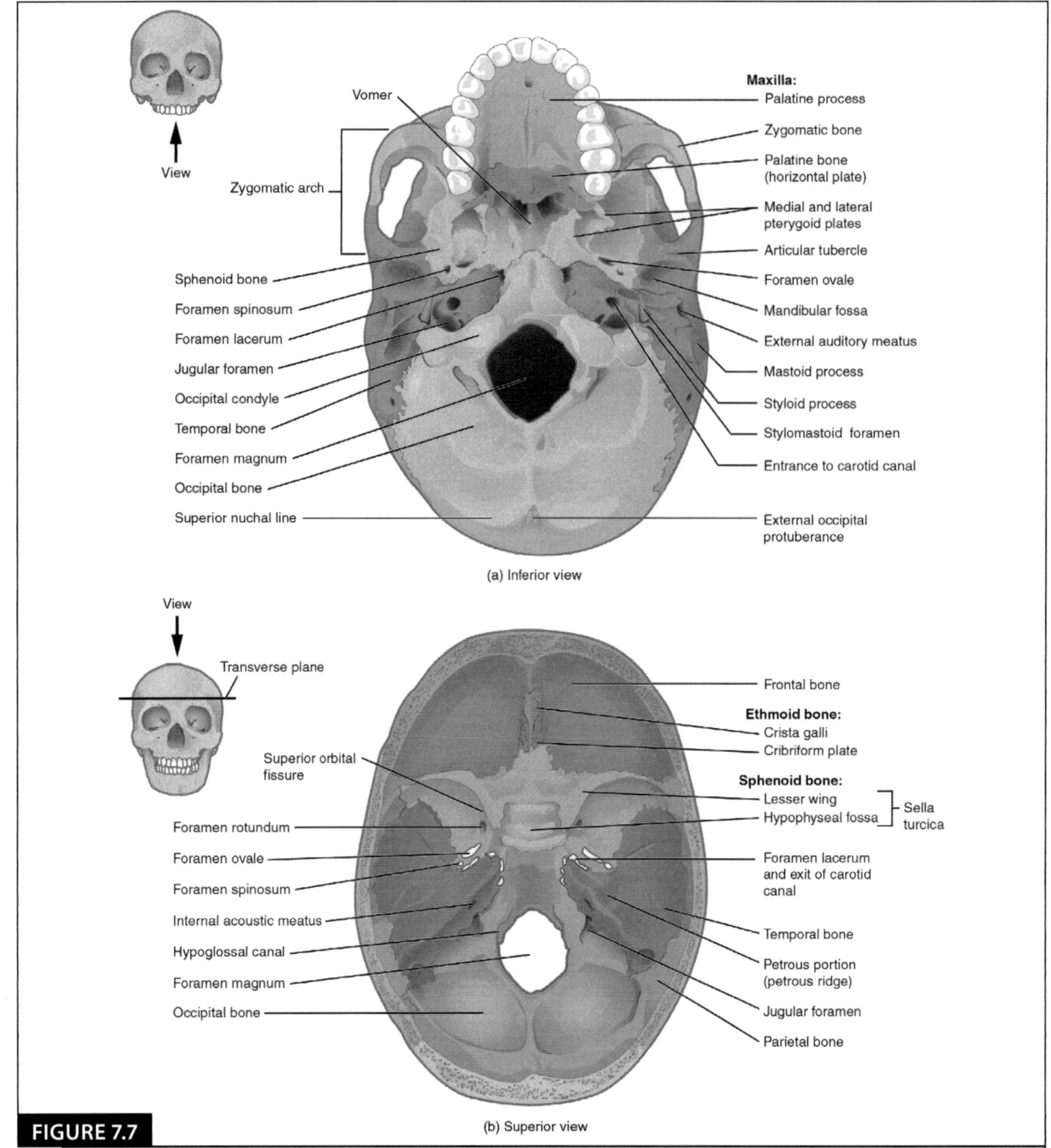


**FIGURE 7.7**

**Human skull—inferior and superior views.** Bones labeled include frontal bone, ethmoid bone, sphenoid bone, temporal bone, parietal bone, occipital bone, maxilla bone, and their bone markings.

OpenStax College [CC BY 3.0 (https://creativecommons.org/licenses/by/3.0)]

## IMPORTANT LAB QUESTIONS FOR LAB TEST STUDY

1. What gland does the sphenoid bone hold?

2. What receptors extend through the ethmoid bone?

3. What special sense organ is housed in the temporal bone (within the petrous portion)?

4. What openings allow the jugular veins to exit the skull?

5. What structure is above the foramen magnum? What structure is below the foramen magnum?

6. What single cervical bone articulates with the occipital condyles?

7. What is the purpose of the internal auditory meatus? (What is a meatus?)

8. What two bones makeup the zygomatic arch (seen laterally on the inferior view)?

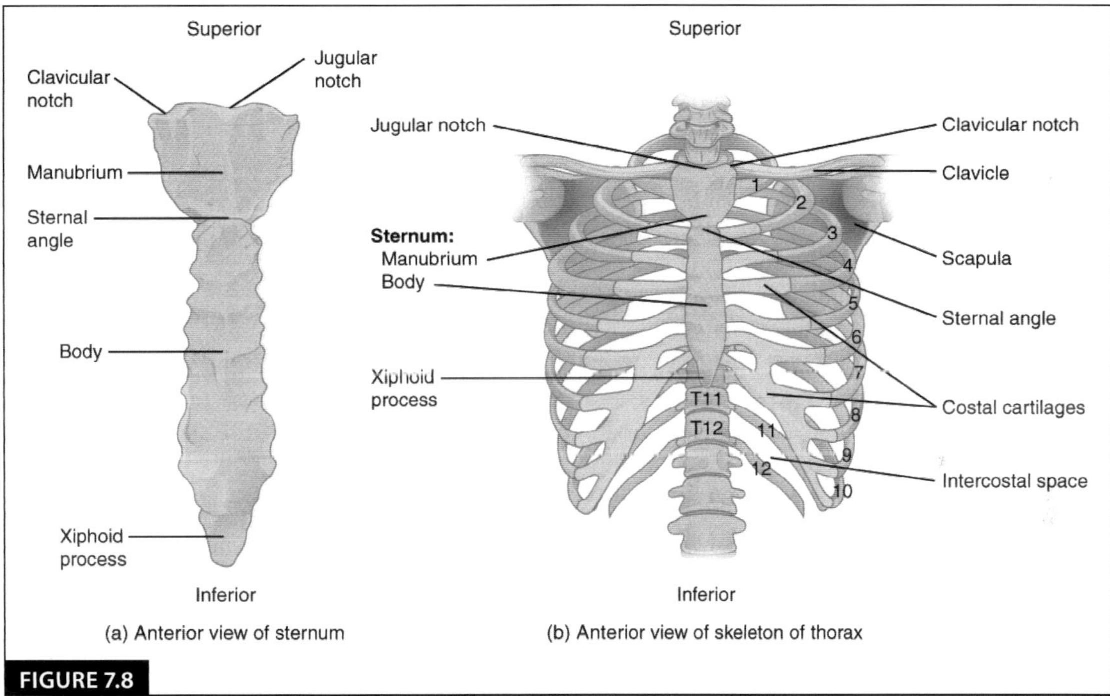


**FIGURE 7.8**

**Anterior views of the sternum and thorax.** Sternum: manubrium, body, xiphoid process.

OpenStax College [CC BY 3.0 (https://creativecommons.org/licenses/by/3.0)]

# 8

## APPENDICULAR SKELETON
### PRE-LAB

Name: _________________________  Section: __________  Date: _________

## LEARNING OBJECTIVES

- Identify the major bones of the appendicular skeleton and the significant bone markings on each.
- Describe the purpose of the appendicular skeleton and its bone markings.

## INTRODUCTION

Of the 206 bones in the human skeleton, the appendicular skeleton comprises 126. Functionally, this skeleton provides locomotion of the axial skeleton and manipulation of objects by the upper limbs. Thus, the bones of the lower limbs are adapted for weight-bearing support and stability as well as for body locomotion via walking or running. In contrast, our upper limbs are not required for these functions. Instead, our upper limbs are highly mobile and can be utilized for a wide variety of activities. The large range of upper limb movements, coupled with the ability to easily manipulate objects with our hands and opposable thumbs (picking up a seashell, building a scaffold, etc.), has allowed humans to construct and manipulate the modern world. Keep in mind, though, that the large range of motion (ROM) of the upper limb also creates many more opportunities for injury. Look at the joints of the upper and lower limbs. Learn these bones, and familiarize yourself with how the two joints differ with respect to their boney connections.

Most of the appendicular skeleton forms during development from cartilage by the process of endochondral ossification. (The flat bones of the axial skeleton form mostly from membranous ossification.)

The appendicular skeleton is divided into six major regions:

1. Pectoral girdles (4 bones)—left and right clavicle (2) and scapula (2).

2. Arms and forearms (6 bones)—left and right humerus (2) (arm), ulna (2) and radius (2) (forearm).

3. Hands (54 bones)—left and right carpals (16) (wrist), metacarpals (10), proximal phalanges (10), middle phalanges (8) and distal phalanges (10).

4. Pelvis (2 bones)—left and right os coxa (hip bone) (2, ossa coxae).

5. Thighs and legs (8 bones)—left and right femur (2) (thigh), patella (2) (knee), tibia (2) and fibula (2) (leg).

6. Feet and ankles (52 bones)—left and right tarsals (14) (ankle), metatarsals (10), proximal phalanges (10), middle phalanges (8) and distal phalanges (10).

It is important to realize that through anatomical variation it is common for the skeleton to have many extra bones (sutural bones in the skull, cervical ribs, lumbar ribs, and even extra lumbar vertebrae).

The appendicular skeleton of 126 bones and the axial skeleton of 80 bones together form the complete skeleton of 206 bones in the human body. Unlike the axial skeleton, the appendicular skeleton is unfused. The connections between the bones of the appendicular skeleton form joints, or articulations, of which there are many types. This allows for a much greater range of motion (ROM). ROM will be discussed with the articulations.

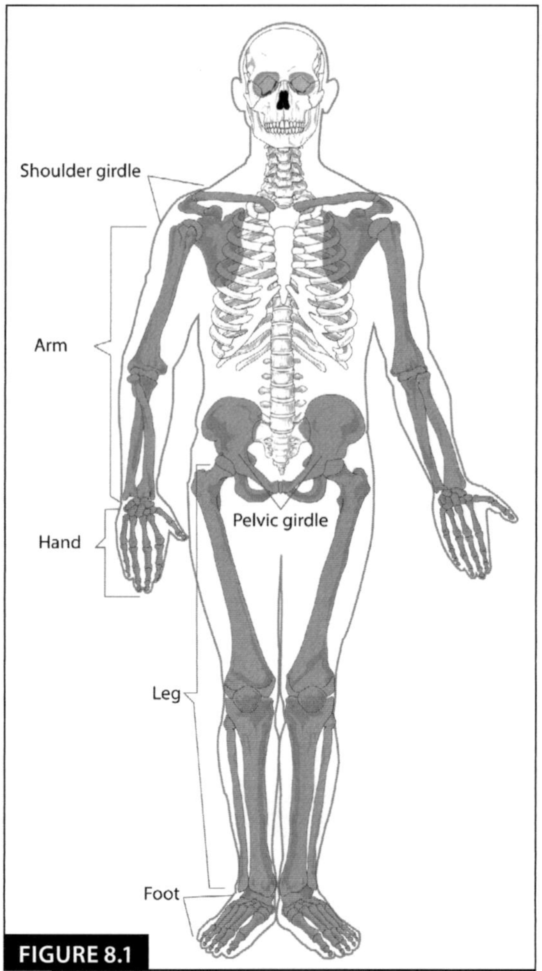

**FIGURE 8.1**

**Human skeleton with the appendicular areas and girdles highlighted.** LadyofHats [Public domain]

(Figure and Intro above adapted from https://courses.lumenlearning.com/ap1/chapter/introduction-to-the-appendicular-skeleton/ and https://en.wikipedia.org/wiki/Appendicular_skeleton)

## PRE-LAB QUESTIONS: FILL-IN-THE-BLANK

1. The two bones that form the pectoral girdle are the ________________________ and the ________________________.

2. The three fused bones that form the pelvic girdle are the ________________________, the ________________________, and the ________________________.

3. Another name for the pelvic bones is the ________________________.

4. The two bones of the forearm are the ________________________ and the ________________________.

5. The bones of the wrist are termed the ________________________ bones. The bones of the palm of the hand are termed the ________________________ bones.

6. An identifying ridge on the anterior surface of the humerus that is used for attachment of a major muscle of the shoulder is the ________________________ tuberosity.

7. The bones that form the ankle are termed the ________________________ bones. The bones of the sole of the foot are termed the ________________________ bones.

8. The thumb of the hand and the hallux (big toe) of the foot have which types of phalanges? ________________________ and ________________________

# 8

# APPENDICULAR SKELETON
## IN-LAB ACTIVITIES

Name: _______________________     Section: __________     Date: _________

## LEARNING OBJECTIVES

- Review the bone tissue model and bone shapes.
- Identify the parts of the long bone.
- Identify the required individual appendicular bones on the skeleton and bones in lab.

## PRE-LAB

Before going to lab, you must complete the following:

1. Read the **Pre-Lab** and answer all Pre-Lab questions.
2. Bring Pre-Lab with you to the lab time.

*Note:* You will spend **2 hr–2 hr and 30 min** in lab at Forsyth Tech to learn and review the axial bones, the compact bone model, and the following list of bones. This amount of time allows you to complete the activities by using the skeletal models and bones and review other models while working with a lab partner. (Add or subtract from the list as your instructor decides.)

## SKELETAL IDENTIFICATION—(APPENDICULAR)

Check off each as you and a lab partner master these, not just observe them, but master them!

## ACTIVITY 1

Identify the following structures on a long (femur) bone:

1. Proximal and distal epiphyses

2. Diaphysis

3. Medullary cavity

4. Epiphyseal line

5. Cancellous osseous connective tissue (spongy bone)

6. Compact osseous connective tissue

## ACTIVITY 2

Identify the following specific bones and bone markings:

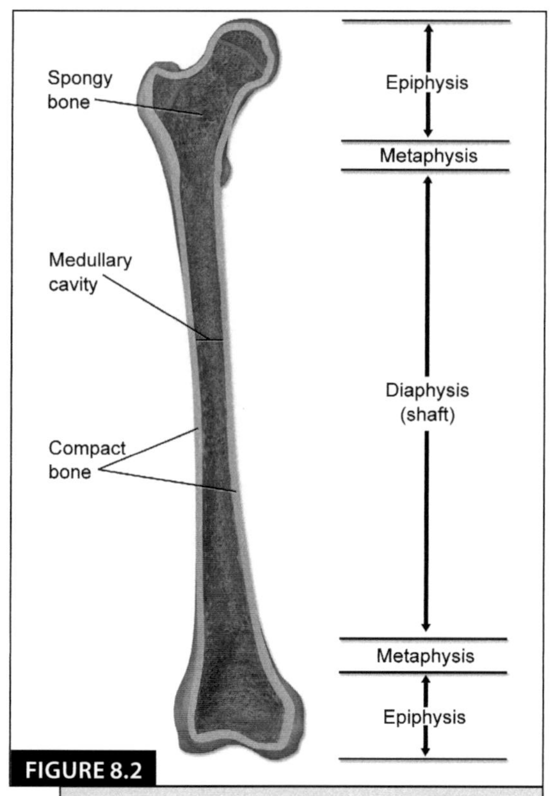


**FIGURE 8.2**

Blausen.com staff (2014). "Medical gallery of Blausen Medical 2014". WikiJournal of Medicine 1 (2). DOI:10.15347/wjm/2014.010. ISSN 2002-4436. [CC BY 3.0 (https://creativecommons.org/licenses/by/3.0)]

### APPENDICULAR SKELETON

1. Pectoral girdle

   a. Clavicle

   b. Scapula

      i. Acromion process (acromion)

      ii. Spine (scapular spine)

      iii. Glenoid cavity (glenoid fossa)

      iv. Coracoid process

      v. Supraspinous fossa

      vi. Infraspinous fossa

2. Upper limb (arm)

   a. Humerus

      i. Head

      ii. Deltoid tuberosity

      iii. Olecranon fossa

      iv. Condyle

         1. Capitulum

         2. Trochlea

      v. Lateral and medial epicondyles

      vi. Greater and lesser tubercles

**b.** Ulna

  **i.** Olecranon process (olecranon)

  **ii.** Semilunar (trochlear) notch

**c.** Radius

  **i.** Head of radius

  **ii.** Radial tuberosity

**d.** Carpal bones [8]

**e.** Metacarpal bones [I–V]

**f.** Phalanges [14] [proximal middle distal]

**3.** Pelvic girdle (os coxa—sing.; ossa coxae—pl.)

  **a.** Ilium

    **i.** Iliac crest

    **ii.** Sacroiliac joint

    **iii.** Anterior superior iliac spine

  **b.** Ischium

    **i.** Ischial tuberosity

    **ii.** Ischial spine

  **c.** Pubis

    **i.** Symphysis pubis (pubic symphysis)

    **ii.** Pubic arch (pubic angle)

  **d.** Obturator foramen

  **e.** Acetabulum

  **f.** Pelvic brim

  **g.** True (lesser) pelvis

  **h.** False (greater) pelvis

  **i.** Greater sciatic notch

**4.** Lower limb

  **a.** Femur

    **i.** Head

    **ii.** Neck

    **iii.** Greater and lesser trochanters

    **iv.** Fovea capitis

    **v.** Lateral and medial condyles and epicondyles

  **b.** Patella

  **c.** Tibia

    **i.** Medial malleolus

    **ii.** Tibial tuberosity

  **d.** Fibula

    **i.** Lateral malleolus

    **ii.** Head

  **e.** Tarsal bones [7]

    **i.** Calcaneus

    **ii.** Talus

  **f.** Metatarsal bones [I–V]

  **g.** Phalanges [14]

    **i.** Proximal

    **ii.** Middle

    **iii.** Distal

## REVIEW

1. The head of the humerus articulates with the _______________________ of the scapula.

2. The head of the femur articulates with the _______________________ of the pelvis.

3. The _______________________ process of the ulna fits into the _______________________ fossa of the humerus when the arm is extended.

4. The patellar ligament attaches to the _______________________________ of the _______________________________ (bone).

5. The _______________________ and the _______________________ form the condyle of the distal end of the humerus.

6. The ankle is made from the ends of the tibia and fibula called the _______________________ _______________________ and the _______________________ _______________________.

**Continue your review in this format for other bones and their bone markings!**

*Note:* Be sure to get your completed work checked off by a member of the lab staff and then keep this handout for your review.

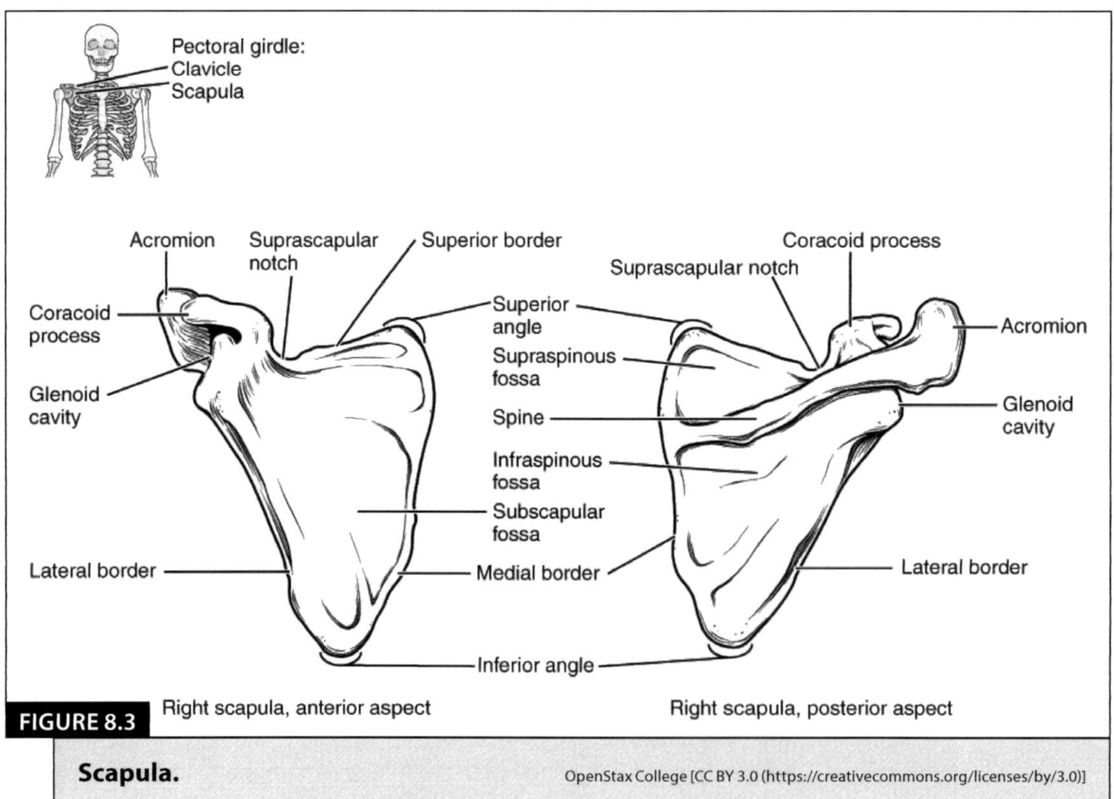


**FIGURE 8.3**

**Scapula.** OpenStax College [CC BY 3.0 (https://creativecommons.org/licenses/by/3.0)]

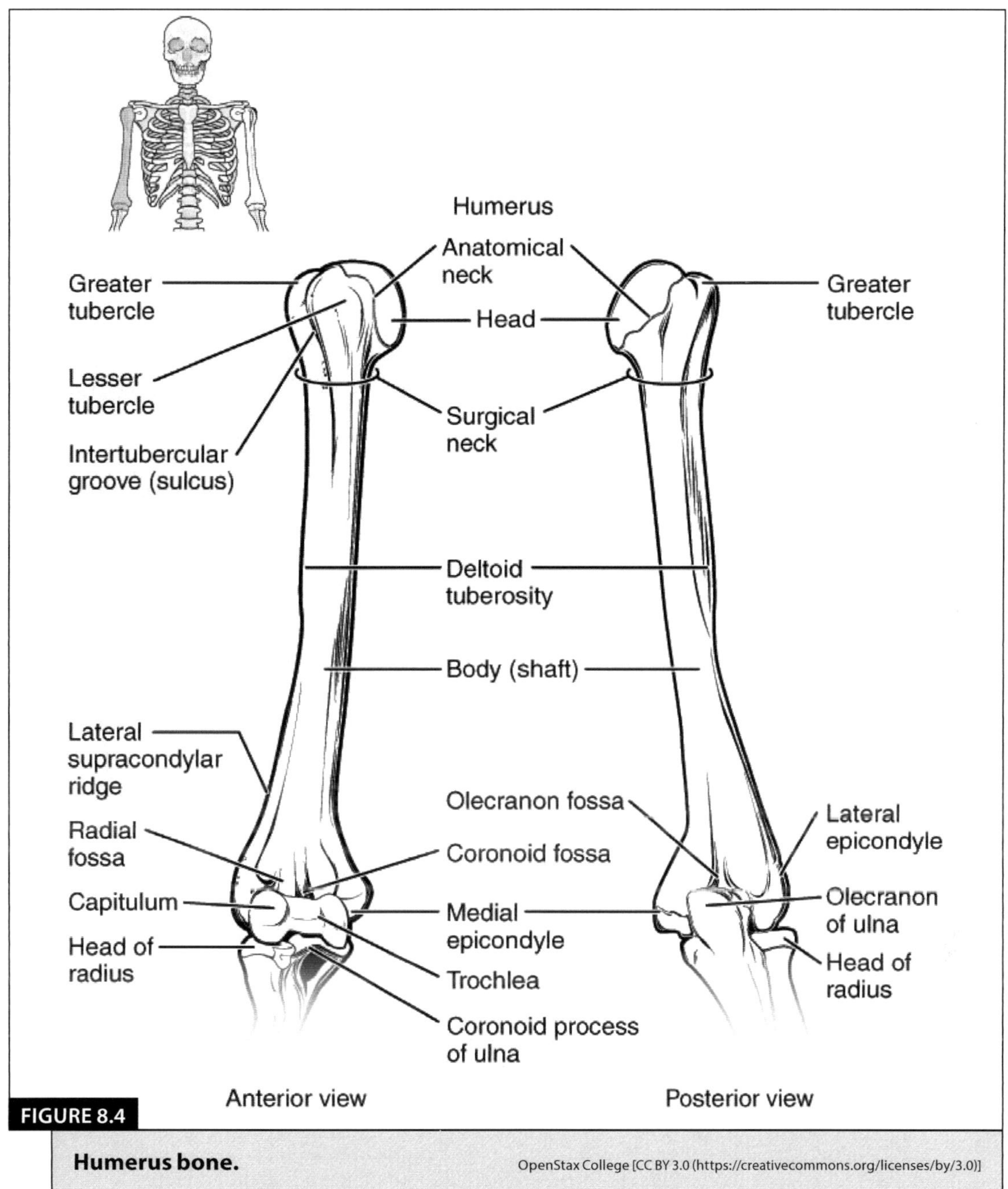


**FIGURE 8.4**

**Humerus bone.** OpenStax College [CC BY 3.0 (https://creativecommons.org/licenses/by/3.0)]

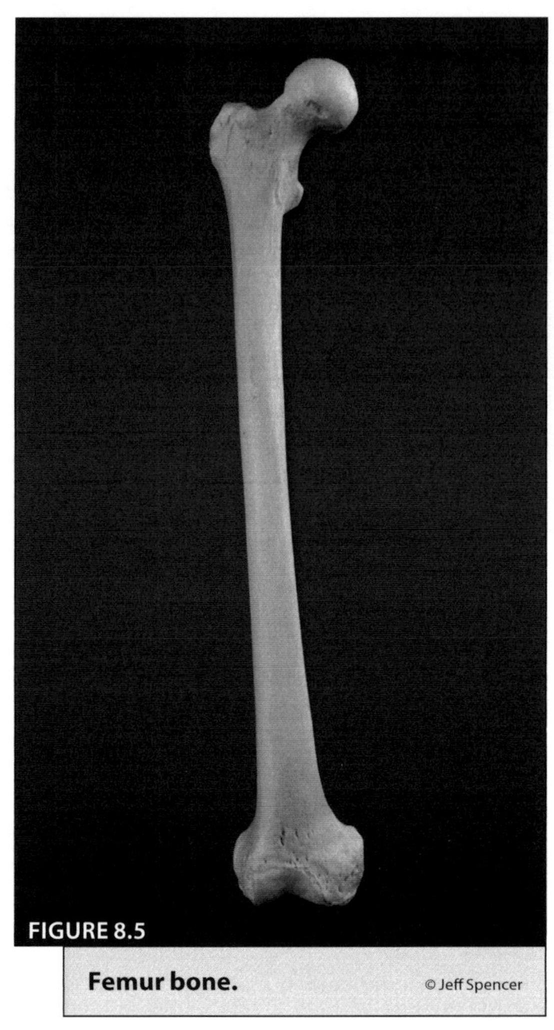

**FIGURE 8.5**

**Femur bone.** © Jeff Spencer

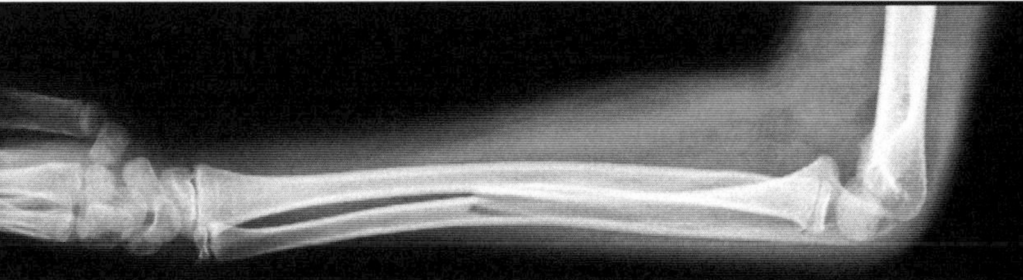

# 9

# JOINTS AND ARTICULATIONS
## PRE-LAB

Name: _______________________    Section: __________    Date: _________

## LEARNING OBJECTIVES

- Discuss both functional and structural classifications for body joints.
- Define and identify the different body movements.
- Discuss the structure of the knee joint.
- Identify certain joint disorders.

## INTRODUCTION

Joints, or articulations, are the location where bones come together. Many articulations allow for movement between the bones. At these joints, the articulating surfaces of the adjacent bones can move smoothly against each other. However, the bones of other joints may be joined to each other by connective tissue or cartilage. These joints are designed for stability and provide for little or no movement. Importantly, joint stability and movement are related to each other. This means that stable joints allow for little or no mobility between the adjacent bones. *Conversely, joints that provide the most movement between bones are the least stable.* Understanding the relationship between joint structure and function will help to explain why particular types of joints are found in certain areas of the body.

The articulating surfaces of bones at stable types of joints, with little or no mobility, are tightly attached to each other. This is called a **synarthrotic** joint. For example, most of the joints of the skull are held together by **fibrous** connective tissue and do not allow for movement between the adjacent bones. This lack of mobility is important because the skull bones serve to protect the brain. Similarly, other joints united by fibrous connective tissue allow for very little movement, which provides stability and weight-bearing support for the body. For example, the tibia and fibula of the leg are tightly united to give stability to the body when standing, but allow for very slight movement (interosseous membrane).

At other joints, the bones are held together by **cartilage,** which permits limited movements between the bones. Limited movement between bones is an **amphiarthrotic** joint. Thus, the fibrocartilage joints of the vertebral column only allow for small movements between adjacent vertebrae, but when added together, these movements provide the flexibility that allows your body to twist, or bend to the front, back, or side. In contrast, at joints that allow for wide ranges of motion, the articulating surfaces of the bones are not directly united to each other. Instead, these surfaces are enclosed within a space filled with lubricating fluid (**synovial** joints), which allows the bones to move smoothly against each other. These joints are called **diarthrotic** and provide greater mobility, but since the bones are free to move in relation to each other, the joint is less stable. Most of the joints between the bones of the appendicular skeleton are this freely moveable diarthrotic type of joint. These joints act as levers allowing the muscles of the body to pull on a bone and thereby produce movement of that body region. Your ability to kick a soccer ball, write your notes, and dance depend on mobility at these types of joints. (Modified from Open Stax https://cnx.org/contents/ndbpDVyl@4/Introduction; Download for free at http://cnx.org/contents/9dd6e90d-5ca5-453c-83ef-280e2c8d3b55@4 )

Answer and fill in the following:

1. Explain what joints are.

2. Describe freely moveable joints. What is their other functional name?

3. What are the types of joints shown below?

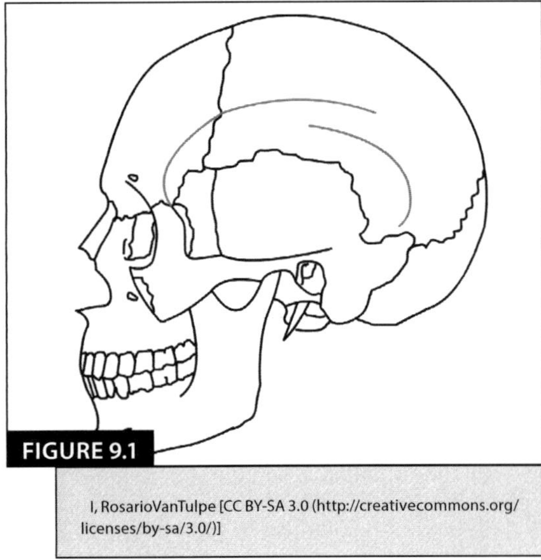

FIGURE 9.1



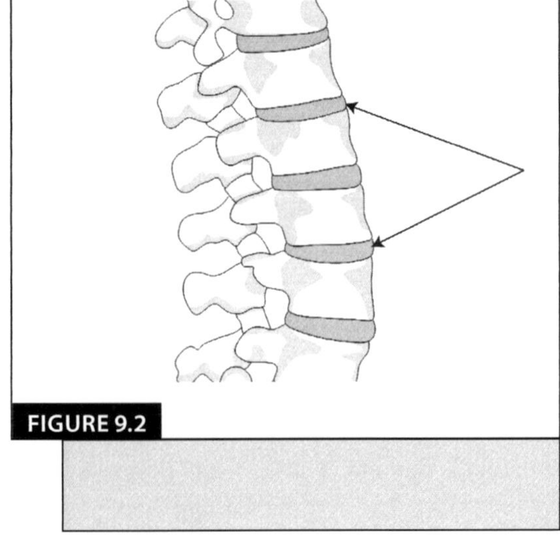

FIGURE 9.2

- Figure 9.1—__________________

- Figure 9.2—__________________

4. **Complete** the following table outlining the types of joints and examples of each in the boxes.

<table>
<tr><td rowspan="2"></td><td colspan="4" align="center">STRUCTURAL</td></tr>
<tr><td></td><td></td><td align="center">Cartilaginous</td><td></td></tr>
<tr><td rowspan="4">FUNCTIONAL</td><td>Synarthrosis</td><td></td><td>Synchondrosis (Example: growth plates)</td><td align="center">X</td></tr>
<tr><td></td><td></td><td>Symphysis (Example: pubic symphysis)</td><td align="center">X</td></tr>
<tr><td>Diarthrosis</td><td align="center">X</td><td align="center">X</td><td></td></tr>
</table>

5. Take a minute to **explain** the reasons why joints differ in their degree of mobility.

This website shows the hand of a child where you can see the *epiphyseal growth plates* in the metacarpals, the proximal phalanges, and the radius and ulna bones.

- http://www.madsci.org/cgi-bin/lynn/image?return=http://www.madsci.org/~lynn/VH/annotated.html&name=hand_wrist&show_all=1&search

6. What kind of joint is at the epiphyseal plates?

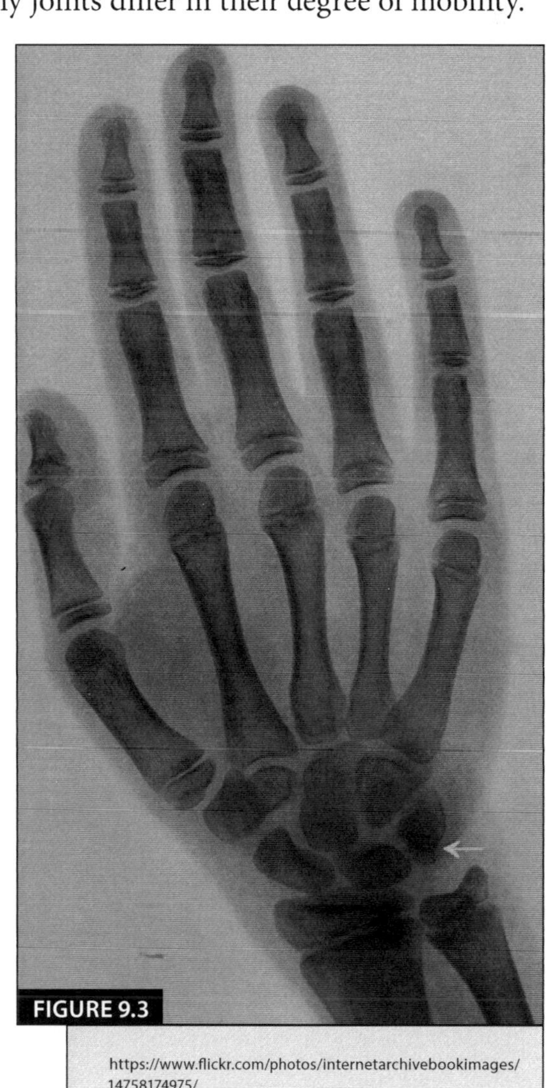

**FIGURE 9.3**

https://www.flickr.com/photos/internetarchivebookimages/14758174975/

7. Tendons (dense regular fibrous connective tissue) connect muscle to bones. What links a bone to another bone and limits the range of movement of the joint?

Watch these videos about the knee's ligaments and their functions.

- https://www.youtube.com/watch?v=RTV5Yo3E7VQ
- https://www.youtube.com/watch?v=SnfEmezg7eY

After watching the video, answer these questions before coming to lab:

8. What is the function of the medial collateral ligament?

9. What is the function of the posterior cruciate ligament?

# 9

# JOINTS AND ARTICULATIONS
## IN-LAB ACTIVITIES

Name: _________________________   Section: __________   Date: _________

## LEARNING OBJECTIVES

- Discuss both functional and structural classifications for body joints.
- Define and identify the different body movements.
- Discuss the structure of the knee joint.
- Identify certain joint disorders.

## PRE-LAB

Before going to lab, you must complete the following:

1. Read the **Pre-Lab** and answer all Pre-Lab questions.

*Note:* You will spend **1 hr and 30 min** in lab at Forsyth Tech to complete the following activities (which may be coupled with other lab activities). This amount of time allows you to complete the activities by using the torso model, knee, and other models as well as working with a lab partner.

## ACTIVITY 1

1. Review the structural and functional ways we classify joints that you read about in the text and filled in the table in the Pre-Lab. **Go over these in the proper categories at least 3 different times, so that they sink into your brain. You need to know these by example and definition for both the lab and lecture/class tests.** Quiz each other, too!

2. Identify the following major types of **JOINTS** and their subgroups. **Be able to identify examples of each in lab.**

### TYPES OF JOINTS

- **Fibrous joints:** two or more bones joined by connective tissue that includes many fibers.
    - Lie between bones that closely contact one another
    - Thin layer of dense fibrous connective tissue joins the bones
    - Suture (skull)
    - Joint in leg between tibia and fibula (interosseous joint)

- **Cartilaginous joints:** two or more bones joined by cartilage
    - Hyaline cartilage connects bones
    - Joints of vertebral column
    - Intervertebral disc: fibrocartilage surrounding a pulpy or gelatinous core
    - Absorbs shocks and helps equalize pressure between adjacent vertebrae when the body moves

- **Synovial joints:** a freely movable joint
    - Most joints are these type
    - Allow free movement
    - Complex structurally more than fibrous or cartilaginous joint types
    - Articular ends covered with hyaline cartilage (articular cartilage) surrounded by a tubular capsule of dense connective tissue

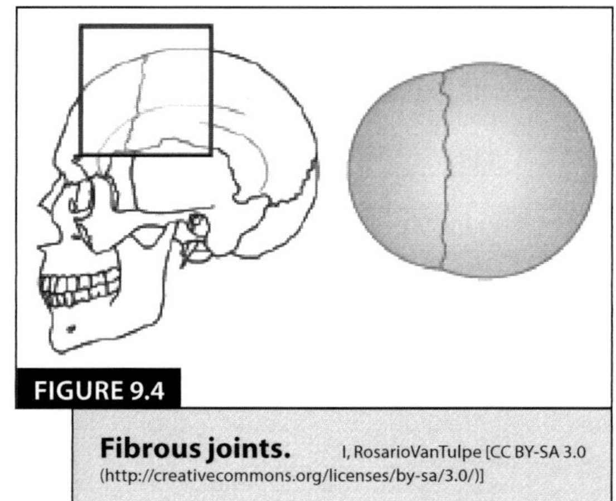

**FIGURE 9.4**

**Fibrous joints.** I, RosarioVanTulpe [CC BY-SA 3.0 (http://creativecommons.org/licenses/by-sa/3.0/)]

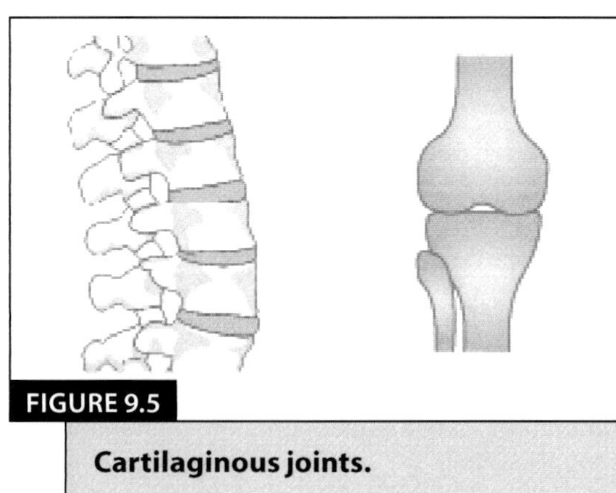

**FIGURE 9.5**

**Cartilaginous joints.**

- Types of synovial joints:

  - **Ball-and-socket joint:** bone with a ball-shaped head that articulates with the cup-shaped cavity of another bone; wider range of motion; movements in all planes

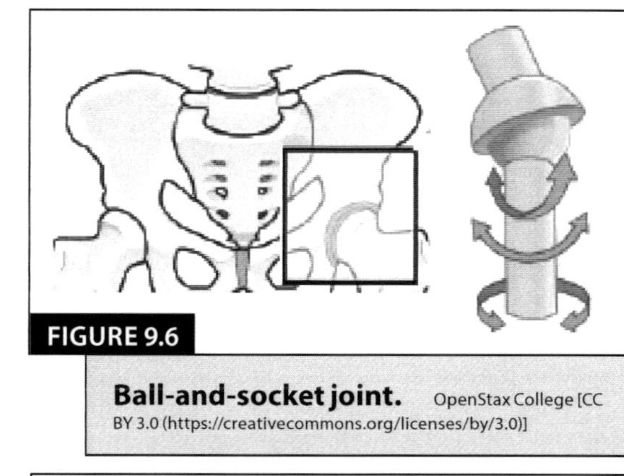

**FIGURE 9.6**

**Ball-and-socket joint.** OpenStax College [CC BY 3.0 (https://creativecommons.org/licenses/by/3.0)]

  - **Condyloid joint:** oval-shaped condyle of one bone fits into an elliptical cavity of another; rotational movement is not possible

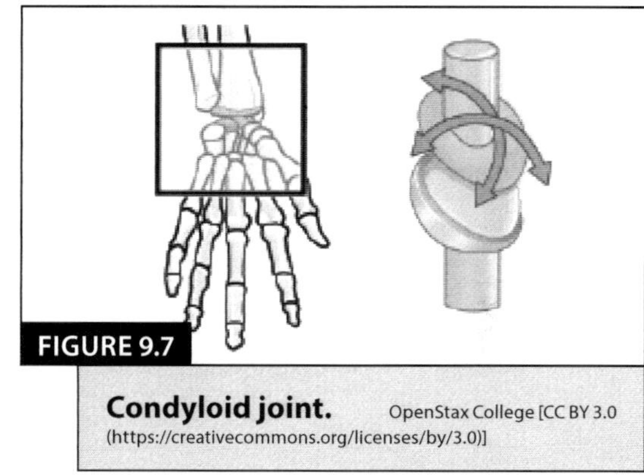

**FIGURE 9.7**

**Condyloid joint.** OpenStax College [CC BY 3.0 (https://creativecommons.org/licenses/by/3.0)]

  - **Gliding joint:** nearly flat, slightly curved; wrist, ankle, vertebrae, scapula to clavicle; allows sliding and twisting

    - **Examples:** Metacarpals and phalanges

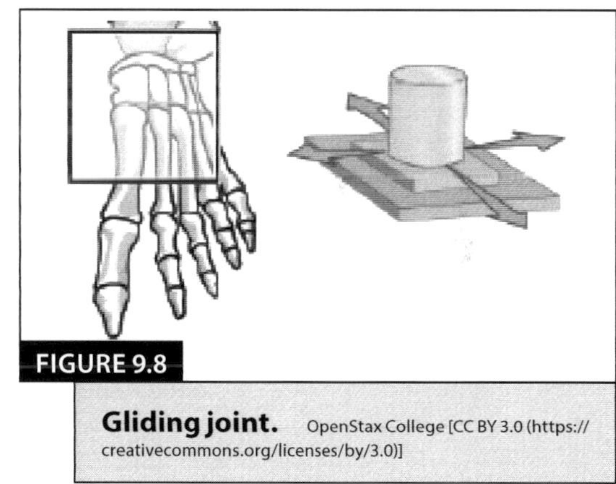

**FIGURE 9.8**

**Gliding joint.** OpenStax College [CC BY 3.0 (https://creativecommons.org/licenses/by/3.0)]

  - **Hinge joint:** convex surface of one bone fits into the concave surface of another

    - **Examples:** Elbow and phalanges

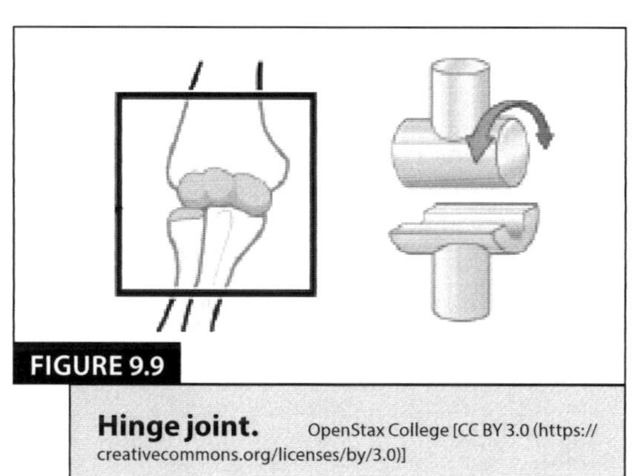

**FIGURE 9.9**

**Hinge joint.** OpenStax College [CC BY 3.0 (https://creativecommons.org/licenses/by/3.0)]

- **Pivot joint:** cylindrical surface of one bone rotates within a ring formed of bone and ligament; rotation around a central axis

  - **Examples:** Proximal end of radius and the ulna

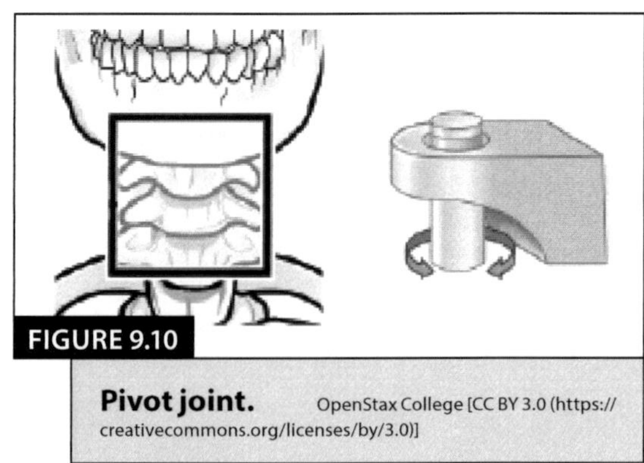


**Pivot joint.**   OpenStax College [CC BY 3.0 (https://creativecommons.org/licenses/by/3.0)]

- **Saddle joint:** between bones whose articulating surfaces have both concave and convex regions

  - **Examples:** Carpal and metacarpal bones of the thumb

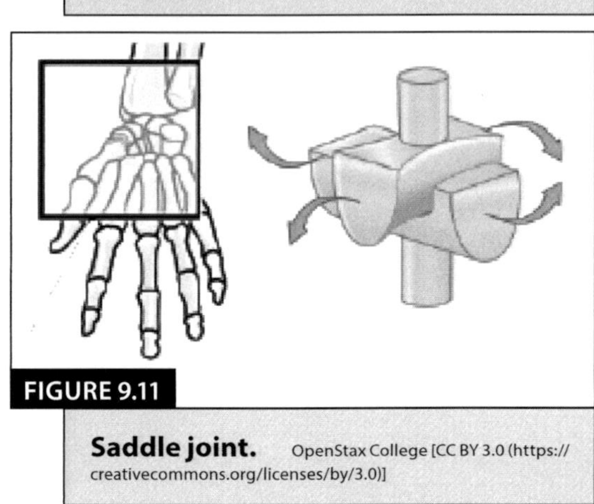


**Saddle joint.**   OpenStax College [CC BY 3.0 (https://creativecommons.org/licenses/by/3.0)]

## COMPLETE THE FOLLOWING

1. Fibrous (immovable/synarthrosis)—syndesmosis, suture, gomphosis—**List** examples of these fibrous joints.

2. Cartilaginous (immovable or slightly moveable/amphiarthrosis)—synchondrosis, symphysis—**List** where each of these can be found in the body.

3. Synovial (freely movable/diarthrosis)—**List** an area in the body where each of these joints can be found:

   **a.** Ball and socket _______________________________________________

   **b.** Hinge _______________________________________________

   **c.** Condyloid _______________________________________________

   **d.** Gliding _______________________________________________

   **e.** Pivot _______________________________________________

   **f.** Saddle _______________________________________________

## ACTIVITY 2: PARTS OF THE SYNOVIAL CAVITY

**Synovial Joints** have distinct parts to them. A lot of you will be working with orthopedic surgeons one day, so make sure that you know these names and their function in the synovial joint (Ex: synovial membrane secretes the synovial fluid).

On the pictures of the human finger joint or a cat dissection, discern the parts of a typical **synovial** joint. Include the articular cartilages and any parts of the primary synovial cavity with capsule (articular capsule = fibrous capsule and the synovial membrane).

1. Obtain a chicken or beef joint to observe by dissecting and finding as many parts of the typical synovial joint as you can. **List which parts you observe.**

2. **DRAW** and **LABEL** below the primary parts of a synovial cavity.

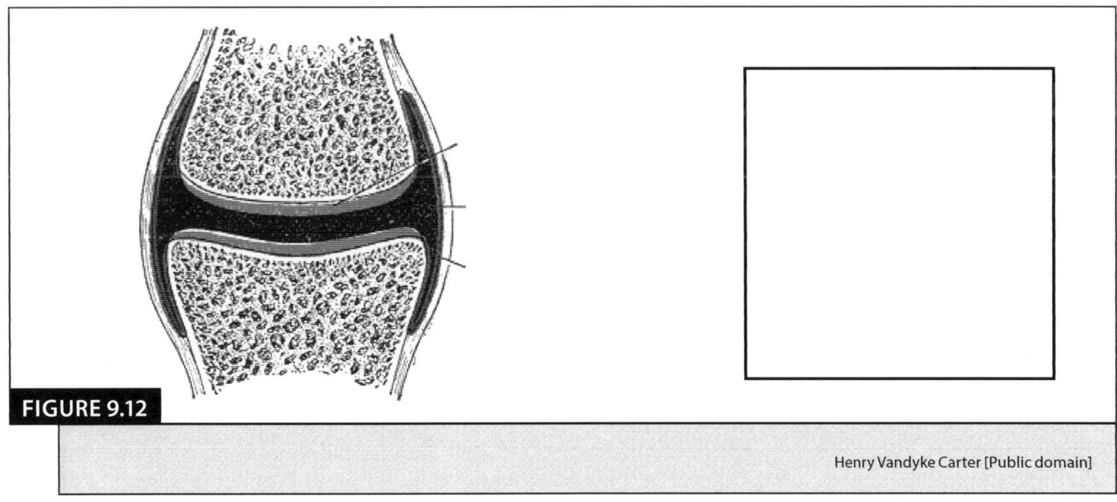

FIGURE 9.12

Henry Vandyke Carter [Public domain]

## ACTIVITY 3: EXAMPLE OF SYNOVIAL JOINT—THE KNEE

On the *human knee model* in lab (or the cat dissection or other dissection), find the following bones, ligaments, and menisci of the human knee articulation. Some models may have the quadriceps tendon and the patellar ligament, while others may only have the patellar ligament. (**The infrapatellar fat pad and the bursae are not on our lab models.**)

1.  Bones
    a.  Femur
    b.  Tibia
    c.  Patella
    d.  Fibula (not part of the knee joint)

2.  Ligaments (remember **not** to use abbreviations on the lab test)
    a.  Patellar ligament
    b.  Lateral (fibular) collateral ligament (LCL)
    c.  Medial (tibial) collateral ligament (MCL)
    d.  Anterior cruciate (means: to cross) ligament (ACL)
    e.  Posterior cruciate (crosses with the ACL) ligament (PCL)

3.  Menisci
    a.  Lateral meniscus
    b.  Medial meniscus

**These structures will be identified on the lab model and not on pictures for the lab test.**

Label Figure 9.13 with the **anterior cruciate ligament, posterior cruciate ligament, medial collateral ligament, lateral collateral ligament, medial meniscus, and lateral meniscus;** also **label** the condyles of the **femur, the tibia, and fibula** bones (the femur has been bent backwards in this view).

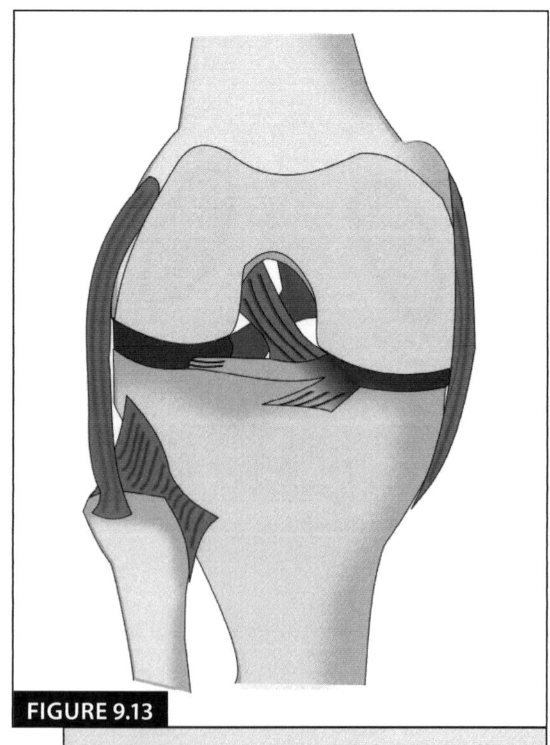

**FIGURE 9.13**

# ACTIVITY 4

**Identify** and **demonstrate** with your lab partner(s) *all* of the following **TYPES OF MOVEMENT:**

See video https://www.youtube.com/watch?v=vdScqySvcxc

1. Flexion: bending parts at a joint so that the angle between them decreases and the parts come closer together.

2. Extension: straightening parts at a joint so that the angle between them increases.

3. Dorsiflexion: bending the foot at the ankle toward the shin.

4. Plantar flexion: bending the foot at the ankle toward the sole.

5. Hyperextension: excess extension of the parts at a joint, beyond the anatomical position (bending the head back beyond the upright position).

6. Abduction: moving a part away from the midline.

7. Adduction: moving a part toward the midline.

8. Rotation: moving a part around an axis.

9. Circumduction: moving a part so that its end follows a circular path. (Note that rotation and circumduction are similar.)

10. Pronation: turning the hand so that the palm is facing downward or posteriorly.

11. Supination: turning the hand so that the palm is facing upward.

12. Eversion: turning the foot so that the sole faces laterally.

13. Inversion: turning the foot so that the sole faces medially.

14. Retraction: moving a part backward.

15. Protraction: moving a part forward.

16. Elevation: raising a part.

17. Depression: lowering a part.

https://yiss-anatomy2010-11.wikispaces.com/Lin+and+Kathryn

**To Help You Review: DESCRIBE** in your own words the 7 movements listed here:

18. Flexion (in sagittal plane)_______________________________________________

19. Extension (in sagittal plane) _____________________________________________

20. Hyperextension (not in the hinge joints, usually) ____________________________

21. Abduction (take away from midline) _______________________________________

22. Adduction ("add" back to the body's midline) _______________________________

23. Circumduction _________________________________________________________

24. Rotation (medial and lateral rotation) _____________________________________

    a. Supination = ________________________________________________________

    b. Pronation = _________________________________________________________

**Identify** the type of movements allowed by the following joints.

| TYPE OF JOINT | MOVEMENT ALLOWED | EXAMPLE OF JOINT |
|---|---|---|
| Ball and Socket | | |
| Hinge | | |
| Pivot | | |
| Condyloid | | |
| Gliding | | |

## JOINT DISORDERS

**1.** What is a sprain?

**2.** What is a strain?

**3.** What is bursitis?

**4.** What is a dislocation?

**5.** What is osteoarthritis? Are there other forms of arthritis?

*Note:* Be sure to get your completed work checked off by a member of the lab staff and then keep this handout for your review.

# 10

# MUSCLE TISSUE, MUSCLE STRUCTURE, MUSCLE OIA
## PRE-LAB

Name: _________________________  Section: __________  Date: _________

## LEARNING OBJECTIVES

- Compare and contrast the characteristics of the three types of muscle tissue.
- Identify the parts of a skeletal muscle fiber.
- Understand the naming system for the skeletal muscle system.

## PRE-LAB

1. Describe a few major characteristics of smooth, skeletal, and cardiac muscle tissue.

   a. Smooth—

   b. Skeletal—

   c. Cardiac—

2. The _________________________ is the functional unit of the skeletal muscular system and the contractile unit of the muscle fiber/cell.

3. The covering on the outside of the muscle itself (muscle belly) is the ______________; the covering for the groups of muscle fibers/cells (the fascicle) within the muscle is the _________________________; the covering around the muscle fiber itself is the _________________________.

4. Define the following terms:

    **a.** Muscle origin—

    **b.** Muscle insertion—

    **c.** Aponeurosis—

    **d.** Tendon—

    **e.** Ligament—

5. Muscles are named for various properties including location, shape, how many attachments, and where those attachments are on the bones. You probably know some of these already; for instance, three attachments for a muscle can be referred to as triceps whereas two attachments for a muscle would be ________________. A shape reference you may know is the triangle or delta shape ($\Delta$) which is used to name the muscle of the shoulder, the _________________________________ muscle.

# 10

# MUSCLE TISSUE, MUSCLE STRUCTURE, MUSCLE OIA
## IN-LAB ACTIVITIES

Name: ___________________________   Section: ___________   Date: __________

## LEARNING OBJECTIVES

- Compare and contrast the characteristics of the three types of muscle tissue.
- Name the connective tissue layers that surround each cell, fascicle, muscle, and group of muscles and indicate the specific type of CT that composes all these layers.
- Identify the parts of a skeletal muscle fiber.
- Understand the naming system for the skeletal muscle system.

## PRE-LAB

Before going to lab, you must complete the following:

**1.** Read the **Pre-Lab** and answer all Pre-Lab questions.

*Note:* You will spend **2 hr–2 hr 30 min** in lab at Forsyth Tech to complete the following activities. This amount of time allows you to complete the activities by using the torso model and other models as well as working with a lab partner.

## HISTOLOGY: MUSCLE TISSUE

Use the designated slides to study the listed structures characteristic of the different muscle tissues.

**Always draw the images you see.** (Slides of all three muscle tissue types together are usually available in labs.)

# ACTIVITY 1: VIEW AND DRAW THE FOLLOWING MUSCLE TISSUE TYPES (SEEN UNDER HIGH POWER)

1. Smooth muscle tissue, c.s. and l.s. (trachea slide, small intestine/duodenum slide, or esophagus/stomach slide)

   **a.** Smooth muscle fibers/ cells

   **b.** Nuclei

   **c.** Connective tissue

2. Skeletal muscle c.s. and l.s. (tongue slide—best under high power lens), l.s. (striated muscle slide or skeletal smooth cardiac slide)

   **a.** Muscle fiber

   **b.** Nuclei

   **c.** A-band

   **d.** I-band

   **e.** Z line

   **f.** Endomysium

   **g.** Perimysium

   **h.** Epimysium

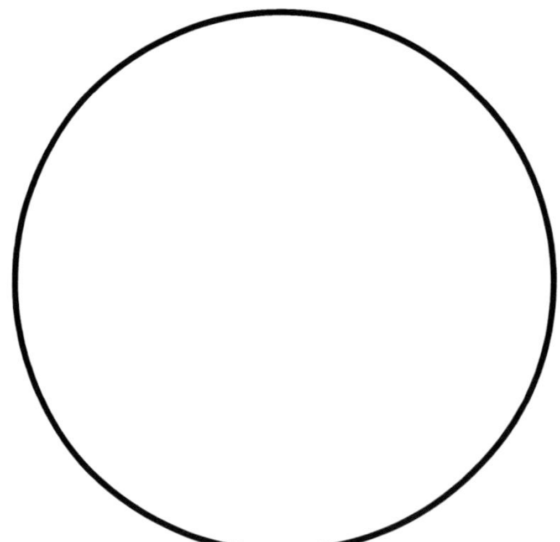

**3.** Cardiac muscle (intercalated discs slide). You can see these darker "lines" under low power, then find them to draw under high power.

**a.** Branching cardiac fiber

**b.** Nuclei

**c.** Intercalated disks

**d.** Connective tissue

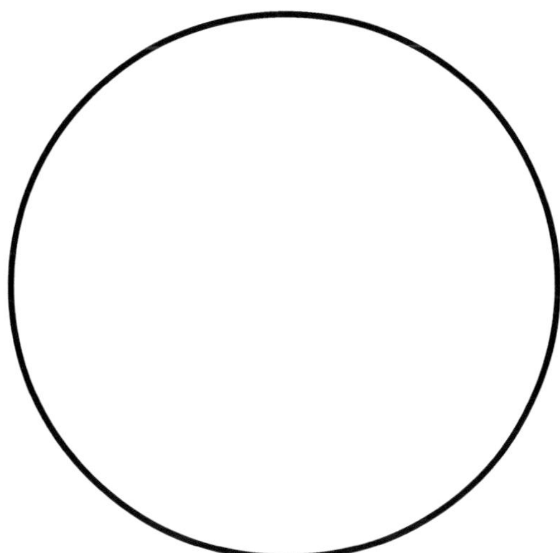

## SKELETAL MUSCLE ORGANIZATION

Each skeletal muscle is an organ that consists of various tissues. These tissues include the skeletal **muscle fibers** (cells), blood vessels, nerve fibers, and connective tissue. Each skeletal muscle has three layers of connective tissue (called "mysia") that enclose it and provide structure to the muscle as a whole, and compartmentalizing the muscle fibers within the muscle into **fascicles** (see Figure below ). The whole muscle is wrapped in a sheath of dense, irregular connective tissue called the **epimysium,** which allows a muscle to contract powerfully while keeping it together.

Inside each skeletal muscle, muscle fibers are organized into individual bundles, each called a **fascicle,** by a middle layer of connective tissue called the **perimysium.** Inside each fascicle, each muscle fiber is encased in a thin connective tissue layer of collagen and reticular fibers called the **endomysium.** The endomysium contains the extracellular fluid and nutrients to support the muscle fiber. These nutrients are supplied via blood to the muscle tissue.

In skeletal muscles that work with tendons to pull on bones, the collagen in the three tissue layers (the mysia) intertwines with the collagen of a tendon. At the other end of the tendon, it fuses with the periosteum coating the bone. The tension created by contraction of the muscle fibers is then transferred though the mysia to the tendon and then to the periosteum to pull on the bone for movement of the skeleton. In other places, the mysia may fuse with a broad, tendon-like sheet called an **aponeurosis,** or to **fascia,** the connective tissue between skin and bones. The broad sheet of connective tissue in the lower back that the latissimus dorsi muscles (the "lats") fuse into is an example of an aponeurosis.

Skeletal muscle cells are long and cylindrical, so they are called muscle **fibers.** During early development, embryonic **myoblasts,** each with its own nucleus, fuse with up to hundreds of other myoblasts to form the multinucleated skeletal muscle fibers (not true of smooth or cardiac muscle fibers seen earlier). Multiple nuclei mean multiple copies of genes, permitting the production of the large amounts of proteins and enzymes needed for muscle contraction.

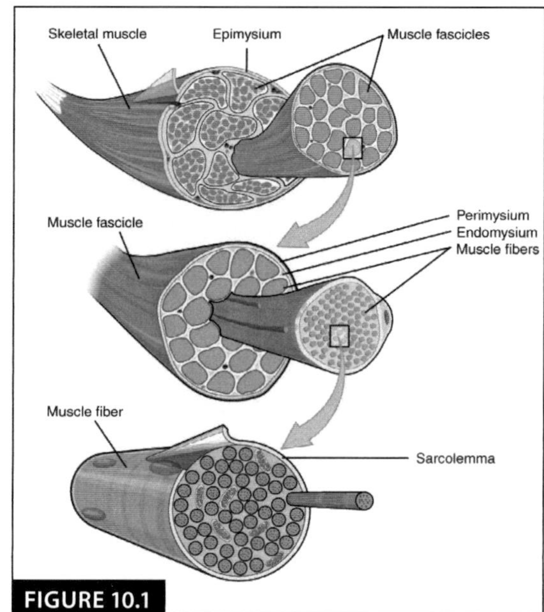


**FIGURE 10.1**

**The whole muscle is covered by the epimysium.** Bundles of muscle fibers called fascicles are covered by the perimysium. Muscle fibers are covered by the endomysium.  OpenStax College [CC BY 3.0 (https://creativecommons.org/licenses/by/3.0)]

Other terminology associated with the muscle fibers contains the prefix *sarco-,* which means "flesh." The fiber's cell membrane is referred to as the **sarcolemma,** the cell's cytoplasm is called **sarcoplasm,** and the storage of cellular calcium is held in the **sarcoplasmic reticulum** (modified smooth endoplasmic reticulum).

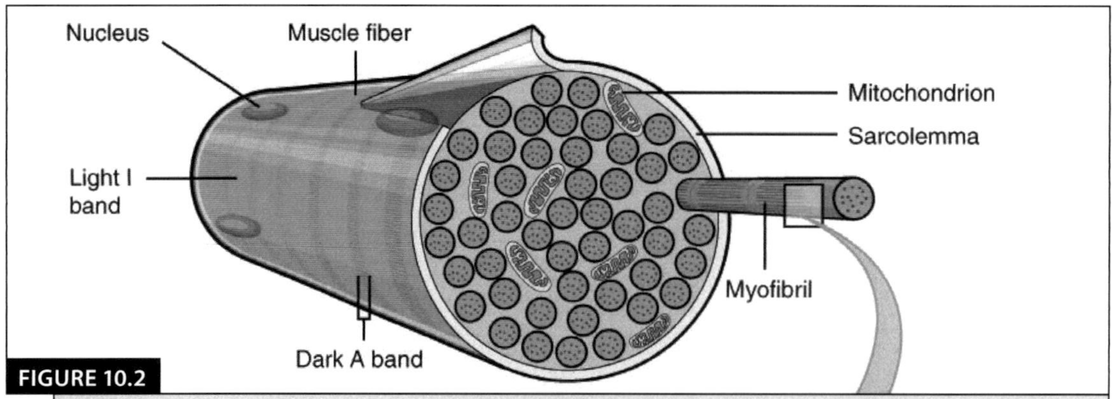


**FIGURE 10.2**

**A skeletal muscle fiber (a cell) is surrounded by a plasma membrane called the sarcolemma, which contains sarcoplasm, the cytoplasm of muscle cells.** A muscle fiber is composed of many fibrils of overlapping proteins, which give the cell its striated appearance.

OpenStax College [CC BY 3.0 (https://creativecommons.org/licenses/by/3.0)]

## REVIEW QUESTIONS

1. What connective tissue layer surrounds the skeletal muscle fiber?

2. What is the fiber's cell membrane called?

3. Contrast the fascia and the aponeuroses of muscles.

4. Compare and contrast the perimysium and the epimysium of muscles.

In lab you may find a model of the skeletal muscle fiber (remember this is the cellular level of skeletal muscle).

## ACTIVITY 2: LOCATE PARTS OF A SKELETAL MUSCLE FIBER—ON THE MODEL IN LAB FIND THE FOLLOWING

- Endomysium
- Sarcolemma
- Sarcoplasm
- Myofibrils (a group of protein filaments arranged into sarcomeres)
- Sarcomeres
- Light band (I-band)

- Dark band (A-Band)
- Z lines
- Multiple nuclei
- The motor neuron and the neuromuscular junction (area where the neuron and the muscle fiber come together, which you will learn about later)

### NAMING SKELETAL MUSCLES

Anatomists name the skeletal muscles according to a number of criteria, each of which describes the muscle in some way. These include naming the muscle after its shape, its size compared to other muscles in the area, its location in the body or the location of its attachments to the skeleton, how many origins it has, or its action.

The skeletal muscle's anatomical **location** or its relationship to a particular bone often determines its name. For example, the frontalis muscle is located on top of the frontal bone of the skull. Similarly, the **shapes** of some muscles are very distinctive and the names, such as orbicularis, reflect the shape. For the buttocks, the **size** of the muscles influences the names: gluteus maximus (largest), gluteus medius (medium), and the gluteus minimus (smallest). Names were given to indicate **length**—brevis (short), longus (long)—and to identify **position** relative to the midline—lateralis (to the outside away from the midline) and medialis (toward the midline). The **direction** of the muscle fibers and fascicles are used to describe muscles relative to the midline, such as the rectus (straight) abdominis or the oblique (at an angle) muscles of the abdomen.

Some muscle names indicate the **number of muscles** in a group. One example of this is the quadriceps, a group of four muscles located on the anterior (front) thigh. Other muscle names can provide information as to how many origins a particular muscle has, such as the biceps brachii. The prefix **bi** indicates that the muscle has two origins and **tri** indicates three origins.

The location of a muscle's **attachment** can also appear in its name. When the name of a muscle is based on the attachments, the **origin** is always named first. For instance, the sternocleidomastoid muscle of the neck has a dual origin on the sternum (sterno) and clavicle (cleido), and it inserts (**insertion**) on the mastoid process of the temporal bone. The last feature by which to name a muscle is its **action.** When muscles are named for the movement they produce, one can find action words in their name. Some examples are flexor (decreases the angle at the joint), extensor (increases the angle at the joint), abductor (moves the bone away from the midline), or adductor (moves the bone toward the midline).

Etymology is the study of how the root of a particular word entered a language and how the use of the word evolved over time. Taking the time to learn the root of the words is crucial to understanding the vocabulary of anatomy and physiology. When you understand the names of muscles, it will help you remember where the muscles are located and what they do (see Table 10.1; you can download for free at http://cnx.org/contents/9dd6e90d-5ca5-453c-83ef280e2c8d3b55@4). Pronunciation of words and terms will take a bit of time to master, but after you have some basic information,the correct names and pronunciations will become easier. (Be sure to get a Naming Muscles Handout if available.)

**Etymology of terminology for naming skeletal muscles and mnemonic devices http://cnx.org/content/col11496/1.6**

**TABLE 10.1**

| EXAMPLE | LATIN OR GREEK TRANSLATION | MNEMONIC DEVICE |
| --- | --- | --- |
| ad | to; toward | ADd back to the body |
| ab | away from | ABduct or take something away from someone |
| sub | under | SUBmarines move under water. |
| ductor | something that moves | A conDUCTOR makes a train move; or fluid moves through a DUCT |
| anti | against | If you are ANTIsocial, you are against engaging in social activities; ANTAgonist is against someone in conversation |
| epi | on top of; above | n/a |
| extensor | increases angle | EXTENd farther away in angle |
| flexor | decreases angle | FLEX arm or leg bends the limb towards the body |
| longissimus | longest | "Longissimus" is longer than the word "long." |
| brevis | short | brief |
| maximus | large | Max; largest |
| medius | medium | "Medius" and "medium" both begin with "med." |
| minimus | tiny; little | mini |
| rectus | straight | To RECTify a situation is to straighten it out. |
| multi | many | If something is MULTIcolored, it has many colors. |
| uni | one | A UNIcorn has one horn. |
| bi/di | two | If a ring is DIcast, it is made of two metals. |
| tri | three | TRIple the amount of money is three times as much. |
| quad | four | QUADruplets are four children born at one birth. |
| externus | outside | EXternal |
| internus | inside | INternal |
| tensor | more rigid | TENSe up your body |

## REVIEW QUESTIONS

1. What action would an adductor group of muscles do?

2. In anatomical position, where would the flexor muscles be on the arm, anterior or posterior side?

3. How many muscle heads would the triceps brachii have connecting it to the bone?

4. How many muscles will you find in the quadriceps group of the lower appendage?

5. Where is the rectus femoris muscle located? In what group is it?

Now ask the opposite of each of the questions above and answer those below.

6. What action would an abductor muscle do?

7. In anatomical position, where would the extensor muscles be on the arm, anterior or posterior side? Why?

8. How many muscle heads would the biceps brachii have connecting it to the bone?

9. How many muscles will you find in the hamstring group of the lower appendage?

10. Where is the biceps femoris muscle located? In what group is it?

11. Compare and contrast the internal oblique and the external oblique muscles.

12. What is different about the transversus abdominis and the rectus abdominis muscles?

**Quiz yourself on all the muscles on the muscle man/woman models before you leave today.**

**Show the staff (or another student if the lab is busy) the specific muscles mentioned. Use the Review Questions above as an exit quiz.**

- Triceps brachii
- Quadriceps group
- Hamstring group
- Rectus femoris
- Biceps femoris

- Internal oblique and the external oblique muscles
- Biceps brachii
- Transversus abdominis
- Rectus abdominis

*Note:* Be sure to get your completed work checked off by a member of the lab staff and then keep this handout for your review.

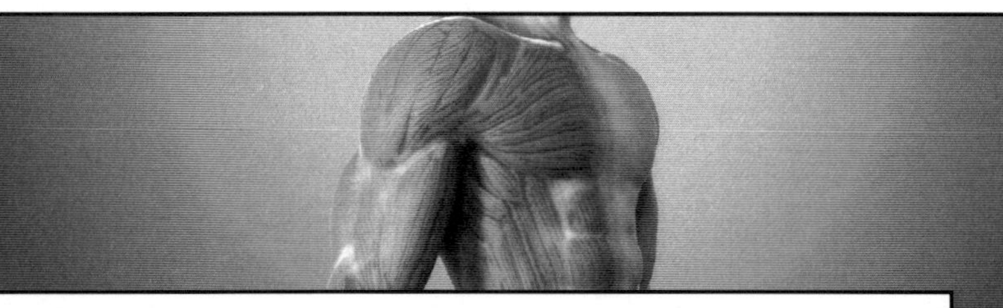

# MUSCULAR SYSTEM NAMES— AXIAL AND APPENDICULAR
## PRE-LAB

Name: _______________________  Section: __________  Date: _________

1. The word rectus means _________________________________________________.

2. The three layers of skeletal muscles that form the abdominal wall are (from outermost to innermost):

   a. _______________________________________________________________

   b. _______________________________________________________________

   c. _______________________________________________________________

3. The four muscles that make up the quadriceps group are :

   a. _______________________________________________________________

   b. _______________________________________________________________

   c. _______________________________________________________________

   d. _______________________________________________________________

4. The three muscles that make up the hamstring group are:

   a. _______________________________________________________________

   b. _______________________________________________________________

   c. _______________________________________________________________

5.  Complete the table below to start learning the muscles and their connection points and actions.

| MUSCLE | ORIGIN | INSERTION | ACTION |
|---|---|---|---|
| Buccinator | | | |
| Sternocleidomastoid | | | |
| Pectoralis major | | | |
| Deltoid | | | |
| Gastrocnemius | | | |

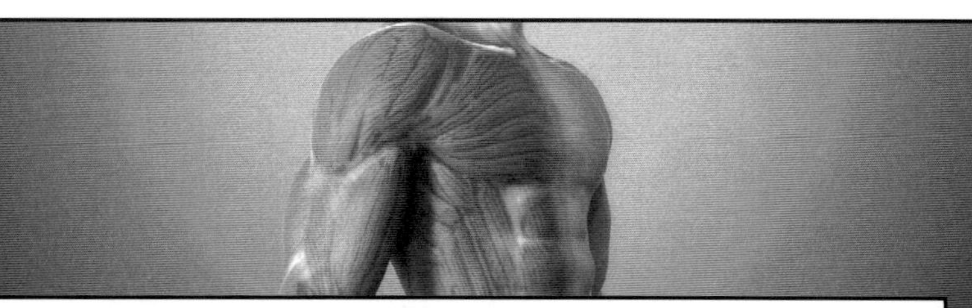

# 11

# AXIAL MUSCULATURE (27 MUSCLES)
## IN-LAB ACTIVITIES

Name: _____________________________  Section: ____________  Date: _________

## LEARNING OBJECTIVE

- Identify the required individual (axial) muscles, and for each with **, know its origin, insertion, and major action (OIA).

## PRE-LAB

Before going to lab, you must complete the following:

**1.** Read the **Pre-Lab** and answer all Pre-Lab questions.

*Note:* You will spend **1 ½–2 hr** (another 1.5 hr in the appendicular skeleton at the least) in lab at Forsyth Tech to complete the following activities. This amount of time allows you to complete the activities by using the muscle models, muscle man model, and other models as well as working with a lab partner.

## INTRODUCTION

Axial musculature is the musculature associated with the axial skeleton. Understanding the actions of individual muscles requires that you first appreciate the role of joint structure and muscle fiber orientation in movement. When you are comfortable with these concepts, use the tables and figures in your **online text** to help you find each of the following muscles on the models, cats, cadavers, and/or the bisected (sagittal) head.

For each, you must learn its major action. For those with **, know the OIA. *Look at the muscles on the models to see in general where these muscles attach. Understand how they move on your own body, then fill in the table in lab.* You only need to put the bones or simplified origin and insertion notes for most of these—see examples in the table.

**Muscles of the face (seen on sagittal heads or other models).**

| TABLE 11.1 | ORIGIN | INSERTION | MAJOR ACTION | OTHER COMMENTS |
|---|---|---|---|---|
| **Orbicularis oris**** | Maxillae and mandible | | | Kissing muscle |
| **Orbicularis oculi** | | Eyelids | | |
| **Buccinator**** | | | Compressing cheeks | Trumpeter muscle |
| **Epicranial aponeurosis (galea aponeurotica)** | | Frontalis | Connective tissue between cranial muscles | Flat white tissue on head/ cranium |
| **Frontalis**** | | Skin of eyebrow, nose | | |
| **Occipitalis**** | Occipital and temporal bones | | | |
| **Zygomaticus major** | | | | |

**Muscles of the mastication—Look at the models in lab to find these! Figure out the attachments, and you will remember them faster and for a longer time.**

| TABLE 11.2 | ORIGIN | INSERTION | MAJOR ACTION | OTHER COMMENTS |
|---|---|---|---|---|
| **Masseter**** | | | | Same action as temporalis |
| **Temporalis** | | Coronoid process | Closes jaw | |

**Muscles of the neck (attachments and actions are obvious by their names).**

**TABLE 11.3**

| | ORIGIN | INSERTION | MAJOR ACTION | OTHER COMMENTS |
|---|---|---|---|---|
| **Sternocleidomastoid**** | Sternum and clavicle | | | Named for attachments |
| **Sternohyoid** | | | | Named for attachments |

**Muscles of the thorax and abdomen.**

**TABLE 11.4**

| | ORIGIN | INSERTION | MAJOR ACTION | OTHER COMMENTS |
|---|---|---|---|---|
| **Pectoralis major**** | | | | |
| **External intercostals (costal = rib)** | Inferior border of each rib | | | Between ribs externally |
| **Internal intercostals** | | Inferior border of superior rib | Depresses ribs | |
| **Transversus thoracis** | Sternum | Ribs | | Depresses ribs for exhale |
| **External oblique** | | Linea alba and iliac crest | | |
| **Internal oblique** | Fascia, iliac crest | | | |
| **Serratus anterior**** | | | | Named for its serrated edge |
| **Transversus abdominis**** | | | | |
| **Diaphragm** | | | | Breathing muscle |
| **Rectus abdominis**** | Pubis (origin) | | | Helps us do "crunches" |
| **Rectus sheath** | X | X | | |
| **Linea alba** | Sternum | Pubis | | Tendinous band of midline |

**Muscles of the back.**

| TABLE 11.5 MUSCLE | ORIGIN | INSERTION | MAJOR ACTION | OTHER COMMENTS |
|---|---|---|---|---|
| **Trapezius**** | | | | Trapezoid shape |
| **Latissimus dorsi**** | | | | |
| **Rhomboideus major (minor is deep)** | Spinous processes | | Adduct scapula | Rhomboid shape |
| **Teres major** | Scapula | Humerus | | Round muscle |
| **Teres minor (rotator cuff)** | | | | |
| **Supraspinatus (rotator cuff)** | | | | Most damaged of 4 |
| **Infraspinatus (rotator cuff)** | | | | In the infraspinous fossa |
| **Subscapularis (rotator cuff)** | | | | |

# STUDY QUESTIONS

1.  **From the skeletal muscle fiber model in lab** (or from the text in Odigia, Lumen, or other), **draw** a picture that includes **all** required lab structures of the sarcomere of a muscle fiber. (Use the tube shape below as a start.)

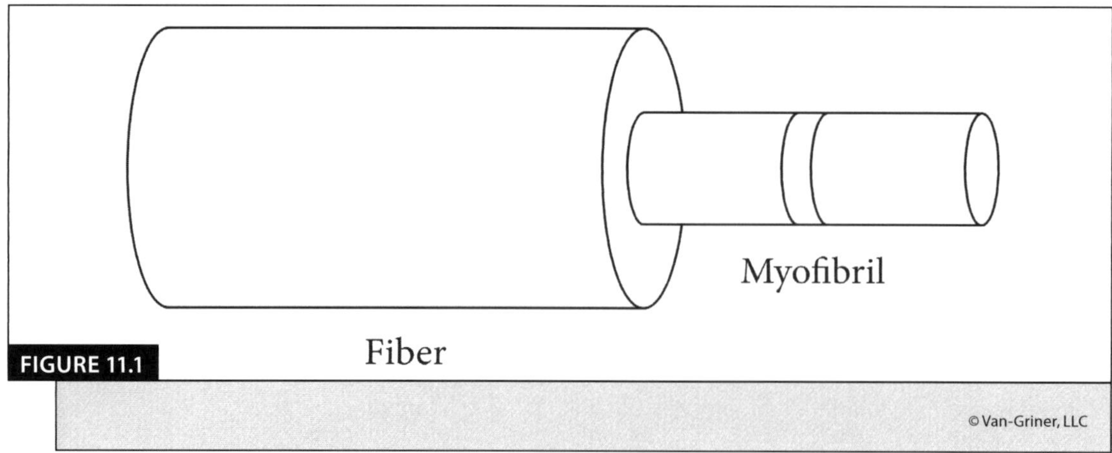


**FIGURE 11.1**

© Van-Griner, LLC

2. If the muscle fiber were to contract and shorten, what would happen to the I-band? The A-band?

3. For each of the following muscles that require attachments and actions, **draw** a quick sketch of the muscle, in addition to the areas on the bones where the muscle attaches. Describe what the muscle does to change the position of the bones when contraction (shortening) takes place (which bone moves and in which direction the bone move when the muscle shortens). Use separate paper.

   a. Masseter

   b. Rectus abdominis

   c. Latissimus dorsi

For study purposes, you can label the muscles pictured here and color in the others on your list. (**Example:** Color the rectus sheath red; color the infraspinatus pink, etc. for the axial muscles)

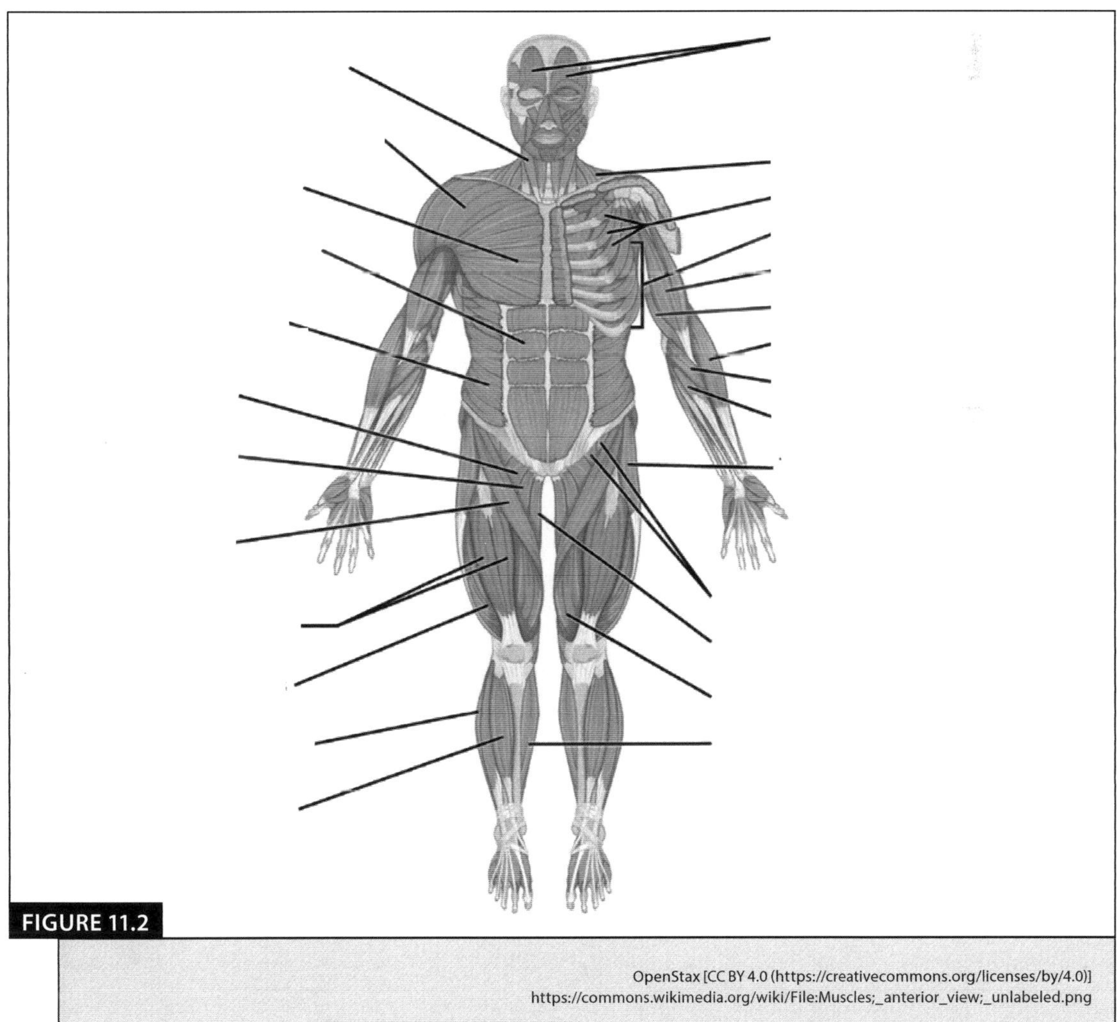

**FIGURE 11.2**



*Note:* Be sure to get your completed work checked off by a member of the lab staff and then keep this handout for your review.

# 12

# APPENDICULAR MUSCLES
## IN-LAB ACTIVITIES

Name: _______________________  Section: __________  Date: _________

## LEARNING OBJECTIVES

- Identify the muscles of the appendicular areas.
- Describe the origins, insertions, and actions of certain muscles.

## PRE-LAB

Before going to lab, you must complete the following:

1. Read the **Pre-Lab** and answer the questions that follow.

*Note:* You will spend **2 hr and 30 min** in lab at Forsyth Tech to complete the following activities. This amount of time allows you to complete the activities by using the muscle models, muscle man models, and other models as well as working with a lab partner.

## ACTIVITY 1

Identify the following skeletal muscles and structures on **models** in lab (or on fetal pig or cat in lab).

Study the list first and find them on pictures/sketches, then in lab find them on 3-D models. Make sure you go over the insertions and origins by pointing to them and saying them **aloud.** Then you can quiz yourself on the **spelling** as review.

**Observe** these muscles by isometrically contracting your muscles for palpation. Locate internal structures with your hands and/or fingers.

- **Biceps brachii**—isometrically flex your forearm with hand supinated. Palpate the muscle and the insertion tendon in the antecubital fossa.

- **Triceps brachii**—put your arm in a strong isometric flexion and then slightly extend your arm while holding the antagonistic flexion. You can palpate the muscle and see its action.

- **Palmaris longus**—make a tight fist and slightly flex at the wrist (isometric contraction). Palpate the wrist flexors and their insertion tendons. You can clearly see the palmaris longus tendon and feel the flexor carpi radialis tendon just lateral to it.

- **Extensor digitorum**—stretch your fingers and abduct them (flared outward) to see this extensor on the posterior aspect of the hand.

- **Quadriceps femoris group**—extend your leg at the knee against resistance (seated, you should also see the patellar tendon).

- **Gastrocnemius**—pull yourself up on your tiptoes to see and palpate the calf muscle.

- **Tibialis anterior**—dorsiflex your foot and palpate the shin muscle lateral to the tibia.

*Note:* Know the origin and insertion of the muscles indicated by **.

**Use models (or cat dissection or digital boards) in the lab to locate the following muscles.**

With a lab partner, find the muscles of the **upper extremity** and their OIA as you fill in this table!

**TABLE 12.1**

| MUSCLES OF THE UPPER EXTREMITY | ORIGIN ATTACHMENT | INSERTION ATTACHMENT | MAJOR ACTION | OTHER |
|---|---|---|---|---|
| Deltoid muscle** | | | | |
| Biceps brachii** | | | | |
| Brachialis | | | | |
| Triceps brachii** | | | | |
| Brachioradialis | | | | |
| Extensor carpi radialis longus (note the brevis) | X | X | | |
| Extensor digitorum | X | X | | |
| Flexor carpi radialis | X | X | | |
| Palmaris longus | X | X | | Medial to flexor carpi radialis |

(Add instructor's choice: flexor carpi ulnaris; extensor carpi ulnaris; pronator teres.)

**Muscles of the pelvic girdle.**

**TABLE 12.2**

| MUSCLE | ORIGIN | INSERTION | MAJOR ACTION | OTHER |
|---|---|---|---|---|
| Iliopsoas | X | X | ** | Iliacus and psoas muscles |
| Gracilis (adductor group) | Ischiopubic ramus | Tibia | | |
| Adductor magnus | | | | |
| Sartorius** | | | | |
| Gluteus maximus | | | | |
| Gluteus medius | Outer surface of the ilium | Greater trochanter of the femur | Abducts thigh at the hip. Medially and laterally rotates the hip. | Place for IM shots |

**Muscles of the lower extremity.**

| TABLE 12.3 | | | | |
|---|---|---|---|---|
| **MUSCLE** | **ORIGIN** | **INSERTION** | **MAJOR ACTION** | **OTHER** |
| *Quadriceps group* | X | X | | Four muscles of anterior thigh |
| Rectus femoris** | | | | |
| Vastus intermedius | X | X | X | Located deep to the femoris |
| Vastus lateralis | X | X | X | |
| Vastus medialis | X | X | X | |
| Quadriceps tendon | X | X | | Tendon holds the patellar bone |
| Tensor fasciae latae muscle | | | | |
| Fascia latae (iliotibial tract, or it band) | | | | |
| *Hamstring group* | X | X | | Three muscles of the posterior thigh |
| Biceps femoris** | | | | |
| Semitendinosus | X | X | | |
| Semimembranosus | X | X | | |
| Tibialis anterior** | | | | |
| Gastrocnemius** | | | | |
| Calcaneal tendon** (Achilles tendon) | | | | |
| Soleus | | | | |

# REVIEW QUESTIONS

1.  What is the agonist (prime mover) in forearm extension?

2.  What is the agonist or prime mover in hyperextension of the thigh?

3.  What is the agonist for arm abduction?

4.  State the criteria for naming the following muscles:
    a.  Rectus abdominis _______________________________________________
    b.  Deltoid _______________________________________________________
    c.  Flexor carpi radialis ____________________________________________
    d.  Gluteus medius _________________________________________________
    e.  Pectoralis minor ________________________________________________
    f.  Biceps brachii __________________________________________________
    g.  Extensor digitorum ______________________________________________
    h.  Pronator teres __________________________________________________

5.  Label these muscles of the arm from the lab list

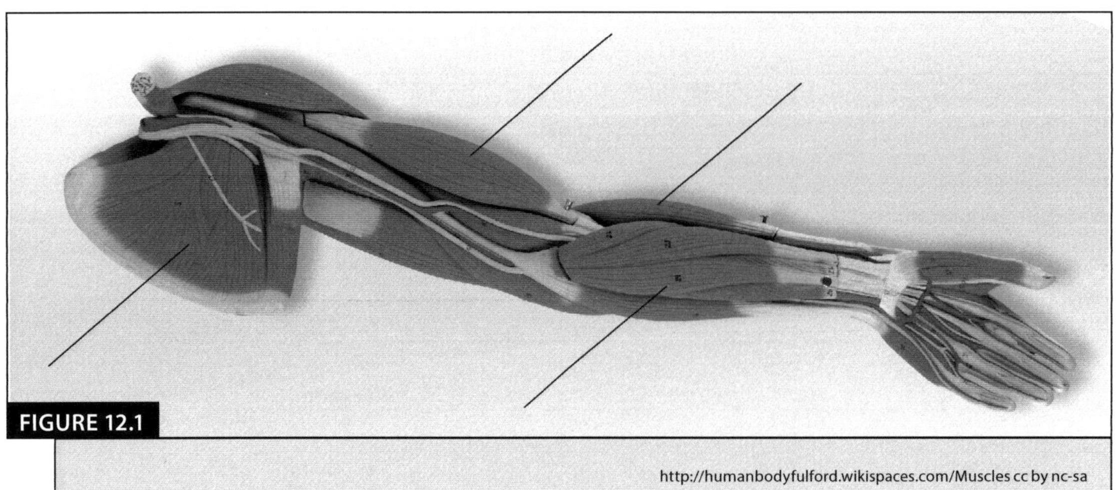

**FIGURE 12.1**

http://humanbodyfulford.wikispaces.com/Muscles cc by nc-sa

**6.** Which muscle(s) perform each action listed below?

**a.** Smiling muscle (paired) ___________________________

**b.** Kissing muscle ___________________________

**c.** Muscle that flexes head and rotates it to the side (paired) ___________________________

**d.** Muscle that closes the mouth (prime mover or agonist) ___________________________

**e.** Extends, adducts, and medially rotates the arm ___________________________

**f.** Flexes forearm at the elbow ___________________________

**g.** Pronates the forearm ___________________________

**h.** Dorsiflexes foot ___________________________

**i.** Plantar flexes foot and flexes leg ___________________________

**j.** Three muscles that flex the leg and extend the thigh

    **i.** ___________________________

    **ii.** ___________________________

    **iii.** ___________________________

**Palpation is a technique used to locate internal structures with your hands and/ or fingers.**

**7.** Show your lab partner how to palpate these structures on *your body:*

**a. Frontalis**—raise your eyebrows and palpate

**b. Masseter**—close the mouth while clenching your teeth

**c. Sternocleidomastoid**—looking in a mirror, turn your face laterally to the left or right to palpate the origin and insertion points on the neck

**d. Iliac crests**—hands on hips, then palpate the gluteus medius inferior to them.

**e. Infraspinatus muscle**—inferior to the scapular spine, palpate there

**f. Quadriceps muscles**

**g. Hamstring muscles**

**h. Tibialis anterior**—palpate the tibial tuberosity inferior to the knee and dorsiflex the foot to palpate the muscle

**i. Gastrocnemius**

Here is a website that will help you review skeletal muscle structure, muscle contraction, the girdles, some muscle disorders, and various muscle groups!

- http://www.sportsinjuryclinic.net/anatomy/human-muscles

*Note:* Be sure to get your completed work checked off by a member of the lab staff and then keep this handout for your review.

# 13

# NERVOUS TISSUE AND SPINAL CORD
## PRE-LAB

Name: _______________________     Section: __________     Date: _________

## LEARNING OBJECTIVES

- Describe nervous tissue and the anatomy of the neuron.
- Read the introductory material in your Open Source Text then fill in the questions below.

## INTRODUCTION

Nervous tissue contains two major cell types, neurons and glial cells. **Neurons** are the cells responsible for communication through electrical signals, so they are referred to as the functional unit of the nervous system. **Glial cells** are supporting cells, maintaining the environment around the neurons. Neurons are polarized cells, based on the flow of electrical signals along their membrane. Signals received at the dendrites are passed along the membrane of the cell body and propagate along the axon towards the target, which may be another neuron, muscle tissue, or a gland. A lipid-rich substance called myelin insulates many axons. Specific types of glial cells provide this insulation. We will focus on the Schwann cells of the peripheral nervous system in the lab activities.

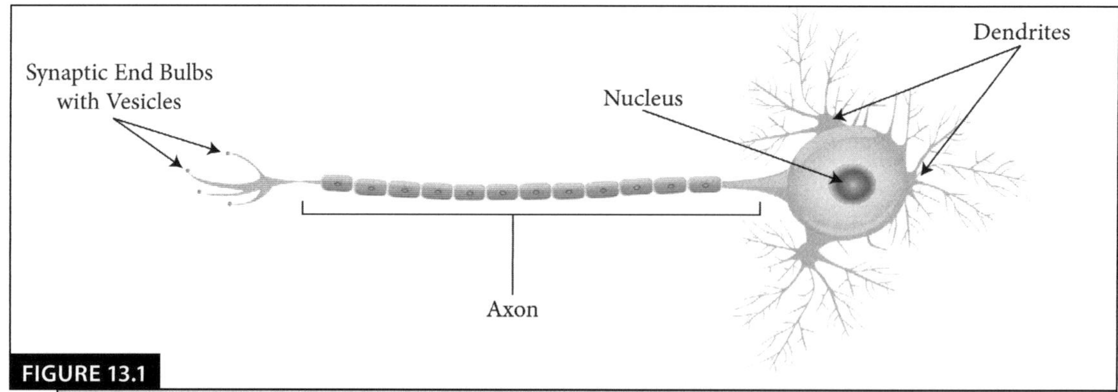


**FIGURE 13.1**

**Anatomy of a multipolar neuron.** Parts of the neuron are labeled: axon dendrites, nucleus, soma (cell body with nucleus) and the synaptic end bulbs at the end of the axon. (Created by c3bc)

## PRE-LAB QUESTIONS

**Use the terms listed below to fill in these sentences.** Not all words will be used, so you must read the text material provided in your Open Source book to answer these. You will find these anatomy parts on models in the lab, so familiarize yourself with them ahead of lab.

- Cell body (soma) (perikaryon)
- Nucleus
- Nissl bodies
- Dendrites
- Axon
- Axonal hillock
- Node of Ranvier
- Schwann cell
- Myelin sheath
- Unmyelinated
- Subarachnoid space

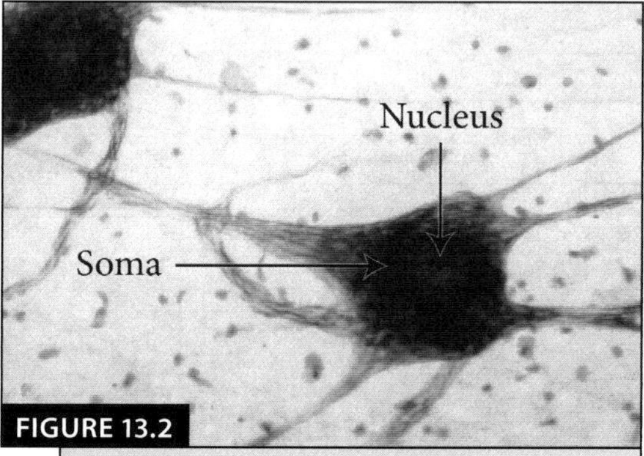


**FIGURE 13.2**

**The cell body (soma) of a neuron.** The other dots around the cell are the glial cell's nuclei. These are the support cells for the neuron.

- Ventricles
- Choroid plexus
- Dura mater
- Arachnoid mater
- Pia mater
- Oligodendrocyte
- Myelinated

1. The functional unit of the nervous system responsible for communication signals is the _______________ (cell).

2. The three important parts of a neuron are multiple extensions called _______________ that **receive** signals from other neurons, the _______________ that sends signals away, and the cell's central mass—_______________(or soma).

3. _______________ cells create a myelin sheath on peripheral neurons (PNS) while _______________ are cells that create a myelin sheath on neurons within the central nervous system (CNS).

4. The modified rough endoplasmic reticulum found in neurons are called _______________ _______________.

5. The three meningeal membranes (meninges) that cover the central nervous system are the _______________, the _______________, and the _______________.

6. Cerebrospinal fluid is produced by the _______________ _______________ (modified blood vessels) located in the _______________ of the brain.

7. Cerebrospinal fluid circulates within the _______________ space.

8. Gray matter in the central nervous system is made up of _______________ neurons while white matter is made up of _______________ neurons.

9. The _______________ nerve root of the spinal cord carries *afferent* or _______________ impulses while the **ventral** nerve root carries *efferent* or _______________ impulses.

# 13

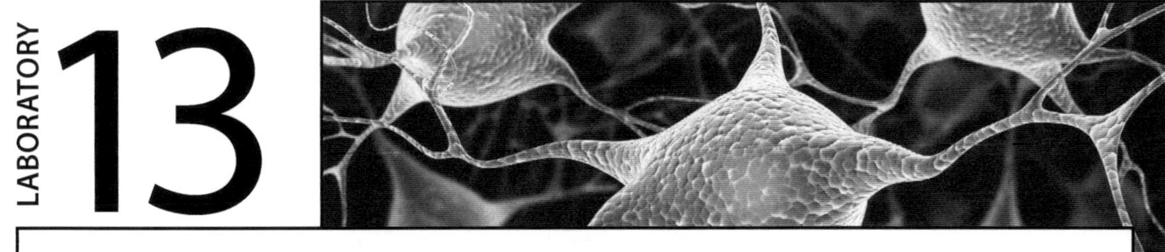

# NERVOUS TISSUE AND SPINAL CORD
## IN-LAB ACTIVITIES

Name: _______________________  Section: __________  Date: _________

## LEARNING OBJECTIVES

- Describe the anatomy of a neuron—the functional unit of the Nervous System.
- Describe CNS tissue and PNS tissues, including myelination.
- Identify the three meninges of the spinal cord (and Brain).
- Identify the parts of the spinal cord.

## PRE-LAB

Before going to lab, you must complete the following:

1. Read the **Pre-Lab** and answer the questions that follow.

*Note:* You will spend ~**2 hr** in lab at Forsyth Tech to complete the following activities. This amount of time allows you to complete the activities by using the motor neuron slide, spinal cord models, spinal cord dissection, and other models as well as working with a lab partner.

**You will find these anatomy parts on models and/or dissections in the lab, so familiarize yourself with them ahead of lab.**

- Cell body (soma) (perikaryon)
- Nucleus
- Nissl bodies
- Dendrites
- Axon
- Axonal hillock
- Node of Ranvier
- Schwann cell
- Myelin sheath
- Unmyelinated
- Subarachnoid space
- Ventricles
- Choroid plexus
- Dura mater
- Arachnoid mater
- Pia mater
- Oligodendrocyte
- Myelinated

## ACTIVITY 1

Draw and label the motor neuron as seen on the neuron **model** in lab below:

- Alternatively take a picture of the model, post that here, and label the picture.
- Include the anatomical parts of the neuron listed above.

## ACTIVITY 2

View the *Motor Neuron slide* under the microscope. Start with the scanning objective to find the stained cell bodies. Move to low power to find the large motor neuron.

1. Draw and label the structures you see, including motor neuron **cell body,** processes (**dendrites** and **axon,** but often you cannot tell the difference between these two types), and **neuroglial cell nuclei** (dots around the neurons of these support cells).

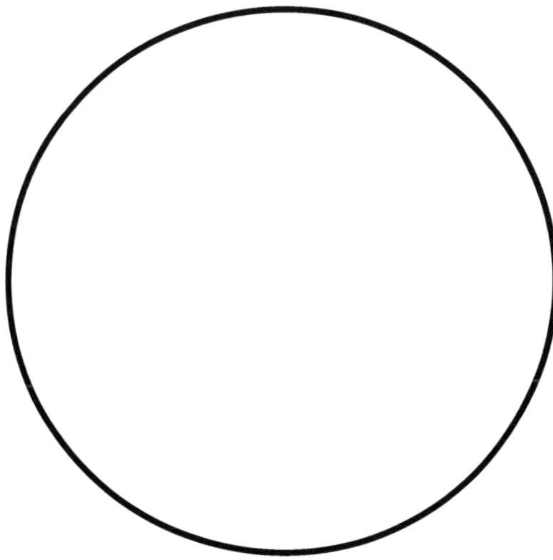

2. **List** and **describe** all the glial cells and functions found in the nervous system. Indicate where you would expect to FIND these different types of cells.

## ACTIVITY 3: MYELIN SHEATH

1. **Draw** an axon covered with a myelin sheath from a *Schwann cell* (PNS). See model in lab as your example.

2. What is the functional significance of myelination? Of nodes of Ranvier?

## ACTIVITY 4: SPINAL CORD DISSECTION

*Note:* Always use PPE for lab work: wear safety glasses and gloves when handling preserved or fresh tissue. Always wash hands thoroughly when you're done.

**Material:** Use a preserved cow (or sheep) spinal cord or a fresh spinal cord from a butcher. Preserved specimens will look different and be more firm than fresh specimens are.

## PROCEDURE

1. After putting on your gloves, observe the *posterior structures* (see figure and models in lab), and place the **spinal cord** into the dissecting pan.

2. Gently use forceps (probes) to separate the **spinal meninges** from the **outer cord.**

3. Find the **dura mater** and the **arachnoid mater** (often too attached to the dura to separate the arachnoid from it).

4. To detach the **pia mater,** use pin or a sharp probe to push gently under the pia mater and pull it from the cord. **Can you find the denticulate ligaments?** These are also seen on the Somso nerve board (green board in lab).

5. Peel back the **meninges** to expose the **posterior root** and find the **rootlets** attached to the spinal cord. Try to find the **dorsal (posterior) root ganglion** to distinguish it from the **ventral root.**

6. Cut a *transverse* section of the spinal cord.

7. Find the **posterior median sulcus** and the **anterior median fissure.** Distinguish the white columns from the gray horns and the gray commissure.

## REVIEW

What do white columns have that make them white that is missing from the gray horns? What is located in the gray matter of the CNS?

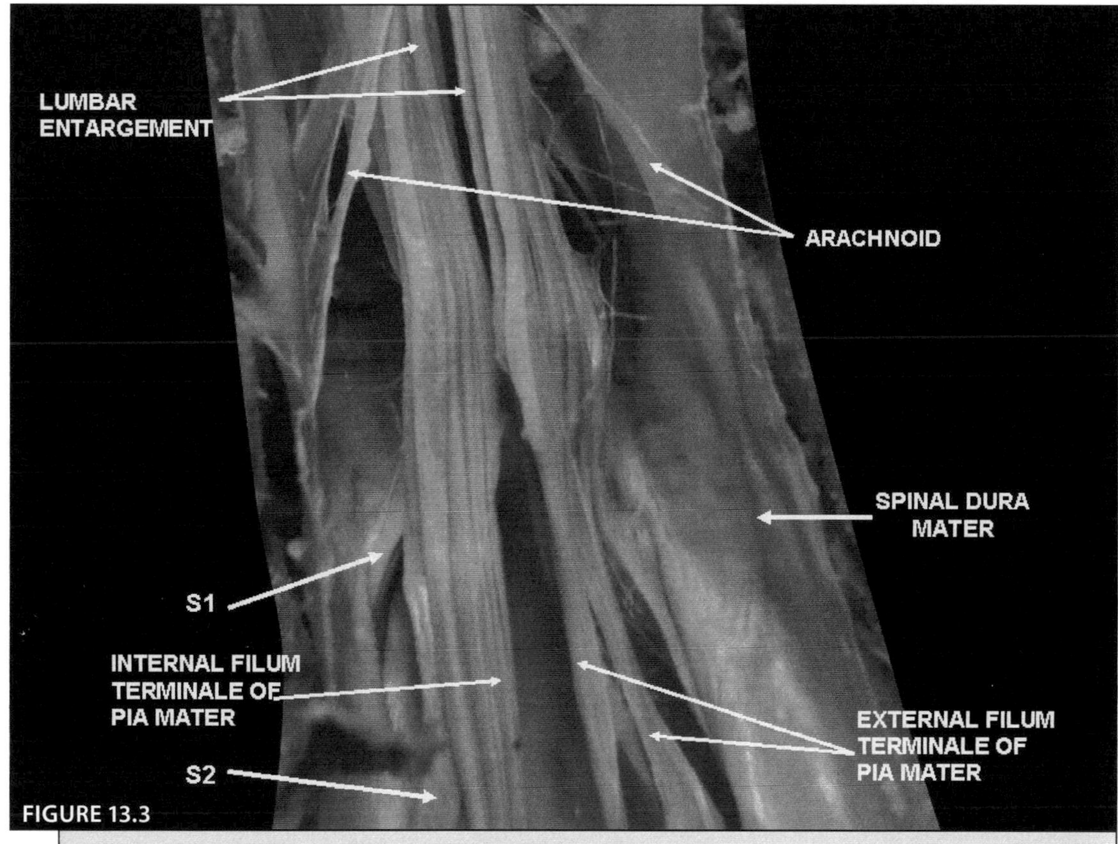


**Lumbar enlargement and meninges labeled on a cow spinal cord dissection.** Also seen are spinal nerves S1 and S2, as well as the filum terminale. https://en.wikipedia.org/wiki/Lumbar_enlargement#/media/File:Slide5sese.GIF

Anatomist90 [CC BY-SA 3.0 (https://creativecommons.org/licenses/by-sa/3.0)]

## ACTIVITY 5: SPINAL MENINGES

1. **Draw** the *transverse section* of the spinal cord and **label** the *3 spinal cord meninges* as seen in lab on the 5th cervical vertebra model (and the spinal cord dissection) below:

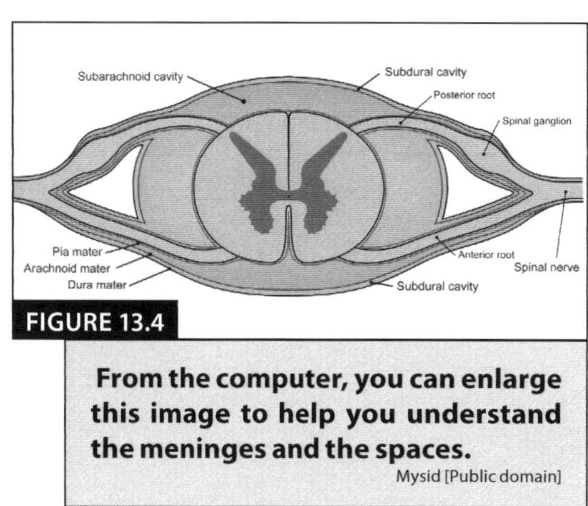


**From the computer, you can enlarge this image to help you understand the meninges and the spaces.**

Mysid [Public domain]

## REVIEW

1.  The functional unit of the nervous system is the ________________________________.

2.  ________________________________ cells create a myelin sheath on peripheral neurons while ________________________________ are cells that create a myelin sheath on neurons within the central nervous system.

3.  The rough endoplasmic reticulum found in neurons is called ________________________.

4.  The three meningeal membranes that cover the central nervous system are the ________________________________, the ________________________________, and the ________________________________.

5.  The spinal cord begins at the ________________________________ and ends between ________________________________.

6.  The ________________________________ ________________________________ anchors the spinal cord to the coccyx bone.

*Note:* Be sure to get your completed work checked off by a member of the lab staff and then keep this handout for your review.

# 14

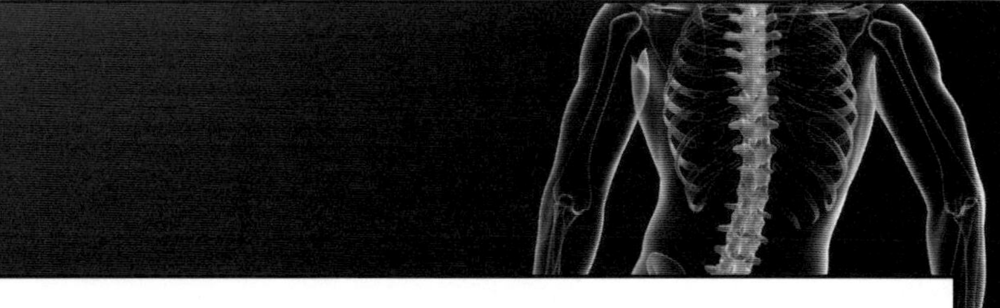

# SPINAL NERVES
## PRE-LAB

Name: _______________________   Section: __________   Date: _________

## LEARNING OBJECTIVES

- Identify the names and location of spinal nerves.
- Identify a primary nerve emerging from each nerve plexus of the spinal cord.

## PRE-LAB ACTIVITY 1

Read the information below and define the terms that follow. Continue to define and study these terms until you no longer need to refer back to the reading material.

## INTRODUCTION

The significance of the nervous system is tied to its ability to provide for rapid intercellular communications. *Intercellular communications* are necessary so that cells, tissues, and organs can do what they need to do, when and where they need to do it. Using electrical properties, your nervous system can send signals from your foot to your brain, interpret those signals, and send signals back to your leg within a fraction of a second. These communications might allow you to specifically withdraw your left foot before you do serious damage by continuing to step on a sharp or hot object. Most cells in the nervous system are found within the skull and vertebral canal in soft structures called the brain and spinal cord, respectively.

The brain and spinal cord communicate with the rest of the body using nervous system structures called nerves. *Nerves* consist of hundreds to millions of long, extremely thin extensions of cytoplasm that emerge from cells called **neurons.** These thin extensions are called nerve fibers or more specifically, *axons.* The axons are held together by supporting non-neuron cells and cell products. Some of these non-nerve cells are called

*Schwann cells,* and they surround many of the individual axons in a nerve with an electrically insulating material called **myelin.** It is often useful to think of axons as electrical wires, some of which are electrically insulated better than others. Using this analogy, the nerves would be electrical cables consisting of thousands of wires with electrical insulation provided by Schwann cells. A third cell type, **fibroblasts,** provides materials that give structural strength to these biological cables.

Nerves extend from the brain and spinal cord to nearly all parts of the body. Nerves extending from the brain are called **cranial nerves,** and nerves extending from the spinal cord are called *spinal nerves.* Here, we will focus on the spinal nerves. The spinal nerves are themselves formed from much smaller nerves. Nerves called *rootlets* emerge directly from the spinal cord, one set of these from the dorsal side of the spinal cord and one set from the ventral side of the spinal cord. The dorsal rootlets join with each other periodically to form *dorsal roots.* The ventral rootlets do the same to form *ventral roots.* At each vertebral level, a new dorsal and ventral root are formed. These roots join to form a single large nerve called a **spinal nerve** on each side of the body at each vertebral level, except for the coccygeal vertebrae. There is normally only one coccygeal spinal nerve on each side. The spinal nerve exits the vertebral column through an *intervertebral foramen* on each side of each vertebra. The spinal nerves are named for the vertebral level at which they form. As the spinal nerves extend further from the spinal cord, their fibers merge to form a network of nerves called a *nerve plexus,* but they only do this in specific regions along the length of the vertebral column. For instance, the thoracic spinal nerves do not form a nerve plexus.

An **axon** in a nerve carries electrical signals in one direction only—either toward (*sensory axons*) or away from (*motor axons*) the brain and spinal cord. Sensory axons and motor axons are intermixed in spinal nerves so spinal nerves are known as *mixed nerves.* Cranial nerves can also be mixed nerves. However, some cranial nerves consist entirely of axons carrying sensory signals (sensory nerves) to the brain, and some cranial nerves consist entirely of axons carrying signals away from the brain (*motor nerves*). Even though a spinal nerve is mixed, the dorsal and ventral roots that form it are not mixed.

The dorsal root is always sensory (signals travel toward the spinal cord), and the ventral root is always motor (signals travel away from the spinal cord). The cell bodies of the motor neurons that send axons into the ventral root are found in the *ventral and lateral horns* of the spinal cord. The cell bodies of sensory neurons are found in *dorsal root ganglia,* which are single enlarged regions of the dorsal roots. The spinal nerves are short, branching quickly into an *anterior ramus* and a smaller diameter *posterior ramus* as they extend from the intervertebral foramina. There are also smaller branches of the spinal nerves, called *rami communicantes,* that connect to parts of the autonomic nervous system. The white rami are found only between the T1 and L2 vertebral levels.

Define the terms below:

1. Nerve

2. Spinal nerve

3. Nerve plexus

4. Intervertebral foramen

5. Cranial nerve

6. Dorsal root

7. Ventral root

8. Rootlets

9. Anterior ramus

10. Posterior ramus

11. Rami communicantes (white and gray)

12. Dorsal root ganglion

13. Anterior and lateral horns

14. Mixed nerve

15. Sensory nerve

16. Sensory neuron

17. Motor nerve

18. Motor neuron

19. Axon

# 14

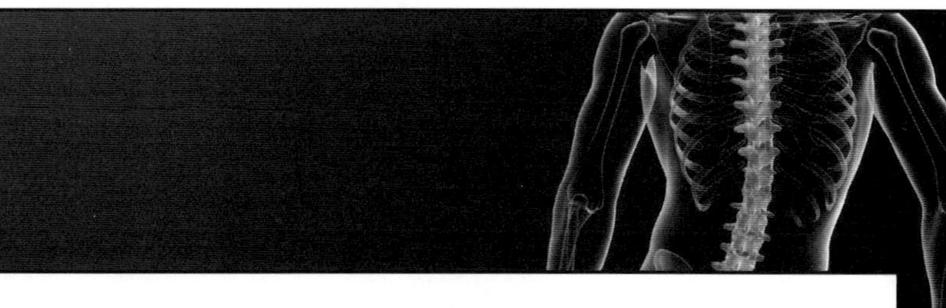

# SPINAL NERVES
## IN-LAB ACTIVITIES

Name: ________________________    Section: __________    Date: _________

## LEARNING OBJECTIVES

- Identify the names and location of spinal nerves.
- Identify a primary nerve emerging from each nerve plexus of the spinal cord.

## PRE-LAB

Before going to lab, you must complete the following:

1. Read the **Pre-Lab** and answer the questions that follow.

*Note:* You will spend **1.5–2 hr** in Lab at Forsyth Tech to complete the following activities. This amount of time allows you to complete the activities by using the nerve board models, spinal cord cross section model in lab, and other models as well as working with and reviewing with a lab partner.

## ACTIVITY 1

### PART A

1. Locate the models of **vertebral column cross sections** in the lab. There are some with the vertebrae and some of just the spinal cord with nerves emerging from cord.

2. **Study** the models with the **definitions** from the Spinal Nerves Pre-lab Handout in front of you.

3. Patiently, associate each definition with a structure on the models.

4. Once you are satisfied with your structure identification, check yourself with the keys/legend to the models in lab, then **quiz yourself** using the models without the definitions in front of you. If a classmate is with you, quiz each other.

## PART B

5. **Draw** the images of the models. Illustrate **all the terms** defined in the Pre-lab handout.

6. Indicate the direction of travel of electrical signals in the nerves (nerves with axons carrying signals toward the spinal cord, away from the spinal cord, and mixed nerves). It is better to make many crude drawings than to make one perfect drawing.

7. **Place your best drawing on the top half of the back of this page.**

# ACTIVITY 2

## PART A

1. Locate models of **anterior views of the vertebral column** with emerging spinal nerves and/or anterior rami (green board in lab), and the **hanging vertebral column** should be used if available.

2. Learn the numbering scheme for the spinal nerves. C1 through C8 spinal nerves start **above the C1 vertebra** and end **after the C7 vertebra.** All other spinal nerves emerge inferior to the vertebra of the same name. **For example,** the T3 spinal nerve emerges from the intervertebral foramen between the T3 and T4 vertebra.

3. **Identify** regions where the spinal nerves form rami. You will find the **cervical, brachial, lumbar, and sacral rami.**

4. **Identify** one major **peripheral nerve** that emerges from each plexus. **For example,** the phrenic nerve emerges from the cervical plexus (primarily).

   (If using the long Somso green board model of the spinal cord, the phrenic nerve can be found on the upper left (of the model) just inferior to the cervical plexus.)

5. **Quiz yourself** or work with a friend thereby using repetition and comparison to remember the relevant structures in the anterior view of vertebral column models.

## PART B

6. **Draw** the images of the **anterior view of vertebral column models.** You should illustrate all the structures mentioned in Activity 2: Part A. It is better to make many crude drawings than to make one perfect drawing.

7. **Place your best drawing on the bottom half of the back of this page.**

## ACTIVITY 3

In addition to these spinal anatomical parts, find the following **spinal nerves on the nerve models** in the lab. Quiz yourself on the models since we use these on our lab tests.

1. **Spinal nerves—31 pairs (one figure)**
   a. Cervical nerves (C1–C8)
   b. Thoracic nerves (T1–T12)
   c. Lumbar nerves (L1–L5)
   d. Sacral nerves (S1–S5)
   e. Coccygeal nerves (Co1)

2. **Plexuses**
   a. Cervical plexus (C1–C4 spinal nerves)
   b. Brachial plexus (C5–T1 spinal nerves)
   c. Lumbosacral plexus (T12–S5 spinal nerves) (some books = lumbar & sacral separate)

3. **Intervertebral foramen**

4. **Sympathetic chain ganglion**

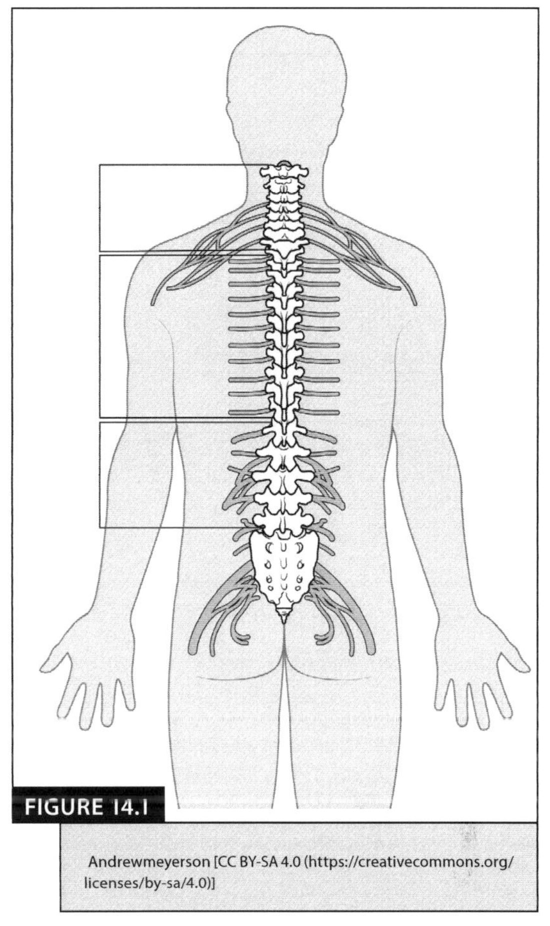

**FIGURE 14.1**

Andrewmeyerson [CC BY-SA 4.0 (https://creativecommons.org/licenses/by-sa/4.0)]

## ACTIVITY 4

1. Identify the following **nerves and from which plexus they arise.** In lab use the white board of nerves and the long spinal cord green board, if available, or the hanging vertebrae/spinal cord
   a. **Phrenic nerve** (from C3–C5 to the diaphragm; remember this: "C3,C4,C5 keep diaphragm alive")
   b. **Axillary nerve**
   c. **Ulnar nerve**
   d. **Radial nerve**
   e. **Median nerve** [carpel tunnel syndrome pain producer]
   f. **Sciatic nerve**
   g. **Femoral nerve**
   h. **Intercostal nerve** (thoracic nerves)

**2.** In the diagram below, indicate the location of each of the spinal nerves listed.

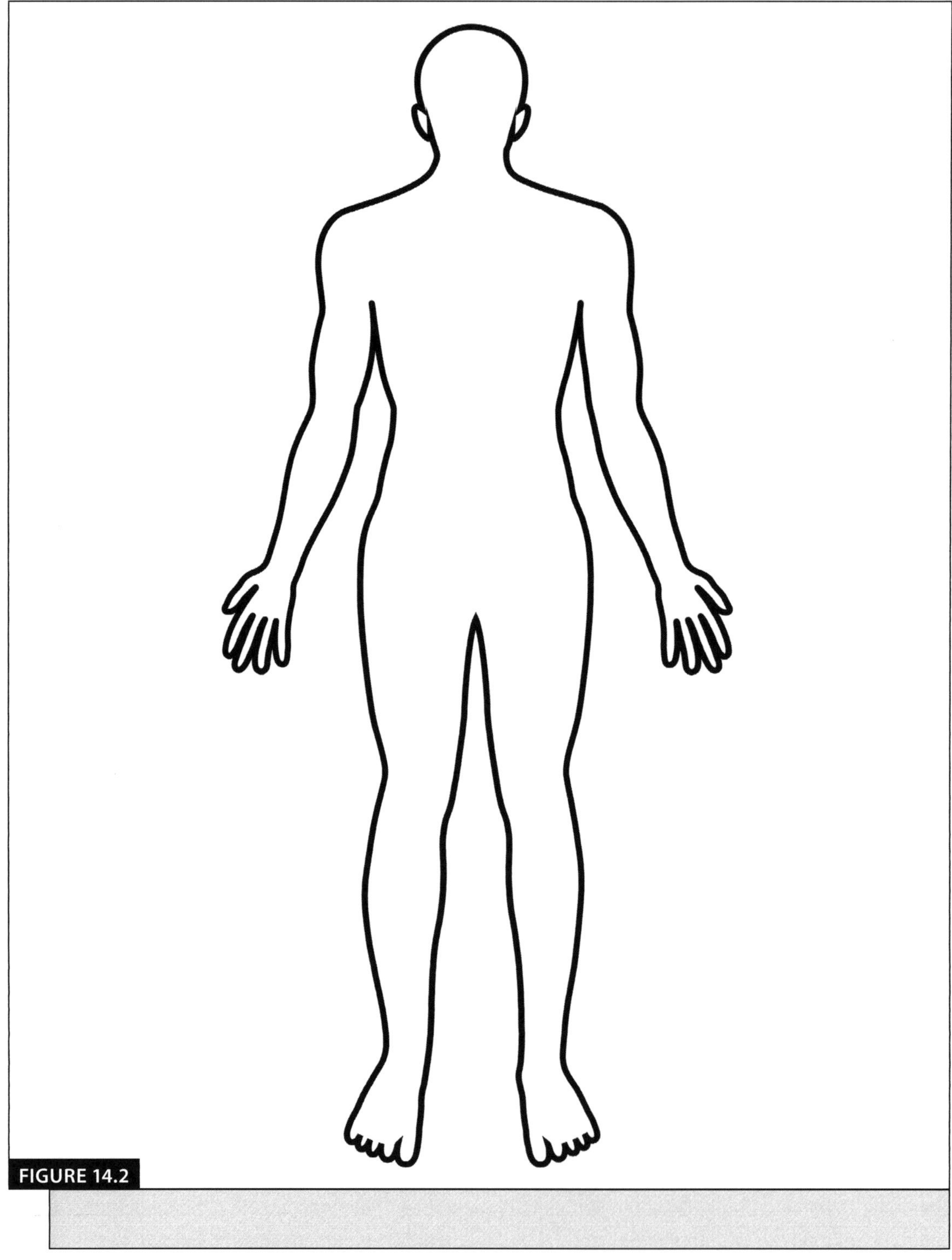

**FIGURE 14.2**

*Note:* Be sure to get your completed work checked off by a member of the lab staff and then keep this handout for your review.

# 15

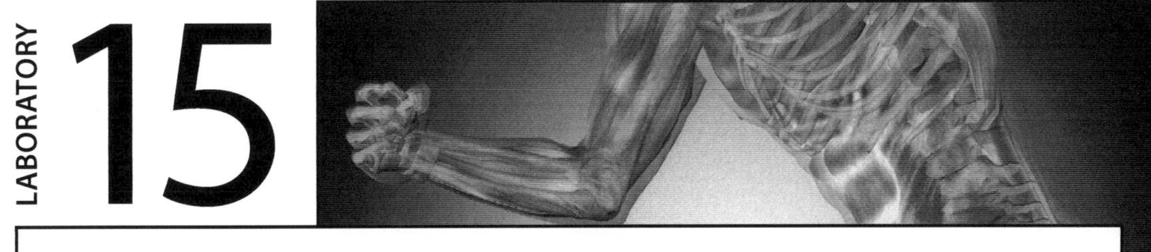

# SOMATIC REFLEXES
## PRE-LAB

Name: _______________________   Section: __________   Date: _________

## LEARNING OBJECTIVES

- Classify reflexes.
- Identify the parts of a reflex arc.
- Learn reflex testing and undergo several reflex tests in lab.

## INTRODUCTION

Reflexes can be classified based on the location of their integration center and the types of effectors that are stimulated by the motor neuron. If a reflex has its integration center located in the brain or brain stem, it is called a **cranial reflex.** If its integration center is located in the spinal cord, it is called a **spinal reflex.** Reflexes that stimulate skeletal muscles are called **somatic reflexes,** while those that stimulate cardiac muscle, smooth muscles, or glands are called **autonomic reflexes.**

## PRE-LAB ACTIVITY

1. Log in to your Blackboard site or LMS for your course.

2. Read Unit 8.5 or the Spinal Reflexes section or concept:

   Objectives:

   - What is the anatomy of the spinal cord and spinal nerves?
   - What is a reflex arc?

3. Read Reflexes in the Open Stax Sensory and Motor Exams [https://cnx.org/contents/FPtK1zmh@8.26:2r012ntk@3/The-Sensory-and-Motor-Exams] or in your text provided.

Answer the following questions and label the following picture:

1. **Read** in your open source text and do some research.

    a.  Give some examples of autonomic reflexes and somatic reflexes.

    b.  What effectors are associated with somatic reflexes?

    c.  What effectors are associated with autonomic reflexes?

2.  What is the difference between a cranial reflex and a spinal reflex? Give some examples of a spinal reflex and a cranial reflex.

3.  Reflex arcs that contain sensory receptors and effectors on **opposite** sides of the body are called ______________________. Reflex arcs where the sensory receptors and effectors are on the **same** side of the body are called ______________________.

4.  In this lab, you will be testing the deep tendon reflexes and a superficial reflex. Research which common reflex tests are the deep tendon reflexes.

    a.  What are the receptors and their location in the **deep** tendon reflexes?

    b.  Where are the receptors for the **superficial** reflex located?

5. **Read** the following website (https://www.youtube.com/watch?v=fwHdYk7NogU) and briefly describe in your own words the following associated with reflexes:

   **a.** Reciprocal inhibition

   **b.** Flexor withdrawal reflex along with the crossed-extensor reflex

6. **Label and describe** the parts of a reflex arc beginning with **stimulus,** the **sensory receptor, sensory neuron, integrating center, motor neuron, and effector.**

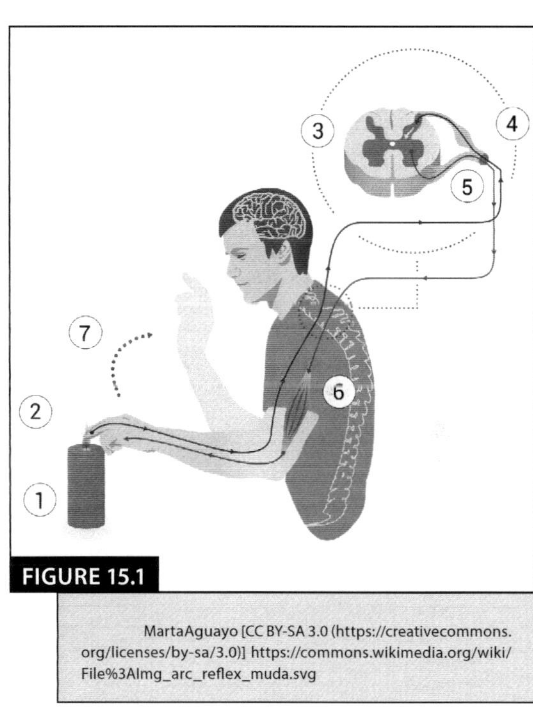

**FIGURE 15.1**

MartaAguayo [CC BY-SA 3.0 (https://creativecommons.
org/licenses/by-sa/3.0)] https://commons.wikimedia.org/wiki/
File%3AImg_arc_reflex_muda.svg

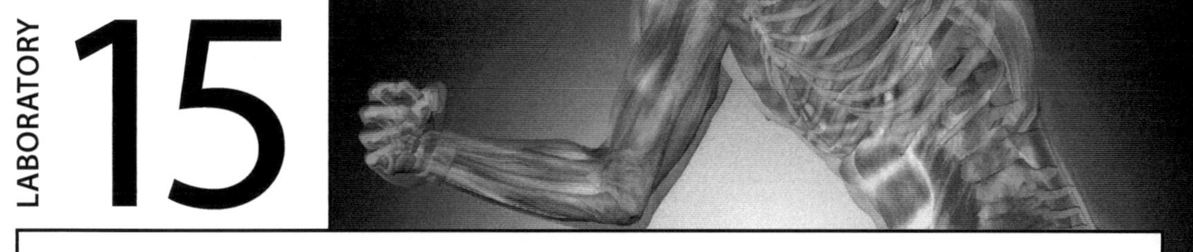

**LABORATORY**

# 15

# SOMATIC REFLEXES
## IN-LAB ACTIVITIES

Name: _________________________   Section: ___________   Date: __________

## LEARNING OBJECTIVES

- Classify reflexes.
- Identify the parts of a reflex arc.
- Learn reflex testing and undergo several reflex tests in lab.
- Explore other ways reflexes are initiated.

## PRE-LAB

Before going to lab, you must complete the following:

**1.** Read the **Pre-Lab** and answer the questions that follow.

*Note:* You will spend **2 hr and 30 min** in lab at Forsyth Tech to complete the following activities. This amount of time allows you to complete the activities by using models in lab as well as working with a lab partner.

**Use this handout to help you learn and perform somatic reflexes.**

## INTRODUCTION

If you remember back to the introductory material, when the concept of homeostasis or the maintenance of a relatively stable internal environment was first introduced, there was also a discussion of feedback control mechanisms. One of the major feedback control mechanisms was negative feedback. This control system contained the following components: a receptor, afferent pathway, control center, efferent pathway, and an effector. In this lab, you will notice how this basic pattern can also be seen in automatic responses called reflexes. These reflexes follow the same basic pattern as a feedback loop but instead we called these components the **sensory receptor,** the afferent pathway (represented by a **sensory neuron**), a control center, (our **integration center,** which is either in the brain or spinal cord), an efferent pathway, (a **motor neuron**), and **effectors,** (a muscle or a gland that responds to motor neuron).

Reflexes can be classified based on the location of their integration center and the types of effectors that are stimulated by the motor neuron. If a reflex has its integration center located in the brain or brain stem, it is called a **cranial reflex.** If its integration center is located in the spinal cord, it is called a **spinal reflex.** Reflexes that stimulate skeletal muscles are called **somatic reflexes,** while those that stimulate cardiac muscle, smooth muscles, or glands are called **autonomic reflexes.**

# ACTIVITY 1: CLASSIFYING REFLEXES

**Do some research and answer the following questions:**

1.  Identify the following as a spinal reflex or a cranial reflex and whether it is an autonomic or somatic reflex.

    a.  Your pupils constrict in bright light. What nerve is involved in this reflex?

    b.  Your toes curl under when someone strokes the bottom of your foot.

    c.  You blink when a bug flies into your eye.

    d.  You withdraw your hand when you pick up a hot pot. As something to think about, what kind of response might cause you to hold on to the hot pot despite it burning your hand?

    (**Hint:** What might allow you to consciously override a muscle contraction?)

## ACTIVITY 2: IDENTIFYING THE PARTS OF A BASIC SPINAL REFLEX ARC

1. Draw and label the basic parts of a spinal reflex arc. Include the following components. Also, look at a cross-section model of the spinal cord and identify the following components of the reflex arc.

    a. **Sensory receptor**—Where are the sensory receptors located for a somatic reflex?

    b. **Sensory neuron**—Looking at the cross-section of the spinal cord, where would the cell bodies for the sensory neurons be located?

    c. **Integrating center**—Where is the integrating center in the spinal cord located?

    d. **Motor neuron**—Where do the motor neurons that are associated with somatic reflexes originate in the spinal cord?

    e. **Effector**—What are the effectors for a somatic reflex arc?

*Draw* **reflex arc here.**

## ACTIVITIES 3–7: REFLEX TESTING

Most of the skeletal muscles are innervated by spinal nerves. From a previous lab, remember that there are 31 pairs of spinal nerves that are coming off of different segments of the spinal cord. Damage to either regions of the spinal cord or the spinal nerves will affect the function of the corresponding muscle that is innervated by the nerves. The activity of reflexes of the spinal nerves is often tested in a clinical situation. **Spinal reflexes** combine the spinal sensory and motor components with a sensory input that directly generates a motor response. The reflexes that are tested in the neurological exam are classified into two groups. A **deep tendon reflex** is commonly known as a **stretch reflex** and is elicited by a strong tap to a tendon, such as in the knee-jerk reflex. A **superficial reflex** is elicited through gentle stimulation of the skin and causes contraction of the associated muscles.

For the arm, the common reflexes to test are the **biceps, brachioradialis, triceps, and flexors for the digits.** For the leg, the **knee-jerk reflex (patellar reflex)** of the quadriceps is common, as is the **ankle reflex (Achilles reflex)** for the gastrocnemius and soleus muscles. The tendon at the insertion for each of these muscles is struck with a rubber mallet. The muscle is quickly stretched, resulting in activation of the muscle spindle that sends a signal into the spinal cord through the dorsal root. The fiber synapses directly on the ventral horn motor neuron that activates the muscle, causing contraction. The reflexes are physiologically useful for stability. If a muscle is stretched, it reflexively contracts to return the muscle to compensate for the change in length.

Also remember from the muscle lab that muscles work in opposing pairs with one group of muscles (the agonist) performing the primary movement, while another group of muscles performs the opposing action (antagonist). Therefore, when a stretch reflex like the deep tendon reflexes are activated, not only must the main agonist contract to perform the reflex but the opposing muscle must relax and is therefore inhibited so that it does not contract against the muscle carrying out the reflex. This is a concept called **reciprocal inhibition.** (Summarized from Neuroscience online: an electronic textbook for the neurosciences http://neuroscience.uth.tmc.edu/s3/chapter02.html)

The most common superficial reflex in the neurological exam is the plantar reflex that tests for the Babinski sign on the basis of the extension or flexion of the toes at the plantar surface of the foot. The plantar reflex is commonly tested in newborn infants to establish the presence of neuromuscular function. To elicit this reflex, an examiner brushes a stimulus, usually the examiner's fingertip, along the plantar surface of the infant's foot. An infant would present a positive Babinski sign, meaning the foot dorsiflexes and the toes extend and splay out. As a person learns to walk, the plantar reflex changes to cause curling of the toes and a moderate plantar flexion. If superficial stimulation of the sole of the foot caused extension of the foot, keeping one's balance would be harder. The descending input of the corticospinal tract modifies the response of the plantar reflex, meaning that a negative Babinski sign is the expected response in testing the reflex. Other superficial reflexes are not commonly tested, though a series of abdominal reflexes can target function in the lower thoracic spinal segments.

**These reflexes are not just tested for their presence or absence but also for their level of activity. This is subjectively rated using a four-point scale:**

The following table is reproduced from Reflex [https://en.wikipedia.org/wiki/Reflex#cite_note-6]

| GRADE | DESCRIPTION |
| --- | --- |
| 0 | Absent |
| 1+ | Hypoactive |
| 2+ | Normal |
| 3+ | Hyperactive without clonus |
| 4+ | Hyperactive with clonus |

The normal reflex is in the range of 2+. (Clonus is an erratic, involuntary, and rhythmic muscle contraction and relaxations.)

1. Using a partner and a reflex hammer, perform the following reflexes.

2. Grade the response of your partner using the above scale. Record the results in the table below.

3. Using the laptops (if) available in lab **(watch a video of these reflexes to get an idea of how to perform them.)**

   **For a good overview of the major deep tendon reflexes, watch the following:** Deep Tendon Reflexes (https://www.youtube.com/watch?v=eqOpNQH09pA).

The deep tendon reflexes include the patellar reflex, biceps reflex, triceps reflex, and Achilles reflex. Please note that it also includes the brachioradialis reflex and flexors for the digits, but you do not have to perform these reflexes in the lab.

# ACTIVITY 3: PATELLAR REFLEX (KNEE-JERK REFLEX)

The patellar reflex, also called the knee jerk reflex, is stimulated by the stretching of the quadriceps muscle, particularly the rectus femoris. This reflex is particular important for maintaining an upright position.

## PROCEDURE

1. Have your partner sit on a chair that allows the legs to freely move.

2. Find the patellar ligament that is located just below the patella but above the tibial tuberosity.

3. With the tapered end of the reflex hammer, firmly tap the patellar ligament. Using the above scale, grade/**record** the movement of this reflex.

## ACTIVITY 4: BICEPS REFLEX

The biceps reflex occurs when the biceps tendon is stretched.

### PROCEDURE

1. To perform this reflex, locate the biceps tendon in the antecubital fossa. Feel for a cordlike structure in this area. If you are unsure about the location, ask your partner to flex their biceps brachii muscle and feel for a cord-like structure that tenses in the antecubital fossa.

2. Put your thumb over the located biceps tendon, and using the tapered part of the reflex hammer, gently tap your thumb. Look for a response in both the muscle and the forearm.

3. **Record** the response that you get.

## ACTIVITY 5: TRICEPS REFLEX

This reflex results in the contraction of the triceps brachii muscle when the triceps tendon is tapped.

### PROCEDURE

1. To test for this reflex, ask your partner to be seated and relaxed.

2. Locate the triceps reflex; this reflex is just proximal to the elbow. If you are having a hard time finding this reflex, ask your partner to extend their forearm and feel for the area that tightens or becomes taut.

3. Either with your partner with the forearm relaxed or supported by you, gently tap the triceps tendon with the tapered end of the reflex hammer.

4. Look for the response and record it based on the grading scale.

## ACTIVITY 6: ACHILLES REFLEX
## (ANKLE JERK; SEE VIDEO)

The Achilles reflex tests for movement in the gastrocnemius and soleus muscles.

### PROCEDURE

1. Ask your partner to sit on a chair so that the legs are freely moveable.

2. Locate the Achilles or calcaneal tendon. This tendon is just proximal to the calcaneus.

3. Have your partner or yourself slightly dorsiflex the foot.

4.  Use the tapered end of the reflex hammer; gently tap the calcaneal tendon.

5.  Look for the plantar flexion response and rate it based on the grading scale.

## ACTIVITY 7: PLANTAR REFLEX (IF TIME, OR MAY DO AT HOME; SEE VIDEO)

The most common superficial reflex in the neurological exam is the plantar reflex that tests for the Babinski sign on the basis of the extension or flexion of the toes at the plantar surface of the foot.

**Watch the video demonstrating the Plantar reflex:** [https://www.youtube.com/watch?v=dcJgxuLtHdg]

## PROCEDURE

1.  Have your partner take off their socks and shoes and sit in a seated position with the soles of their feet exposed.

2.  Using the metal end of the reflex hammer, stroke the sole of the foot along the side, up, and down as if forming a J.

3.  Look for the curling of the big toe and digits as a normal reflex response in the adult.

## FOLLOWING COMPLETION OF ACTIVITIES 3–7

For the above reflexes describe the location of the sensory receptor, the muscles involved in the reflex, and the spinal nerves that are being tested in the reflex. For the deep tendon reflexes, also include the antagonistic muscles that are inhibited while the reflex action is occurring.

| REFLEX | SENSORY RECEPTOR | SPINAL NERVE(S) | MUSCLES (S) | ANTAGONISTIC MUSCLES RECIPROCALLY INHIBITED |
|---|---|---|---|---|
| Patellar reflex | | | | |
| Biceps reflex | | | | |
| Triceps reflex | | | | |
| Achilles reflex | | | | |
| Plantar reflex | | | | |

1.  Is the Babinski sign normal or abnormal in adults? Briefly describe it.

Reflexes are also initiated by pain such as would occur in the withdrawal reflex or flexor reflex.

**Read the paragraph about this flexor reflex (or withdrawal reflex) from Neuroscience online:** (http://neuroscience.uth.tmc.edu/s3/chapter02.html—under the Figure 2.4 on that page)

## ANSWER THE FOLLOWING QUESTIONS

1.  What are the neurons involved in this reflex? Briefly describe the pathway.

2.  What are the receptors in this reflex?

3.  In the lower limbs, balance must also be maintained while removing the opposite leg from the painful stimulus, which is called the cross-extensor reflex. Briefly describe the pathway for this.

*Note:* Be sure to get your completed work checked off by a member of the lab staff and then keep this handout for your review.

# 16

# BRAIN (AND CRANIAL NERVES)
## PRE-LAB

Name: _______________________     Section: ___________     Date: _________

## LEARNING OBJECTIVES

- Locate regions and lobes of the cerebrum by common anatomical landmarks.
- Differentiate between the gray matter and white matter of the brain.
- Relate the structures of the mammalian brain with their functions.
- Describe the protective coverings of the CNS and how they protect the brain and spinal cord.
- Observe the anatomy and learn the function of the ventricular system of the adult brain.
- Identify the locations of the 12 cranial nerves.

## INTRODUCTION

Read the text provided (Odigia or Lumen, etc.) to give you a more complete view of the anatomy and physiology of the brain before you observe and dissect the brain in lab.

The iconic ridges of the human brain, which appear to make up most of the mass of the brain, form the **cerebrum.** The outer wrinkled portion is composed of gray matter (cell bodies, axon terminals, and short unmyelinated axons) called the **cerebral cortex,** and the rest of the structure is beneath that outer covering. The ridges are the **gyri** (gyrus, singular) and the surrounding shallow depressions are the **sulci** (sulcus, singular). There is a large separation between the two sides of the cerebrum called the **longitudinal fissure.** It separates the cerebrum into two distinct halves, a right and left **cerebral hemisphere.** Deep within the cerebrum, the white matter of the **corpus callosum** provides the major connection and pathway for communication between the two hemispheres of the cerebral cortex. This white matter, as other white matter, contains myelinated axons carrying signals between the two cerebral hemispheres.

The other primary regions of the brain include the **diencephalon,** the **brain stem** and the **cerebellum.** The diencephalon has multiple functions in its various areas. These areas include the **thalamus, epithalamus** (with **pineal gland**), and **hypothalamus** from which the pituitary gland (endocrine gland) is connected by the funnel-shaped infundibulum. The brain stem is the deepest and most fundamental of the regions, including the **midbrain, pons,** and **medulla oblongata.** The cerebellum, or little brain, forms from the hindbrain (rhombencephalon) and is connected to the rest of the brain by the pons (meaning "bridge"). The five lobes of the brain include the **frontal lobe, parietal lobe, occipital lobe, temporal lobe,** and the deeper **insula.**

The **central sulcus** separates the frontal lobe from the parietal lobe (named for the skull bones) on the superior surface of the brain. The gyrus that forms the anterior of the central sulcus is the **precentral gyrus** and regulates signals from the cortex involved in the planning, control, and execution of voluntary movements (primary motor cortex). The **postcentral gyrus** in the parietal lobe receives sensory signals from the **thalamus** (a relay center) and is called the somatosensory cortex.

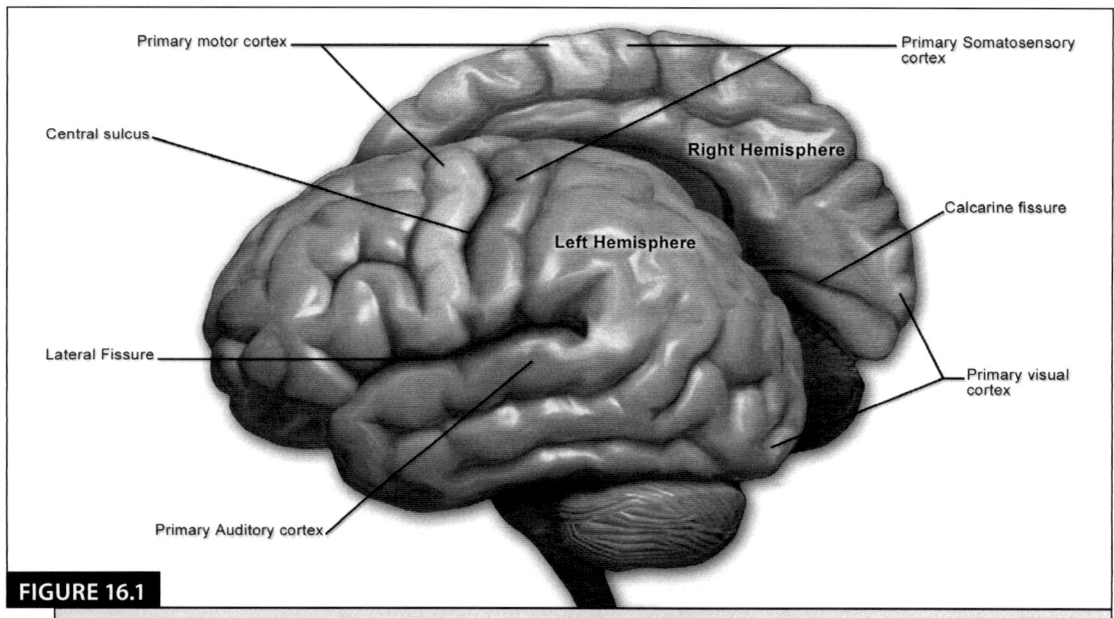


**FIGURE 16.1**

**Human brain showing the primary motor cortex and the somatosensory cortex.** Also shown are the primary auditory cortex and the primary visual cortex. Clearly seen are the gyri and sulci of the brain, as are the cerebellum and part of the brain stem. Extensive folding increases the surface area available for cerebral functions. Blausen.com staff (2014). "Medical gallery of Blausen Medical 2014". WikiJournal of Medicine 1 (2). DOI:10.15347/wjm/2014.010. ISSN 2002-4436. [CC BY 3.0 (https://creativecommons.org/licenses/by/3.0)]

1. The __________________ __________________ separates the two cerebral hemispheres.

2. The __________________ __________________ separates the cerebellum from the cerebrum.

3. Raised areas of the brain surface are called __________________ while shallow depressions are called __________________.

4. The primary **motor** cortex in the brain is located within the ___________________ gyrus while the primary **sensory** cortex is located within the ___________________ gyrus.

5. The brainstem is composed of the ________________, the ________________, and the ________________.

6. The parts of the diencephalon of the brain include the ________________, the ________________, and the ________________.

7. The ________________ ________________ is composed of neuronal pathways that allow communication between the right and left cerebral hemispheres.

8. The ________________ ________________ is an endocrine gland that extends inferiorly from the hypothalamus and sits in the sella turcica.

9. The white matter of the cerebellum is called the ________________ ________________ or "white tree."

10. The **five** lobes of the brain are the ________________, ________________, ________________, ________________, and ________________.



**FIGURE 16.2**

**Midsagittal view of the human brain.** Labels include Frontal lobe, Parietal lobe, Occipital lobe, Parieto-occipital sulcus, cerebellum, spinal cord, midbrain, pons, medulla oblongata (brain stem is colored gold with each portion outlined), thalamus, hypothalamus (gold colored), corpus callosum, and the central sulcus.



**FIGURE 16.3**

**Sheep brain midsagittal view with labels of anatomy mentioned above.** © Van-Griner, LLC

Sheep brain dissection done in lab. Follow directions from your instructor or biology supply house.

# 16

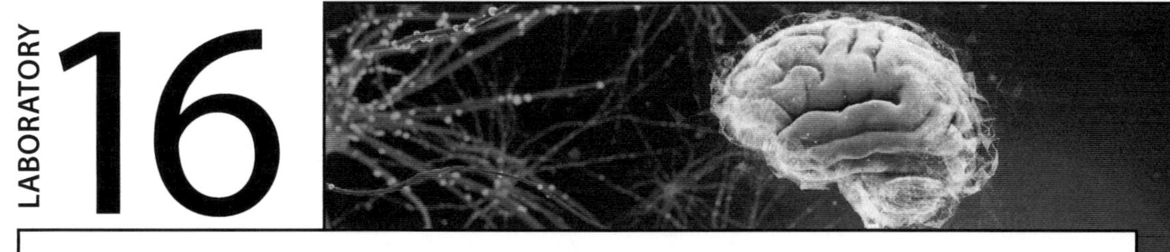

# BRAIN (AND CRANIAL NERVES)
## IN-LAB ACTIVITIES

Name: _______________________     Section: __________     Date: _________

## LEARNING OBJECTIVES

- Identify the lobes and major regions of the brain.
- Differentiate between the gray matter and white matter of the brain.
- Relate the structures of the mammalian brain with their functions.
- Describe the protective coverings of the CNS and how they protect the brain and spinal cord.
- Observe the anatomy and learn the function of the ventricular system of the adult brain.
- Identify the locations of the 12 cranial nerves.

## PRE-LAB

Before going to lab, you must complete the following:

1. Read the **Pre-Lab** and answer the questions that follow.

## INTRODUCTION

The brain and the spinal cord are the central nervous system, and they represent the main organs of the nervous system. The spinal cord is a single structure, whereas the adult brain is described in terms of four major regions: the cerebrum, the diencephalon, the brain stem, and the cerebellum.

## THE CEREBRUM AND CEREBRAL CORTEX

The cerebrum is covered by a continuous layer of gray matter that wraps around either side of the forebrain—the cerebral cortex. This thin, extensive region of wrinkled gray matter is responsible for the higher functions of the nervous system. A **gyrus** (plural = gyri) is the ridge of one of those wrinkles, and a **sulcus** (plural = sulci) is the groove between two gyri. The pattern of these folds of tissue indicates specific regions of the cerebral cortex.

The head is limited by the size of the birth canal, and the brain must fit inside the cranial cavity of the skull. Extensive folding in the cerebral cortex enables more gray matter to fit into this limited space. If the gray matter of the cortex were peeled off of the cerebrum and laid out flat, its surface area would be roughly equal to one square meter.

The folding of the cortex maximizes the amount of gray matter in the cranial cavity. The cortex can be separated into five major regions, or lobes. The **lateral sulcus** separates the **temporal lobe** from the other lobes. Superior to the lateral sulcus are the **parietal lobe** and **frontal lobe,** which are separated from each other by the **central sulcus.** The posterior region of the cortex is the **occipital lobe,** which has no obvious anatomical border between it and the parietal or temporal lobes. From the medial surface, an obvious landmark separating the parietal and occipital lobes is called the parietooccipital sulcus. The fact that there is no obvious anatomical border between these lobes is consistent with the functions of these regions being interrelated. The fifth lobe is deep to the parietal lobe and the temporal lobe; called the **insula,** it houses the basal nuclei.

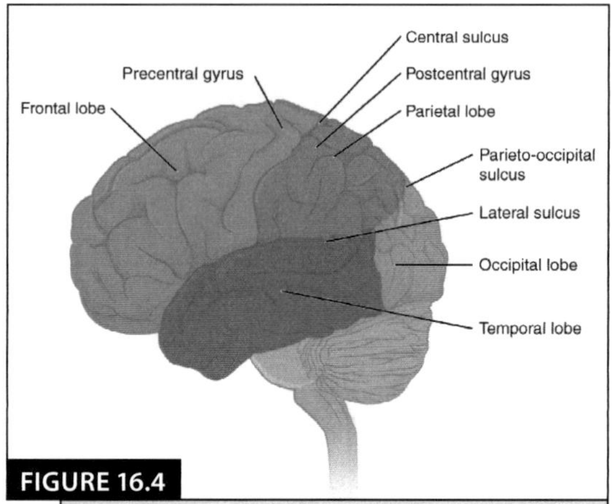



**FIGURE 16.4**

**Lobes of the Cerebral Cortex.** The cerebral cortex is divided into five lobes. Frontal lobe, Parietal lobe, and Occipital lobe are on the crown, and the temporal lobe is inferior and lateral to the frontal and parietal lobes. The fifth lobe, called the insula, is not pictured here but is deep to the temporal and parietal lobes. Extensive folding increases the surface area available for cerebral functions.

OpenStax College [CC BY 3.0 (https://creativecommons.org/licenses/by/3.0)]

## THE DIENCEPHALON

During embryonic development, the **diencephalon** is engulfed by the rapidly growing telencephalon. The diencephalon is comprised of the thalamus, the epithalamus with the pineal gland, and the hypothalamus. This deep area of the brain has a variety of functions. The **thalamus** is a relay center or switchboard for nerve impulses from the spinal cord to the cerebral cortex, directing the signals to where on the cortex they will be interpreted (or integrated with an association neuron or motor neuron). All sensory information, except for the sense of smell, passes through the thalamus before processing by the cortex. The cerebrum also sends information down to the thalamus. The **epithalamus** houses the **pineal gland,** the endocrine gland that secretes melatonin for sleep and wake cycles. The **hypothalamus** regulates both the nervous and endocrine systems, helping to regulate the body's homeostasis. Other parts of the hypothalamus are involved in memory and emotion as part of the limbic system.

## THE BRAIN STEM

This deepest portion of the brain is the most important for the body's survival. It is the most primitive area of the brain and controls what medical personnel call the patient's vitals. The midbrain coordinates sensory representations of the visual, auditory, and somatosensory perceptual spaces. The pons is the main connection with the cerebellum. The pons and the medulla regulate several crucial functions, including the cardiovascular and respiratory systems and rates ("vitals"). Attached to the brain stem, but considered a separate region of the adult brain, is the cerebellum.

## THE CEREBELLUM

The **cerebellum,** as the name suggests, is the "little brain." The cerebellum is largely responsible for comparing information from the cerebrum with sensory feedback from the periphery through the spinal cord. By comparing this information, the cerebellum helps coordinate motor movements from the cerebral cortex to the body via the pons.

## THE CRANIAL NERVES

The cranial nerves connect through the brain stem and provide the brain with the sensory input and motor output associated with the head and neck, including most of the special senses. The major ascending and descending pathways between the spinal cord and brain, specifically the cerebrum, pass through the brain stem.

*Note:* You will spend **2 hr and 30 min** in lab at Forsyth Tech to complete the following activities. This amount of time allows you to complete the activities by using models in lab as well as working with a lab partner.

# ACTIVITY 1

**Identify** the following features of the **brain** on models in lab and the **dissection of the sheep brain** (if available).

1. Cerebrum
   a. Cerebral hemispheres
      i. Major fissures
   b. Longitudinal fissure
   c. Transverse fissure
      i. Convolutions (gyrus/gyri and sulcus/sulci)
      ii. Major sulci
2. Central sulcus
3. Lateral sulcus
   a. Lobes
4. Frontal lobe
   a. Precentral gyrus (primary motor cortex)
   b. Prefrontal cortex
5. Parietal lobe
   a. Postcentral gyrus (primary sensory cortex)
6. Occipital lobe
7. Insula lobe
8. Temporal lobe
   a. Cerebral cortex
   b. Corpus callosum

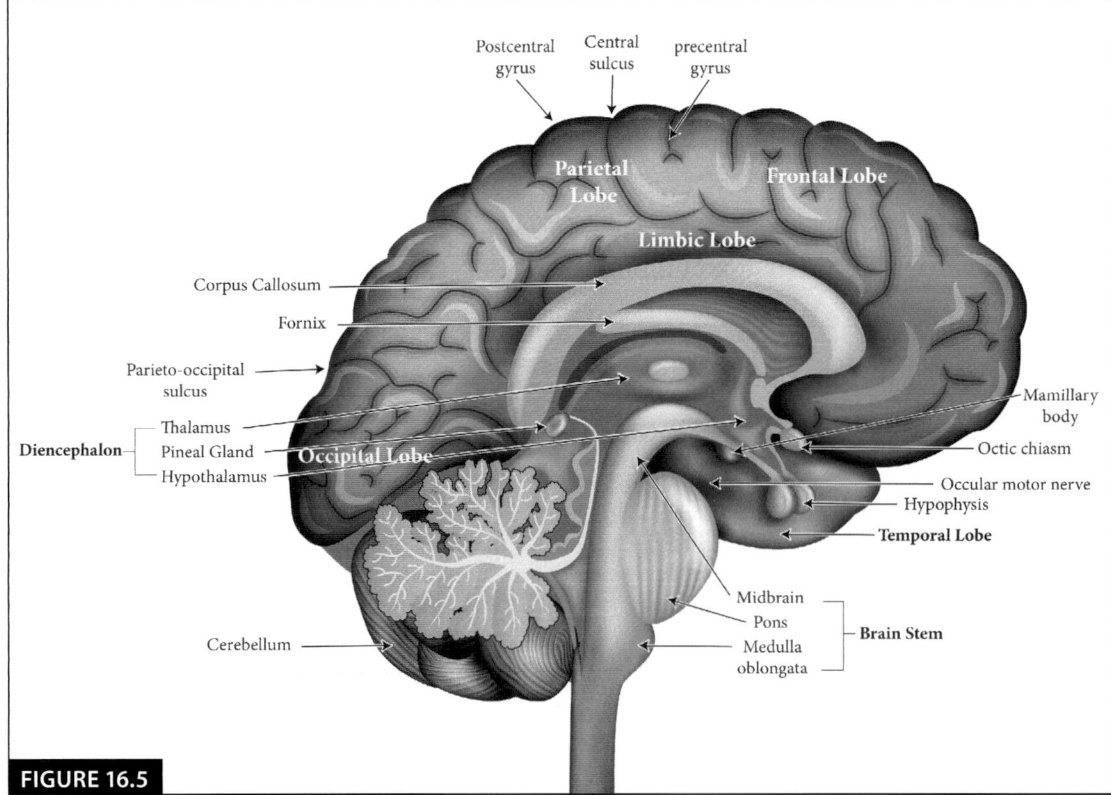


**FIGURE 16.5**

**Primary anatomical structures of the brain.** Lobes: frontal lobe, parietal lob, occipital lobe, temporal lobe (not seen – insula lobe). Diencephalon: thalamus, pineal gland, hypothalamus. Brain stem: midbrain pons, medulla oblongata.

## LIMBIC SYSTEM

*Note:* See a basic picture to show where its parts are located in the brain.

9. **Diencephalon**
   a. Thalamus
      i. Intermediate mass of thalamus (interthalamic adhesion)
   b. Hypothalamus
      i. Pituitary gland (hypophysis)
      ii. Infundibulum of pituitary gland
   c. Epithalamus
      i. Pineal gland (body) [bulb at posterior end]

10. **Mammillary body**

11. **Brainstem**
    a. Midbrain (mesencephalon)
    b. Pons
    c. Medulla oblongata

12. **Cerebellum**
    a. Cerebellar hemispheres
    b. Arbor vitae
    c. Cerebellar cortex

13. **Meninges**
    a. Dura mater
       i. Falx cerebri
       ii. Tentorium cerebelli
       iii. Falx cerebelli
    b. Arachnoid mater /subarachnoid space /arachnoid villi (which drains fluid from subar. Space)

14. **Ventricles** (see model of ventricles in lab)
    a. Right lateral ventricle
    b. Left lateral ventricle (together right and left are called the lateral ventricles)
    c. Third ventricle
    d. Cerebral aqueduct
    e. Fourth ventricle
    f. Choroid plexus of each ventricle

15. **Vessels of the brain** (see model of base of skull in lab and a brain model with blood vessels)
    a. Right internal carotid artery
    b. Left internal carotid artery
    c. Right internal jugular vein
    d. Left internal jugular vein

16. **Cranial nerves** (structures marked with * should be identified on models for next test)
    a. Olfactory nerves (I)*
       i. Olfactory bulbs
    b. Optic nerves (II)*
       i. Optic chiasma
    c. Oculomotor nerves (III)
    d. Trochlear nerves (IV)
    e. Trigeminal nerves (V)*
    f. Abducens nerves (VI)
    g. Facial nerves (VII)
    h. Auditory nerves (VIII)
    i. Glossopharyngeal nerves (IX)
    j. Vagus nerves (X)*
    k. Accessory nerves (XI)

## ACTIVITY 2: DISSECTION OF THE SHEEP BRAIN

**Follow directions given by your instructor or biology supply house or follow the website:** https://www.biologycorner.com/anatomy/sheepbrain/sheep_brain_dissection_guide.html

**You should be able to find the following structures to prepare for your lab test.** As you cut through the brain, you will notice the inner **white matter** of the brain and the external layer of **gray matter** called the cortex. Other gray matter exists in the brain called basal nuclei.

1. **Cerebrum**
   a. Cerebral hemispheres
   b. Major fissures
      i. Longitudinal fissure
      ii. Transverse fissure
   c. Convolutions (gyrus/gyri and sulcus/sulci)
   d. Major sulci
      i. Central sulcus (ask instructor for help)
      ii. Lateral sulcus
   e. Lobes
      i. Frontal lobe
      ii. Parietal lobe
      iii. Occipital lobe
      iv. Temporal lobe
   f. Cerebral cortex
   g. Corpus callosum

2. **Diencephalon**
   a. Thalamus
      i. Intermediate mass of thalamus (interthalamic adhesion)
   b. Hypothalamus
      i. Pituitary gland
   c. Epithalamus
      i. Pineal gland (body) (bulb at posterior end)

3. **Mammillary body**

4. **Brainstem**
   a. Midbrain (mesencephalon)
   b. Pons
   c. Medulla oblongata

5. **Cerebellum**
   a. Cerebellar hemispheres
   b. Arbor vitae
   c. Cerebellar cortex

6. **Meninges**
   a. Dura mater
      i. Falx cerebri
      ii. Tentorium cerebelli

## ACTIVITY 3

Review sheep brain dissection and label the following diagram.

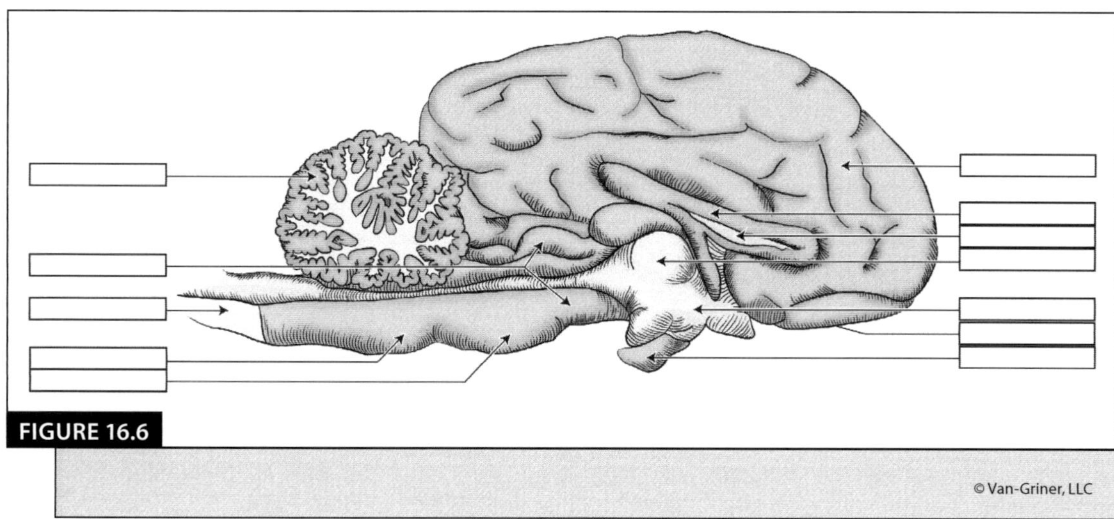

**FIGURE 16.6**



***Note:*** Be sure to get your completed work checked off by a member of the lab staff and then keep this handout for your review.

# 17

# CRANIAL NERVES
## PRE-LAB

Name: _________________________  Section: __________  Date: _________

## LEARNING OBJECTIVE

- Identify the cranial nerves and their functions.

**Using your reference text, fill in the blanks as requested for each one of the following activities.**

## PRE-LAB ACTIVITY

Answer the following questions before attending the lab.

1. We identify cranial nerves using a given name and a Roman numeral. Anatomists numbered them in order from the first cranial nerve under the cerebrum to the last one from the lower medulla of the brain stem. **Write down the name of each one of the 12 cranial nerves.**

    a. _________________________________________________

    b. _________________________________________________

    c. _________________________________________________

    d. _________________________________________________

    e. _________________________________________________

    f. _________________________________________________

    g. _________________________________________________

    h. _________________________________________________

    **i.** _______________________________________________

    **j.** _______________________________________________

    **k.** _______________________________________________

    **l.** _______________________________________________

**2.** Associate the cranial nerve names with the following *special* senses.

    **a.** Sense of smell _______________________________________

    **b.** Sense of vision _______________________________________

    **c.** Sense of taste _______________________________________

    **d.** Sense of hearing _______________________________________

    **e.** Sense of balance and equilibrium _______________________

**3.** Cranial nerves can be classified as being entirely **s**ensory, entirely **m**otor, or **b**oth sensory and motor. You can learn these by making up a mnemonic sentence with each first letter being either S, M, or B for sensory, motor, or both for each of the 12 cranial nerves. Here is an example: "**S**ome **s**ay **m**arry **m**oney, **b**ut **m**y **b**rother **s**ays **b**ad **b**usiness **m**arry **m**oney." Now you try to make up a mnemonic:

**4.** Identify the 3 **sensory** cranial nerves by **name and number:**

    **a.** _______________________________________________

    **b.** _______________________________________________

    **c.** _______________________________________________

**5.** **Decide** if the following lists are correct or not:

Make changes only if not correct.

    **a.** Motor nerves: Oculomotor, Trochlear, Abducens, Facial, Vagus

    **b.** Mixed/Both function nerves: V1, V2 (sensory) and V3 (motor); Accessory; Glossopharyngeal

# 17

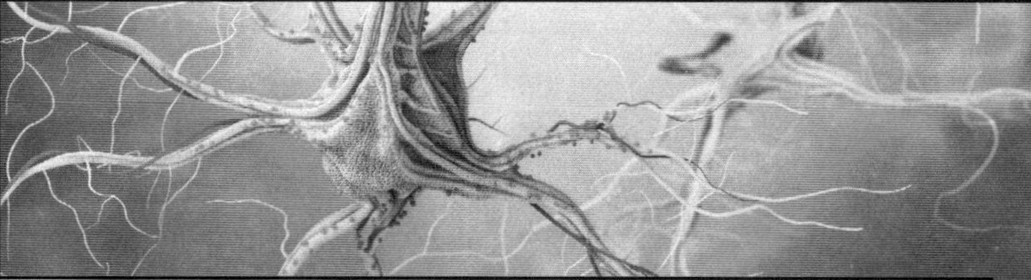

## CRANIAL NERVES
### IN-LAB ACTIVITIES

Name: _________________________  Section: __________  Date: _________

## LEARNING OBJECTIVES

- Identify the cranial nerves and their functions, paths, and innervations.
- Perform Cranial Nerve Tests and suggest diagnoses for each.

## PRE-LAB

Before going to lab, you must complete the following:

Read the **Pre-Lab** and answer the questions that follow.

You will spend **between 45 min and 1 hr 30 min** in lab at Forsyth Tech to complete the following activities (after the lab test). This amount of time allows you to complete the activities by using models in lab as well as working with a lab partner.

## ACTIVITY 1: IDENTIFY THE ORIGIN, PATH, AND INNERVATION OF THE CRANIAL NERVES

For each one of the cranial nerves, **identify** the following important facts using anatomical models, pictures, and the reference/Lumen textbook.

1. Cranial nerves are identified first from anterior to posterior, then from medial to lateral

2. They can start at an organ, or their origin can appear at the lateral fissure of the cerebrum, the midbrain, the pons, the pons-medulla border, and the medulla oblongata.

3. They exit passing through openings (foramina, fissures, meatus, or canals) on the anterior cranial fossa, the middle cranial fossa, and the posterior cranial fossa.

4. Sensory branches (afferent) will originate at a special sense organ.

5. Motor branches (efferent) will originate from the brain/brain stem.

6. Finally, they will carry the special sensory modality to a specialized region of the brain, or they will innervate organs carrying the motor commands.

Fill in Table 17.1 with the requested information from each Cranial Nerve:

**TABLE 17.1**

| CRANIAL NERVE | WHERE IS THE ORIGIN? | AT THE CRANIUM OPENING TO PASS THROUGH? (SEE FIGURE) | WHAT DOES THE CN INNERVATE (MOTOR) OR WHERE IT ENDS IN THE BRAIN (SENSORY)? |
|---|---|---|---|
| Olfactory | | | |
| Optic | | | |
| Oculomotor | | | |
| Trochlear | Midbrain | | Extrinsic eye muscles |
| Trigeminal | | | |
| Abducens | | | Extrinsic eye muscles |
| Facial | | | Muscles of the face (motor) (sensory?) |
| Vestibulocochlear | | | |
| Glossopharyngeal | | | |
| Vagus | | | |
| Accessory | | | |
| Hypoglossal | | | |

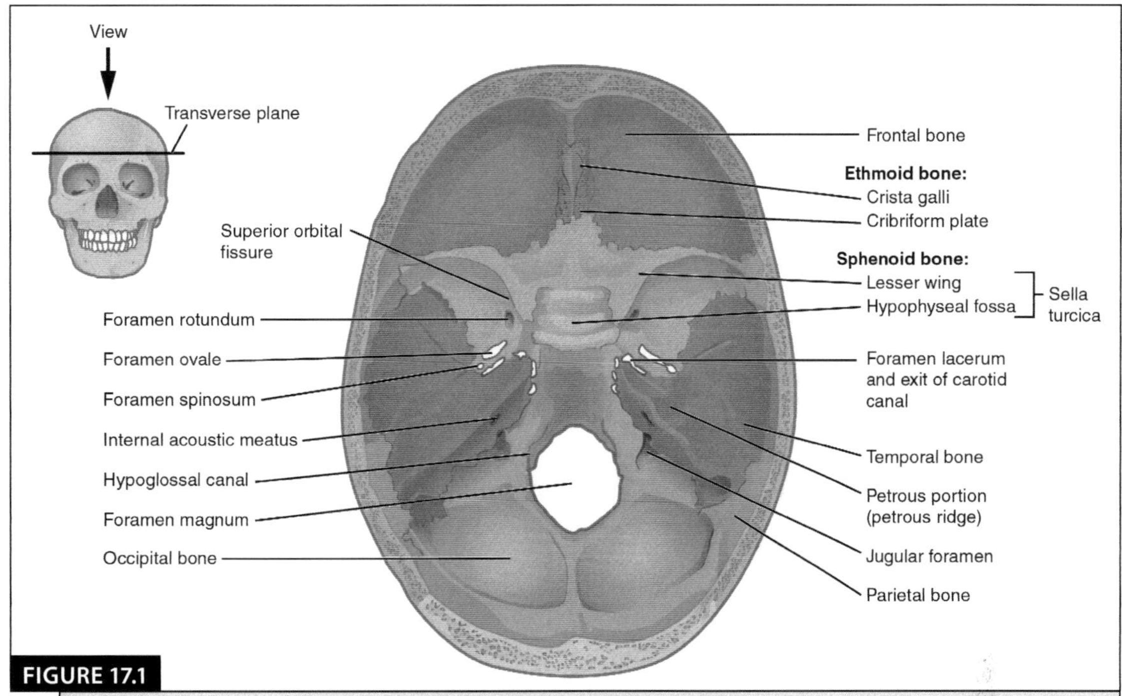


**FIGURE 17.1**

**Superior view cranial fossa and foramina for blood vessels and cranial nerves.**
OpenStax College [CC BY 3.0 (https://creativecommons.org/licenses/by/3.0)]

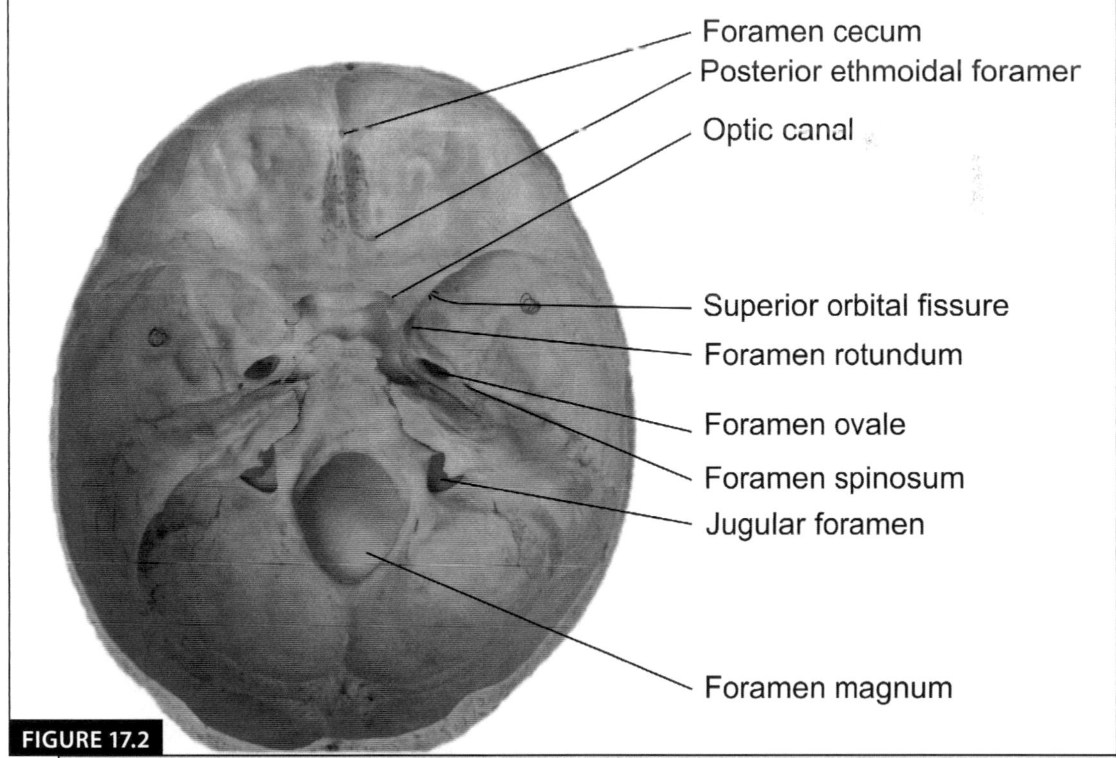


**FIGURE 17.2**

**Superior view cranial fossa and foramina for blood vessels and cranial nerves.** Not all foramina for the cranial nerves are labeled. Schädelbasis1.jpg: Welleschik derivative work: Mcstrother [CC BY-SA 2.5 (https://creativecommons.org/licenses/by-sa/2.5)]

# ACTIVITY 2: ANALYSIS OF THE CRANIAL NERVE FUNCTION

For this section you will be working with a lab partner or another adult as a test subject. You will be asked to perform simple tests working with a laboratory partner. If time is a concern, choose the special senses as your basic tests.

## THE CRANIAL NERVE EXAM

Cranial nerves can be evaluated to test their normal function and the possibility of some type of alteration. The cranial nerves can be separated into four major groups associated with the subtests of the cranial nerve exam.

1. First are the sensory nerves, then

2. The nerves that control eye movement,

3. The nerves of the oral cavity and superior pharynx, and

4. The nerve that controls movements of the neck.

   a. Sensory: The olfactory, optic, and vestibulocochlear nerves are strictly sensory nerves for smell, sight, balance, and hearing, whereas the trigeminal, facial, and glossopharyngeal nerves carry somatosensation of the face, and taste—separated between the anterior two-thirds of the tongue and the posterior one-third. Special senses are tested by presenting the particular stimuli to each receptive organ.

   b. Eye movement: The oculomotor, trochlear, and abducens nerves control the extraocular muscles and are connected by the medial longitudinal fasciculus to coordinate gaze. Testing conjugate gaze is as simple as having the patient follow a visual target, like a pen tip, through the visual field ending with an approach toward the face to test convergence and accommodation.

   c. Oral cavity and pharynx: Along with the vestibular functions of the eighth nerve (CN VIII), the vestibulo-ocular reflex stabilizes gaze during head movements by coordinating equilibrium sensations with the eye movement systems. The trigeminal nerve controls the muscles of chewing, which are tested for stretch reflexes. Motor functions of the facial nerve are usually obvious if facial expressions are compromised, but can be tested by having the patient raise their eyebrows, smile, and frown. Movements of the tongue, soft palate, or superior pharynx can be observed directly while the patient swallows, while the gag reflex is elicited, or while the patient says repetitive consonant sounds. The motor control of the gag reflex is largely controlled by fibers in the vagus nerve and constitutes a test of that nerve because the parasympathetic functions of that nerve are involved in visceral regulation, such as regulating the heartbeat and digestion.

   d. Neck: Movement of the head and neck using the sternocleidomastoid and trapezius muscles is controlled by the accessory nerve. Flexing of the neck and strength testing of those muscles reviews the function of that nerve.

Fill in Table 17.2. For each one of the cranial nerves, perform the following test. Fill in the results from your lab partner(s).

**TABLE 17.2**

| CRANIAL NERVE | REFERENCE | TESTS/DIRECTIONS | RESULT |
|---|---|---|---|
| Olfactory | | Identify substances, spices, fruit, etc. | |
| Optic | Vision test. Snellen chart | | |
| Oculomotor | | Dim room lights. Hold a hand vertically between the eyes to shield one eye from direct light. Shine flashlight to one eye and observe pupil reaction and the opposite site as well. | |
| Trochlear | | Move finger up and down and side to side in front | |
| Trigeminal | | Cotton touch test; push up on chin of open mouth to see resistance | |
| Abducens | | Follow object along horizontal plan | |
| Facial | | Sugar test<br>Wink test<br>Smile & whistle test<br>Look up and wrinkle forehead | |
| Vestibulocochlear | Use tuning forks Equilibrium tests | | |
| Glossopharyngeal | Uvula—midline, normal | Subject says "Ah" | . |
| Vagus | Swallow reflex | | |
| Accessory | | Shrug shoulders against resistance | |
| Hypoglossal | | Protrude and retract tongue | |

By the end of this section, you will be able to:

- Describe the functional grouping of cranial nerves.
- Suggest diagnoses that would explain certain losses of function in the cranial nerves.

The cranial nerve exam allows directed tests of forebrain and brain stem structures. The twelve cranial nerves serve the head and neck. The vagus nerve (cranial nerve X) has autonomic functions in the thoracic and superior abdominal cavities. The special senses are served through the cranial nerves, as well as the general senses of the head and neck. The movement of the eyes, face, tongue, throat, and neck are all under the control of cranial nerves. Preganglionic parasympathetic nerve fibers that control pupillary size, salivary glands, and the thoracic and upper abdominal viscera are found in four of the nerves. Tests of these functions can provide insight into damage to specific regions of the brain stem and may uncover deficits in adjacent regions.

The olfactory, optic, and vestibulocochlear nerves (cranial nerves I, II, and VIII) are dedicated to four of the special senses: smell, vision, equilibrium, and hearing, respectively. Taste sensation is relayed to the brain stem through fibers of the facial and glossopharyngeal nerves. The trigeminal nerve is a mixed nerve that carries the general somatic senses from the head, similar to those coming through spinal nerves from the rest of the body.

1. **CN I:** Testing smell is straightforward, as common smells are presented to one nostril at a time. The patient should be able to recognize the smell of coffee or mint, indicating the proper functioning of the olfactory system. Loss of the sense of smell is called **anosmia** and can be lost following blunt trauma to the head or through aging. The short axons of the first cranial nerve regenerate on a regular basis. The neurons in the olfactory epithelium have a limited life span, and new cells grow to replace the ones that die off. The axons from these neurons grow back into the CNS by following the existing axons—representing one of the few examples of such growth in the mature nervous system. If all of the fibers are sheared when the brain moves within the cranium, such as in a motor vehicle accident, then no axons can find their way back to the olfactory bulb to reestablish connections. If the nerve is not completely severed, the anosmia may be temporary as new neurons can eventually reconnect. Olfaction is not the pre-eminent sense, but its loss can be quite detrimental. The enjoyment of food is largely based on our sense of smell. Anosmia means that food will not seem to have the same taste, though the gustatory sense is intact, and food will often be described as being bland. However, the taste of food can be improved by adding ingredients (e.g., salt) that stimulate the gustatory sense.

2.  **CN II:** Testing vision relies on the tests that are common in an optometry office. The Snellen chart (Figure 17.3) demonstrates visual acuity by presenting standard Roman letters in a variety of sizes. The result of this test is a rough generalization of the acuity of a person based on the normal accepted acuity, such that a letter that subtends a visual angle of 5 minutes of an arc at 20 feet can be seen. To have 20/60 vision, for example, means that the smallest letters that a person can see at a 20-foot distance could be seen by a person with normal acuity from 60 feet away. Testing the extent of the visual field means that the examiner can establish the boundaries of peripheral vision by simply holding their hands out to either side and asking the patient when the fingers are no longer visible without moving the eyes to track them. If it is necessary, further tests can establish the perceptions in the visual fields. Physical inspection of the optic disk, or where the optic nerve emerges from the eye, can be accomplished by looking through the pupil with an ophthalmoscope.

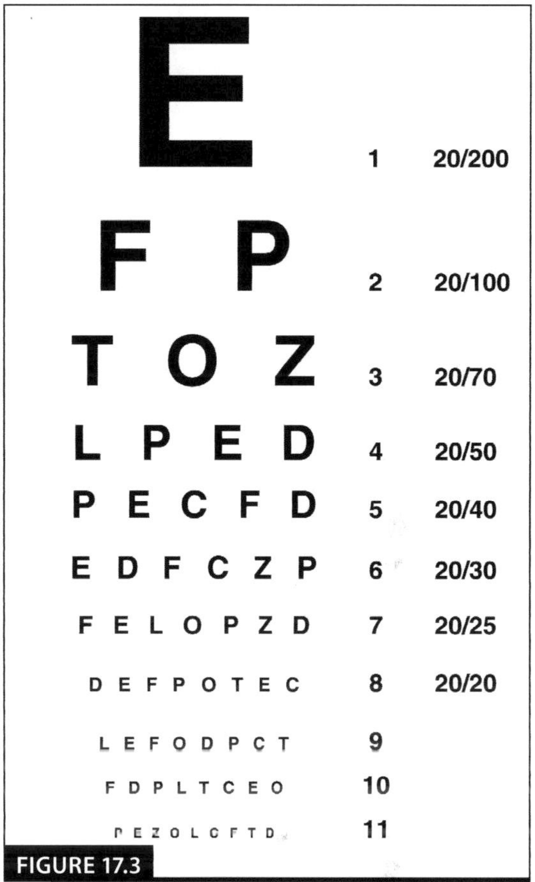

**FIGURE 17.3**

**The Snellen Chart.** OpenStax College [CC BY 3.0 (https://creativecommons.org/licenses/by/3.0)]

The Snellen chart for visual acuity presents a limited number of Roman letters in lines of decreasing size. The line with letters that subtend 5 minutes of an arc from 20 feet represents the smallest letters that a person with normal acuity should be able to read at that distance. The different sizes of letters in the other lines represent rough approximations of what a person of normal acuity can read at different distances. For example, the line that represents 20/20 vision would have larger letters so that they are legible to the person with normal acuity at 200 feet.

The optic nerves from both sides enter the cranium through the respective optic canals and meet at the optic chiasm at which fibers sort such that the two halves of the visual field are processed by the opposite sides of the brain. Deficits in visual field perception often suggest damage along the length of the optic pathway between the orbit and the diencephalon. For example, loss of peripheral vision may be the result of a pituitary tumor pressing on the optic chiasm formed by the axons that decussate in the chiasm from the medial retinae of either eye, and therefore carry information from the peripheral visual field.

3.  **CN II and III:** Penlight Test

    Shining light in one eye will elicit constriction of both pupils. The efferent limb of the pupillary light reflex is bilateral. Light shined in one eye causes a constriction of that pupil, as well as constriction of the contralateral pupil. Shining a penlight in the eye of a patient is a very artificial situation, as both eyes are normally exposed to the same light sources.

    Testing this reflex can illustrate whether the optic nerve or the oculomotor nerve is damaged. If shining the light in one eye results in no changes in pupillary size but shining light in the opposite eye elicits a normal, bilateral response, the damage is associated with the optic nerve on the nonresponsive side. If light in either eye elicits a response in only one eye, the problem is with the oculomotor system. If light in the right eye only causes the left pupil to constrict, the direct reflex is lost and the consensual reflex is intact, which means that the right oculomotor nerve (or Eddinger–Westphal nucleus) is damaged. Damage to the right oculomotor connections will be evident when light is shined in the left eye. In that case, the direct reflex is intact, but the consensual reflex is lost, meaning that the left pupil will constrict while the right does not.

4.  **CN VIII:** The vestibulocochlear nerve carries both equilibrium and auditory sensations from the inner ear to the medulla. Though the two senses are not directly related, anatomy is mirrored in the two systems. Problems with balance, such as vertigo, and deficits in hearing may both point to problems with the inner ear. Within the petrous region of the temporal bone is the bony labyrinth of the inner ear. The vestibule is the portion for equilibrium, composed of the utricle, saccule, and the three semicircular canals. The cochlea is responsible for transducing sound waves into a neural signal. The sensory nerves from these two structures travel side-by-side as the vestibulocochlear nerve, though they are really separate divisions. They both emerge from the inner ear, pass through the internal auditory meatus, and synapse in nuclei of the superior medulla. Though they are part of distinct sensory systems, the vestibular nuclei and the cochlear nuclei are close neighbors with adjacent inputs. Deficits in one or both systems could occur from damage that encompasses structures close to both. Damage to structures near the two nuclei can result in deficits to one or both systems.

    Balance or hearing deficits may be the result of damage to the middle or inner ear structures. Ménière's disease is a disorder that can affect both equilibrium and audition in a variety of ways. The patient can suffer from vertigo, a low-frequency ringing in the ears, or a loss of hearing. From patient to patient, the exact presentation of the disease can be different.

Additionally, within a single patient, the symptoms and signs may change as the disease progresses. Use of the neurological exam subtests for the vestibulocochlear nerve illuminates the changes a patient may go through. The disease appears to be the result of accumulation, or over-production, of fluid in the inner ear, in either the vestibule or cochlea.

Tests of equilibrium are important for coordination and gait and are related to other aspects of the neurological exam. The vestibulo-ocular reflex involves the cranial nerves for gaze control. Balance and equilibrium, as tested by the Romberg test, are part of spinal and cerebellar processes and involved in those components of the neurological exam, as discussed later.

5. **CN VIII:** Hearing is tested by using a tuning fork in a couple of different ways.

The Rinne test involves using a tuning fork to distinguish between conductive hearing and sensorineural hearing. Conductive hearing relies on vibrations being conducted through the ossicles of the middle ear. Sensorineural hearing is the transmission of sound stimuli through the neural components of the inner ear and cranial nerve. A vibrating tuning fork is placed on the mastoid process, and the patient indicates when the sound produced from this is no longer present. Then the fork is immediately moved to just next to the ear canal so the sound travels through the air. If the sound is not heard through the ear, meaning the sound is conducted better through the temporal bone than through the ossicles, a conductive hearing deficit is present.

The Weber test also uses a tuning fork to differentiate between conductive versus sensorineural hearing loss. In this test, the tuning fork is placed at the top of the skull, and the sound of the tuning fork reaches both inner ears by travelling through bone. In a healthy patient, the sound would appear equally loud in both ears. With unilateral conductive hearing loss, however, the tuning fork sounds louder in the ear with hearing loss. This is because the sound of the tuning fork has to compete with background noise coming from the outer ear, but in conductive hearing loss, the background noise is blocked in the damaged ear, allowing the tuning fork to sound relatively louder in that ear. With unilateral sensorineural hearing loss, however, damage to the cochlea or associated nervous tissue means that the tuning fork sounds quieter in that ear.

6.  **CN V:** The trigeminal system of the head and neck is the equivalent of the ascending spinal cord systems of the dorsal column and the spinothalamic pathways. Somatosensation of the face is conveyed along the nerve to enter the brain stem at the level of the pons. Synapses of those axons, however, are distributed across nuclei found throughout the brain stem. The mesencephalic nucleus processes proprioceptive information of the face, which is the movement and position of facial muscles. It is the sensory component of the jaw-jerk reflex, a stretch reflex of the masseter muscle. The chief nucleus, located in the pons, receives information about light touch as well as proprioceptive information about the mandible, which are both relayed to the thalamus and, ultimately, to the postcentral gyrus of the parietal lobe. The spinal trigeminal nucleus, located in the medulla, receives information about crude touch, pain, and temperature to be relayed to the thalamus and cortex. Essentially, the projection through the chief nucleus is analogous to the dorsal column pathway for the body, and the projection through the spinal trigeminal nucleus is analogous to the spinothalamic pathway.

    Subtests for the sensory component of the trigeminal system are the same as those for the sensory exam targeting the spinal nerves. The primary sensory subtest for the trigeminal system is sensory discrimination. A cotton-tipped applicator, which is cotton attached to the end of a thin wooden stick, can be used easily for this. The wood of the applicator can be snapped so that a pointed end is opposite the soft cotton-tipped end. The cotton end provides a touch stimulus, while the pointed end provides a painful, or sharp, stimulus. While the patient's eyes are closed, the examiner touches the two ends of the applicator to the patient's face, alternating randomly between them. The patient must identify whether the stimulus is sharp or dull. These stimuli are processed by the trigeminal system separately. Contact with the cotton tip of the applicator is a light touch, relayed by the chief nucleus, but contact with the pointed end of the applicator is a painful stimulus relayed by the spinal trigeminal nucleus. Failure to discriminate these stimuli can localize problems within the brain stem. If a patient cannot recognize a painful stimulus, that might indicate damage to the spinal trigeminal nucleus in the medulla.

    The medulla also contains important regions that regulate the cardiovascular, respiratory, and digestive systems, as well as being the pathway for ascending and descending tracts between the brain and spinal cord. Damage, such as a stroke, that results in changes in sensory discrimination may indicate these unrelated regions are affected as well.

7.  **CN III, CN IV, CN VI:** Gaze Control

    The three nerves that control the extraocular muscles are the oculomotor, trochlear, and abducens nerves, which are the third, fourth, and sixth cranial nerves. As the name suggests, the abducens nerve is responsible for abducting the eye, which it controls through contraction of the lateral rectus muscle. The trochlear nerve controls the superior oblique muscle to rotate the eye along its axis in the orbit medially, which is called intorsion, and is a component of focusing the eyes on an object close to the face. The oculomotor nerve controls all the other extraocular muscles, as well as a muscle of the upper eyelid. Movements of the two eyes need to be coordinated to locate and track visual stimuli accurately. When moving the eyes to locate an object in the horizontal plane, or to track movement horizontally in the visual field, the lateral rectus muscle of one eye and medial rectus muscle of the other eye are both active. The lateral rectus is controlled by neurons of the abducens nucleus in the superior medulla, whereas the medial rectus is controlled by neurons in the oculomotor nucleus of the midbrain. Coordinated movement of both eyes through different nuclei requires integrated processing through the brain stem. In the midbrain, the superior colliculus integrates visual stimuli with motor responses to initiate eye movements. The paramedian pontine reticular formation (PPRF) will initiate a rapid eye movement, or saccade, to bring the eyes to bear on a visual stimulus quickly. These areas are connected to the oculomotor, trochlear, and abducens nuclei by the medial longitudinal fasciculus (MLF) that runs through the majority of the brain stem. The MLF allows for conjugate gaze, or the movement of the eyes in the same direction, during horizontal movements that require the lateral and medial rectus muscles. Control of conjugate gaze strictly in the vertical direction is contained within the oculomotor complex. To elevate the eyes, the oculomotor nerve on either side stimulates the contraction of both superior rectus muscles; to depress the eyes, the oculomotor nerve on either side stimulates the contraction of both inferior rectus muscles.

Purely vertical movements of the eyes are not very common. Movements are often at an angle, so some horizontal components are necessary, adding the medial and lateral rectus muscles to the movement. The rapid movement of the eyes used to locate and direct the fovea onto visual stimuli is called a saccade.

The movements between the nose and the mouth are closest, but still have a slant to them. Also, the superior and inferior rectus muscles are not perfectly oriented with the line of sight. The origin for both muscles is medial to their insertions, so elevation and depression may require the lateral rectus muscles to compensate for the slight adduction inherent in the contraction of those muscles, requiring MLF activity as well.

Testing eye movement is simply a matter of having the patient track the tip of a pen as it is passed through the visual field. Watch this video example: https://www.youtube.com/watch?v=D_y56PQvZZA.

This may appear similar to testing visual field deficits related to the optic nerve, but the difference is that the patient is asked to not move the eyes while the examiner moves a stimulus into the peripheral visual field. Here, the extent of movement is the point of the test. The examiner is watching for conjugate movements representing proper function of the related nuclei and the MLF. Failure of one eye to abduct while the other adducts in a horizontal movement is referred to as internuclear ophthalmoplegia. When this occurs, the patient will experience diplopia, or double vision, as the two eyes are temporarily pointed at different stimuli. Diplopia is not restricted to failure of the lateral rectus because any of the extraocular muscles may fail to move one eye in perfect conjugation with the other.

The final aspect of testing eye movements is to move the tip of the pen in toward the patient's face. As visual stimuli move closer to the face, the two medial recti muscles cause the eyes to move in one nonconjugate movement that is part of gaze control. When the two eyes move to look at something closer to the face, they both adduct, which is referred to as convergence. To keep the stimulus in focus, the eye also needs to change the shape of the lens, which is controlled through the parasympathetic fibers of the oculomotor nerve. The change in focal power of the eye is referred to as accommodation. Accommodation ability changes with age; focusing on nearer objects, such as the written text of a book or on a computer screen, may require corrective lenses later in life. Coordination of the skeletal muscles for convergence and coordination of the smooth muscles of the ciliary body for accommodation are referred to as the accommodation–convergence reflex.

8.  **CN XI:** Muscles test: (Spinal) Accessory Nerve

    To test these muscles, the patient is asked to flex and extend the neck or shrug the shoulders against resistance, testing the strength of the muscles. Lateral flexion of the neck toward the shoulder tests both at the same time. Any difference on one side versus the other would suggest damage on the weaker side. These strength tests are common for the skeletal muscles controlled by spinal nerves and are a significant component of the motor exam. Deficits associated with the accessory nerve may have an effect on orienting the head, as described with the vestibulo-ocular reflex (VOR).

9.  **CN XII:** The test for hypoglossal function is the "stick out your tongue" part of the exam. The genioglossus muscle is responsible for protrusion of the tongue. If the hypoglossal nerves on both sides are working properly, then the tongue will stick straight out. If the nerve on one side has a deficit, the tongue will stick out to that side—pointing to the side with damage. Loss of function of the tongue can interfere with speech and swallowing. Additionally, because the location of the hypoglossal nerve and nucleus is near the cardiovascular center, inspiratory and expiratory areas for respiration, and the vagus nuclei that regulate digestive functions, a tongue that protrudes incorrectly can suggest damage in adjacent structures that have nothing to do with controlling the tongue.

*Note:* Be sure to get your completed work checked off by a member of the lab staff and then keep this handout for your review.

# 18

# AUTONOMIC NERVOUS SYSTEM
## PRE-LAB

Name: ___________________________  Section: ___________  Date: _________

## LEARNING OBJECTIVES

- Identify the major nerve pathways of the two divisions of the autonomic nervous system.

- Explain the reflex arc for ANS vs SNS.

- Describe how organs react when innervated by the PANS and SANS divisions of the ANS.

## INTRODUCTION

The **autonomic nervous system** (**ANS**) is a division of the peripheral nervous system that supplies smooth muscle and glands (effectors), and thus influences the function of internal organs. Within the brain, the autonomic nervous system is regulated by the hypothalamus. The autonomic nervous system has two branches: the **sympathetic** autonomic nervous system (SANS) and the **parasympathetic** autonomic nervous system (PANS). The sympathetic nervous system is often considered the "fight or flight" system, while the parasympathetic nervous system is often considered the "rest and digest" or "feed and breed" system. In many cases, both of these systems have "opposite" actions where usually one system activates a physiological response and the other inhibits it.

The two divisions of the ANS have separate pathways from the somatic nervous system. They are connected to the spinal nerves, though, by nerves called the **rami communicantes** (find these on the nerve board in lab as well). The sympathetic division emerges from the spinal cord at the lateral gray horn in the thoracic and lumbar areas, terminating around L2–3. The parasympathetic division has craniosacral "outflow," meaning that the neurons begin at the cranial nerves (specifically the oculomotor nerve, facial nerve, glossopharyngeal nerve, and vagus nerve) and sacral (S2–S4) spinal cord.

The autonomic nervous system is unique in that it requires a sequential two-neuron efferent (motor neuron) pathway; the preganglionic neuron must first synapse onto a postganglionic neuron before innervating the target organ. The two motor neurons of the autonomic nervous system synapse in "autonomic ganglia." Those of the parasympathetic division are located close to the target organ; however, the ganglia of the sympathetic division are located close to the spinal cord.

Sympathetic and parasympathetic divisions typically function in opposition to each other. But this opposition is better termed complementary in nature rather than antagonistic. For an analogy, one may think of the sympathetic division as the accelerator and the parasympathetic division as the brake. The sympathetic division typically functions in actions requiring quick responses. The parasympathetic division functions with actions that do not require immediate reaction.

However, many instances of sympathetic and parasympathetic activity cannot be attributed to "fight" or "rest" situations. For example, standing up from a reclining or sitting position would entail an unsustainable drop in blood pressure (orthostatic hypotension) if not for a compensatory increase in the arterial sympathetic tone. Another example is the constant, second-to-second modulation of heart rate by sympathetic and parasympathetic influences, as a function of the respiratory cycles. In general, these two systems should be seen as permanently modulating vital functions, in usually antagonistic fashion, to achieve homeostasis.

View the figures and diagrams of the SANS and PANS provided in your OER text to examine the two systems before going to lab to complete the lab activities.

## PRE-LAB ACTIVITY

Answer the following **before** attending lab this week.

1.  What regulates the autonomic NS?

2.  What are the two divisions of the ANS?

3.  How does the ANS differ from the somatic motor neuron system?

4.  What is another "nickname" for the sympathetic nervous system that describes where it emerges from the spinal cord?

5.  If the PANS is the "rest and digest" system, which organs increase their output with nerve signals from this pathway?

6.  If the SANS is the "fight or flight" division, which organs increase their output with stimulation from this pathway?

7.  From what you have read here and in your other textbook source, why is a seesaw or teeter-totter a good analogy for the dual innervation and opposing effects of these two ANS divisions?

# 18

# AUTONOMIC NERVOUS SYSTEM
## IN-LAB ACTIVITIES

Name: ___________________________  Section: ___________  Date: __________

## LEARNING OBJECTIVES

- Compare and contrast the ANS and the SNS.
- Compare and contrast the PANS and SANS divisions.
- Identify the major nerve pathways of the two divisions of the autonomic nervous system.
- Explain the reflex arc for ANS vs SNS.
- Describe how organs react when innervated by the PANS and SANS divisions of the ANS.

The **autonomic nervous system (ANS)** is a division of the peripheral nervous system that supplies smooth muscle and glands, and thus regulates the function of internal organs and blood vessels. The autonomic nervous system is a control system that acts largely unconsciously and regulates bodily functions such as the heart rate, digestion, respiratory rate, pupillary diameter, urination, and sexual arousal. This system is the primary mechanism in control of the fight-or-flight response.

The autonomic nervous system has two branches: the **sympathetic nervous system and the parasympathetic nervous system.** The sympathetic nervous system is often considered the "fight-or-flight" system, while the parasympathetic nervous system is often considered the "rest and digest" or "feed and breed" system. In many cases, both of these systems have "opposite" actions where one system activates a physiological response and the other inhibits it, depending upon the area of the body that is innervated. In heart failure, the sympathetic nervous system increases its activity, leading to increased force of muscular contractions that in turn increases the stroke volume, as well as peripheral vasoconstriction to maintain blood pressure. However, these effects accelerate disease progression, eventually increasing mortality in heart failure.

Although the ANS is also known as the visceral nervous system, the ANS is only connected with the motor side. Most autonomous functions are involuntary, but they can often work in conjunction with the somatic nervous system that provides voluntary control.

# ACTIVITY 1

With a partner in lab, follow the directions below and answer these together.

1.  **Watch these two videos** about the ANS:

    - https://www.youtube.com/watch?v=w56rT2ay07k&list=PL5GRRRmaGVqWEy ICMJOI04coQoR3_vvgh (you can watch the first of Ms. Riggs 6 videos for this lab)

    - https://www.youtube.com/watch?v=I1ikqN3PFdM

    a.  Compare and contrast the ANS to the SNS

| ANS | SNS |
| --- | --- |
|  |  |
|  |  |

    b.  In addition, compare and contrast the PANS and SANS of the ANS.

| PANS | SANS |
| --- | --- |
|  |  |
|  |  |

2.  Identify the major nerves of the PANS in the lab on brain models and nerve boards. What target organs do the nerves innervate?

3.  Identify the pathways and ganglia of the SANS in the lab on the nerve boards. Why are there so many and from which two areas of the spinal cord do they emerge?

## ACTIVITY 2: AUTONOMIC SYSTEM SIGNALING MOLECULES

With a partner in lab, follow the directions below.

| | SYMPATHETIC | PARASYMPATHETIC |
|---|---|---|
| Preganglionic | Acetylcholine → nicotinic receptor | Acetylcholine → nicotinic receptor |
| Postganglionic | Norepinephrine → α- or β-adrenergic receptors<br>Acetylcholine → muscarinic receptor (associated with sweat glands and the blood vessels associated with skeletal muscles only) | Acetylcholine → muscarinic receptor |

1.  Using the table above, ***draw*** 2 simple flow charts of the pathway that shows the pre and post ganglionic fibers and which NT are used in each pathway at the ganglion and at the target organ.

2.  **Draw** and **label** ANS reflex arc.

3.  Use the diagram in Figures 18.1 and 18.2 to answer these questions:

    a.  Where are the ganglia located for the Sympathetic Nervous System pathways?

    b.  Where are the ganglia located for the Parasympathetic Nervous System found? (list 4 specifically and the others in general)

    (For the lab test, be able to name 2 of the four ganglia of the PANS, so pick two of them that make sense in their names or that you think you can recall.)

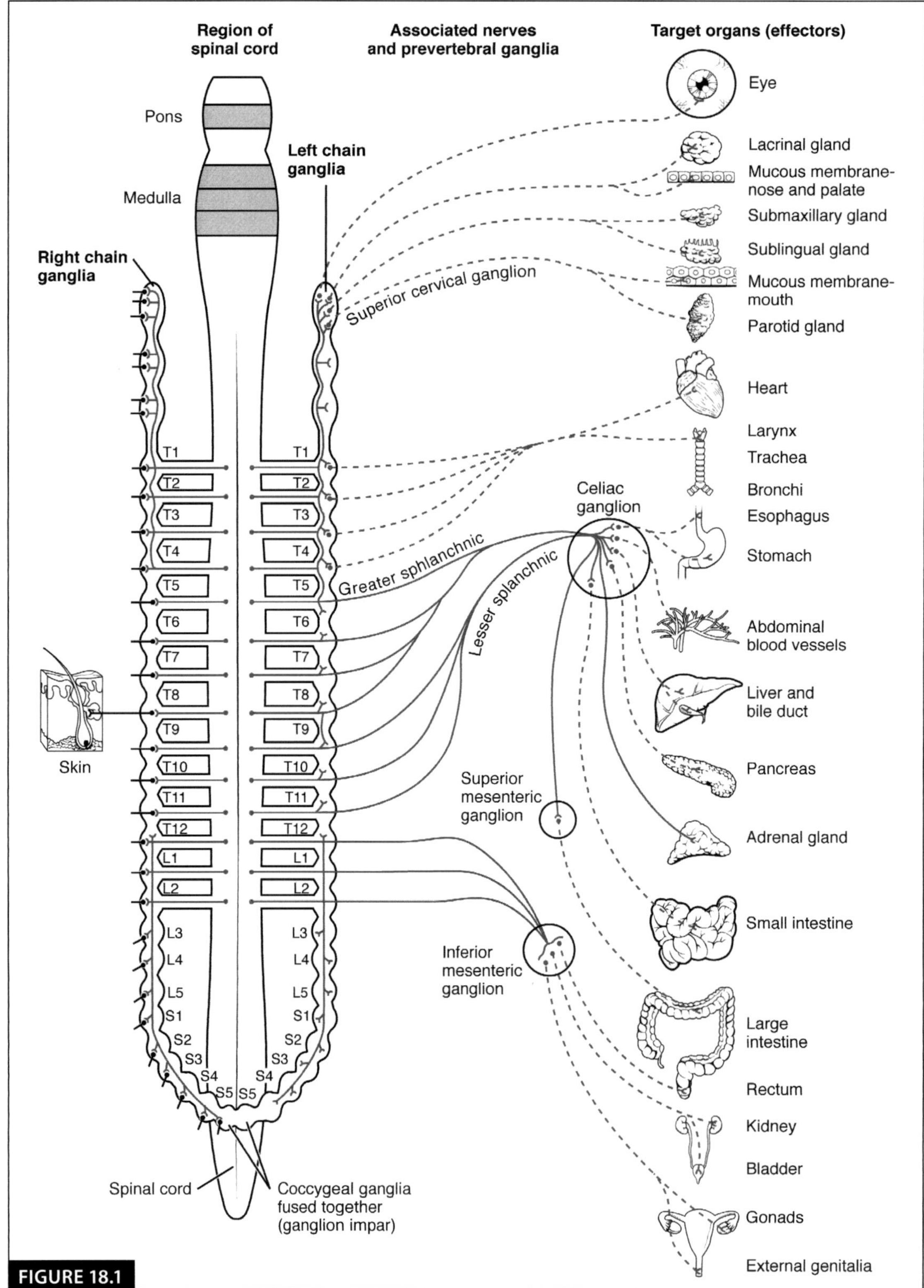


**FIGURE 18.1**

**The target organs of the Parasympathetic Nervous System (PANS).** The sympathetic chain ganglion are shown on either side of the spinal cord as well as the cranial and sacral nerves involved in signals from the PANS. OpenStax College [CC BY 3.0 (https://creativecommons.org/licenses/by/3.0)]

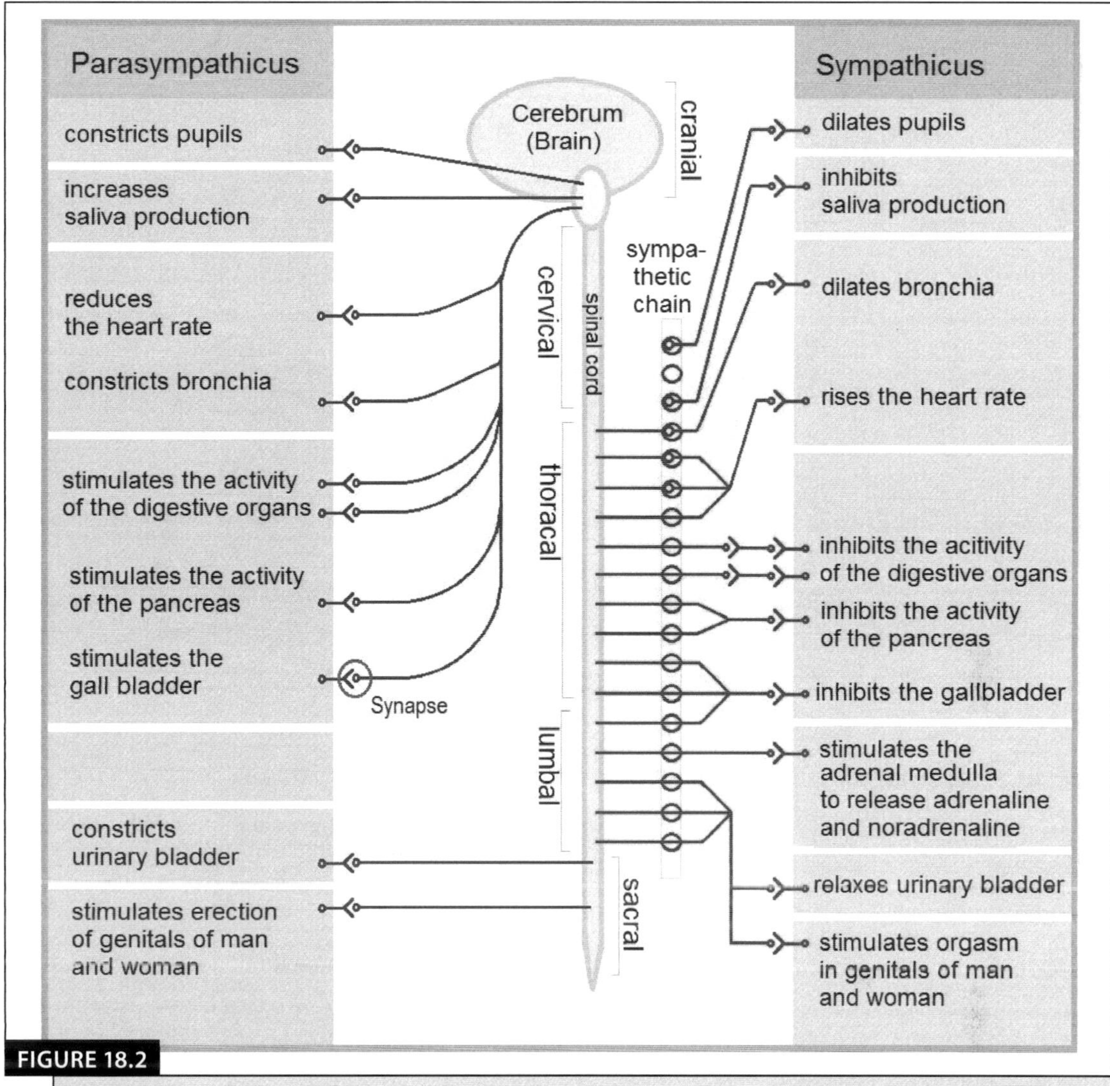


**FIGURE 18.2**

**View of the PANS and SANS of the Autonomic Nervous system where you can see the targets of each division of the PNS.**  Geo-Science-International [CC0]

4. What is the difference in how the PANS and SANS affect these organs?

   a. Pupils

   b. Urinary bladder

   c. Genitals

   d. Bronchia

   e. Saliva production

5. What do these differences tell you about the use of anti-cholinergic drugs during surgeries? (Which system do these drugs decrease in activity?) Think about fluids like saliva and digestive juices.

## ACTIVITY 3

- Perform a few autonomic NS tests with a lab partner. The Valsalva maneuver will be explained but will **not** be tested in the lab.

To show the results of the autonomic NS in action, we could try a simple lie detector test. The autonomic NS is used for lie detection tests called polygraph tests. In a simple example, you can ask a lab partner a few questions while monitoring his/her pupil size, skin temperature, sweat production, and pulse rate. 1) The partner taking the test will think of a number between 1-10. 2) You will ask him/her a series of questions in order to figure out what the number is, but s/he can choose to fool you, or not, by lying about some of the answers (i.e. "Is the number 1?"). 3) Then you can try to guess which responses are the lies by your observations and whether you can guess the number. Observe the effects listed above for each response as much as possible, or choose one or two to focus on in your assessment of the person's responses. In lab, you should find temperature sensors for the skin. Feel for the pulse rate at the radial artery. Pupil dilation and sweat production can be observed (temperature sensor could be placed in the palm, as well). 4) What is the number you guessed? __________ Was it correct? __________

Another test of the ANS used for diagnoses is the Valsalva maneuver. (**Do not** perform this one in lab since we are not privy to each other's health issues.)

The **Valsalva maneuver** is performed by moderately forceful attempted exhalation against a closed airway, usually done by closing one's mouth and pinching one's nose shut while pressing out as if blowing up a balloon. Variations of the maneuver can be used either in medical examinations as a test of cardiac function and autonomic nervous control of the heart, or to "clear" the ears and sinuses (that is, to equalize pressure between them). Initially, heart stroke volume and blood pressure fall, while the pulse rate (HR) increases, then the Cardiac Output (CO) from the heart will return to normal after releasing the resistance. (Valsalva is also used by dentists following extraction of a maxillary molar tooth. They perform the maneuver to determine if a perforation exists.) https://en.wikipedia.org/wiki/Valsalva_maneuver

## ACTIVITY 3: REVIEW QUESTIONS

1. During the lie detector test, were you able to see pupil size changes, or temperature or sweat changes? List which ones, if any.

2. Why would a lie detector test not be reliable?

3. Thinking about the effects of the ANS, why do you think the Valsalva maneuver is used as a test?

## REVIEW QUESTIONS

1. Which of these physiological changes would *not* be considered part of the sympathetic fight-or-flight response?

    **a.** Increased heart rate

    **b.** Increased sweating

    **c.** Dilated pupils

    **d.** Increased stomach motility

2. Which type of fiber could be considered the longest?

    **a.** Preganglionic parasympathetic

    **b.** Preganglionic sympathetic

    **c.** Postganglionic parasympathetic

    **d.** Postganglionic sympathetic

3. Which signaling molecule is *most likely* responsible for an increase in digestive fluids and activity?

    **a.** Epinephrine

    **b.** Norepinephrine

    **c.** Acetylcholine

    **d.** Adrenaline

4. Which of these cranial nerves contains preganglionic parasympathetic fibers?

    **a.** Optic, CN II

    **b.** Facial, CN VII

    **c.** Trigeminal, CN V

    **d.** Hypoglossal, CN XII

5. How many motor neurons are found in an autonomic reflex arc?

    **a.** 1

    **b.** 2

    **c.** 3

    **d.** 0

# 19

# GENERAL SENSES
## PRE-LAB

Name: _________________________    Section: __________    Date: _________

## LEARNING OBJECTIVES

- Explain the difference between general and special senses.
- Describe the pathways of the general senses.
- Define sensory adaptation and referred pain.
- Explain the significance of the homunculus man to the general senses.

## PRE-LAB ACTIVITY

1. Log in to your Blackboard site or other OER textbook.
2. Read Unit 8.8 in Odigia "How are General Senses Defined."
   - Objective: What is the difference between general and special senses?
3. **Watch video** General Senses
   - https://www.youtube.com/watch?v=xvIZzjns4dU

## ANSWER THE FOLLOWING QUESTIONS

1. List all of the general senses here:

2. List a difference between the general senses and special senses.

3. Fill in the blank.

    a. The somas (cell bodies) of the first order neurons are located in the
    _________________ _________________ _________________.

    b. The somas of the second order neurons are located in the _________________
    _________________ _________________.

    c. The somas of the third order neurons are located in the _________________.

    d. The axon terminals of the third order neurons are located in the _________________
    _________________ _________________.

    e. The _________________ order neuron will decussate.

4. Contrast the location of decussation between the posterior column medial lemniscus and spinothalamic tracts.

5. **Research** 2-point discrimination distance *(document your source)* as it pertains to receptor density testing. Then hypothesize a correlation between receptor density and the measured 2-point discrimination distance.

**6.** Explain the homunculus man and its significance in general sense processing.

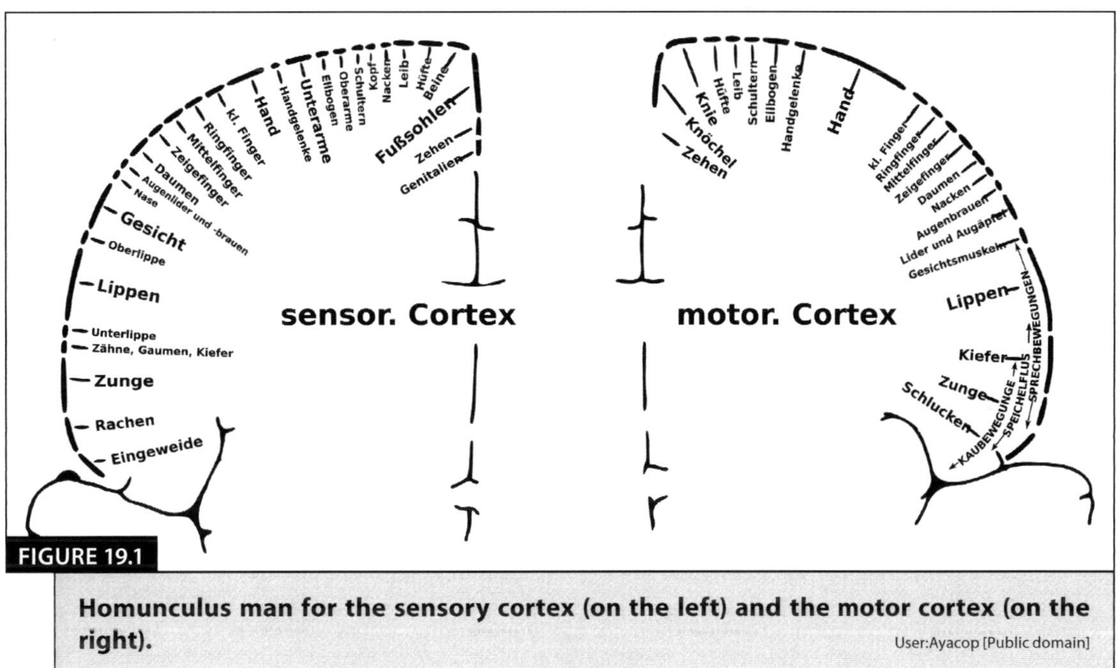


**FIGURE 19.1**

**Homunculus man for the sensory cortex (on the left) and the motor cortex (on the right).** User:Ayacop [Public domain]

**7.** What is sensory adaptation?

**8.** What is referred pain? Give an example.

# 19

# GENERAL SENSES
## IN-LAB ACTIVITIES

Name: _________________________    Section: __________    Date: _________

## LEARNING OBJECTIVES

- Classify general senses.
- Describe the pathways of the general senses.
- Define sensory adaptation and referred pain.
- Explain the significance of the homunculus man to the general senses.

## INTRODUCTION

Senses can be classified as either general senses or special senses. General senses are widespread throughout the body and have simple structured receptors and include tactile (touch) sensations, pain, temperature, proprioception (body position), and internal visceral sensation. Special senses, on the other hand, have their receptors concentrated in specialized sensory organs like the eye for vision, ear for hearing and balance, nose for the sense of smell, and taste buds for the sense of taste. The receptors for the special senses tend to be more complex and include separate sensory receptor cells.

## ACTIVITY 1: IDENTIFYING MECHANORECEPTORS AND OTHER GENERAL SENSE RECEPTORS

The cells that interpret information about the environment can be either (1) a specialized receptor cell, which has distinct structural components that interpret a specific type of stimulus; or (2) a neuron that has an encapsulated ending or free nerve ending with dendrites embedded in tissue that would receive a sensation (see the figure below). The pain and temperature receptors in the dermis of the skin are examples of neurons that have free nerve endings.

Receptors can be classified structurally on the basis of cell type and the type of modality or stimuli they sense.

**Get a model** of the skin and identify the following tactile receptors in the lab:

Free nerve endings, Merkel's discs, Meissner's corpuscles, and Pacinian corpuscles

On the below picture, **label** the lamellated (Pacinian corpuscles) and Meissner's (tactile) corpuscles. Draw in where the free nerve endings and the Merkel's discs would be located.

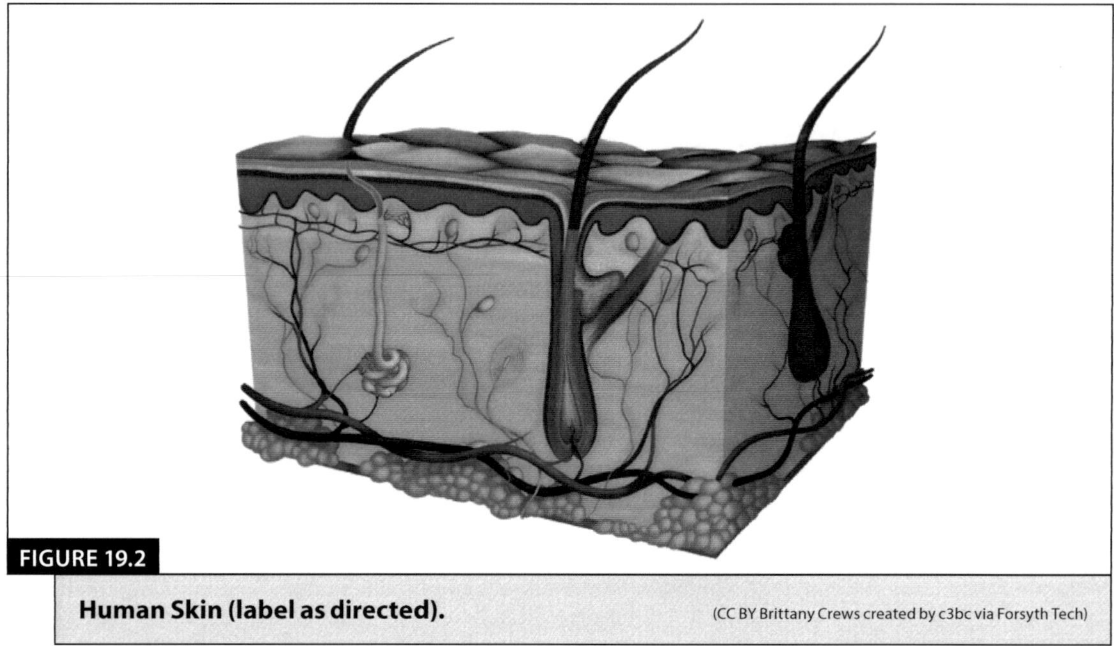

**FIGURE 19.2**

**Human Skin (label as directed).** (CC BY Brittany Crews created by c3bc via Forsyth Tech)

If available, **view the slide** of the skin that shows the lamellated (Pacinian corpuscles) and tactile (Meissner's) corpuscles.

**Draw** a picture of what you see.

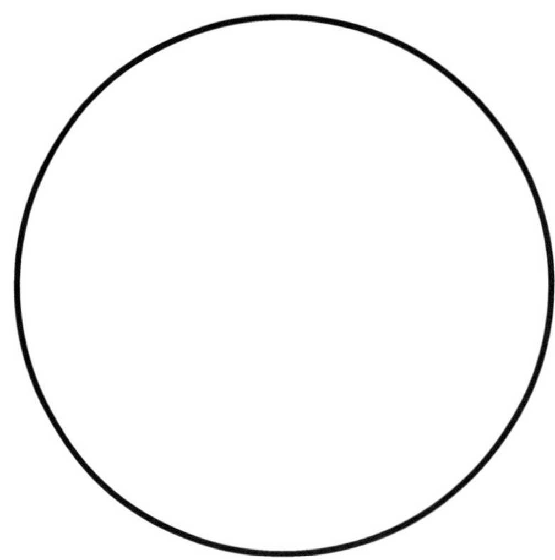

Looking in your course material on the muscles, draw a muscle along with its corresponding tendons in the space provided. Based on the description of muscle spindles and tendon stretch organs, **circle and label** the approximate area of these proprioceptors in your illustration.

**Read** about somatosensation in your course material and **fill in the following table.**

**Mechanoreceptors of somatosensation.**

| TABLE 19.1 | | |
|---|---|---|
| **NAME** | **LOCATIONS** | **STIMULI** |
| Free nerve endings | | |
| Mechanoreceptors (Merkel's discs) | | |
| Tactile (Meissner's) corpuscle | | |
| Lamellated (Pacianian) corpuscle | | |
| Muscle spindle | | |
| Tendon stretch organ (Golgi tendon organ) | | |

## ACTIVITY 2: TRACING SENSORY PATHWAYS (SPINOTHALAMIC AND POSTERIOR COLUMN LEMNISCUS PATHWAYS)

Once any sensory cell transduces (converts) a stimulus into a nerve impulse, that impulse has to travel along sensory axons to reach the CNS. The nerves that convey sensory information from the periphery to the CNS are either spinal nerves connected to the spinal cord or cranial nerves connected to the brain.

Generally, spinal nerves contain afferent axons from sensory receptors in the periphery, such as from the skin, mixed with efferent axons travelling to the muscles or other effector organs. As the spinal nerve nears the spinal cord, it splits into dorsal and ventral roots. The dorsal root contains only the axons of sensory neurons, whereas the ventral roots contain only the axons of the motor neurons. (Remember the words that go together section we already covered?) Typically, spinal nerve systems that connect to the brain are contralateral, in that the right side of the body is connected to the left side of the brain and the left side of the body to the right side of the brain. This crossing over of information from right body to left brain is termed decussation and can happen at two locations: the pyramids of the medulla oblongata and in the white matter of the spinal cord. In the simplest terms, the right hemisphere of the brain receives information from and controls motor output to the left side of the body, and vice versa for the left hemisphere of the brain.

A sensory pathway that carries peripheral sensations to the brain is referred to as an ascending pathway, or ascending tract. The various sensory modalities each follow specific pathways through the CNS. Somatosensory stimuli from below the neck pass along the sensory pathways of the spinal cord, whereas somatosensory stimuli from the head and neck travel through the cranial nerves. The somatosensory pathways are divided into two separate systems on the basis of the location of the receptor neurons. The dorsal column system (also referred to as the medial lemniscus pathway) and the spinothalamic tract are the two major pathways that bring sensory information to the brain. The sensory pathways in each of these systems are composed of three successive neurons.

In your online text material, read about the dorsal column system and the spinothalamic tract and then **complete Activity 2.**

## ACTIVITY

1. **Label** on the following illustrations: the first order neuron, second order neuron, and third order neuron. **Circle and name** the area that decussation takes place for each pathway (***Hint:*** The Dorsal Column System is in the brain stem). ***For a test,*** be sure that ***you could label*** where the first order, second order, and third order neuron originate and terminate.

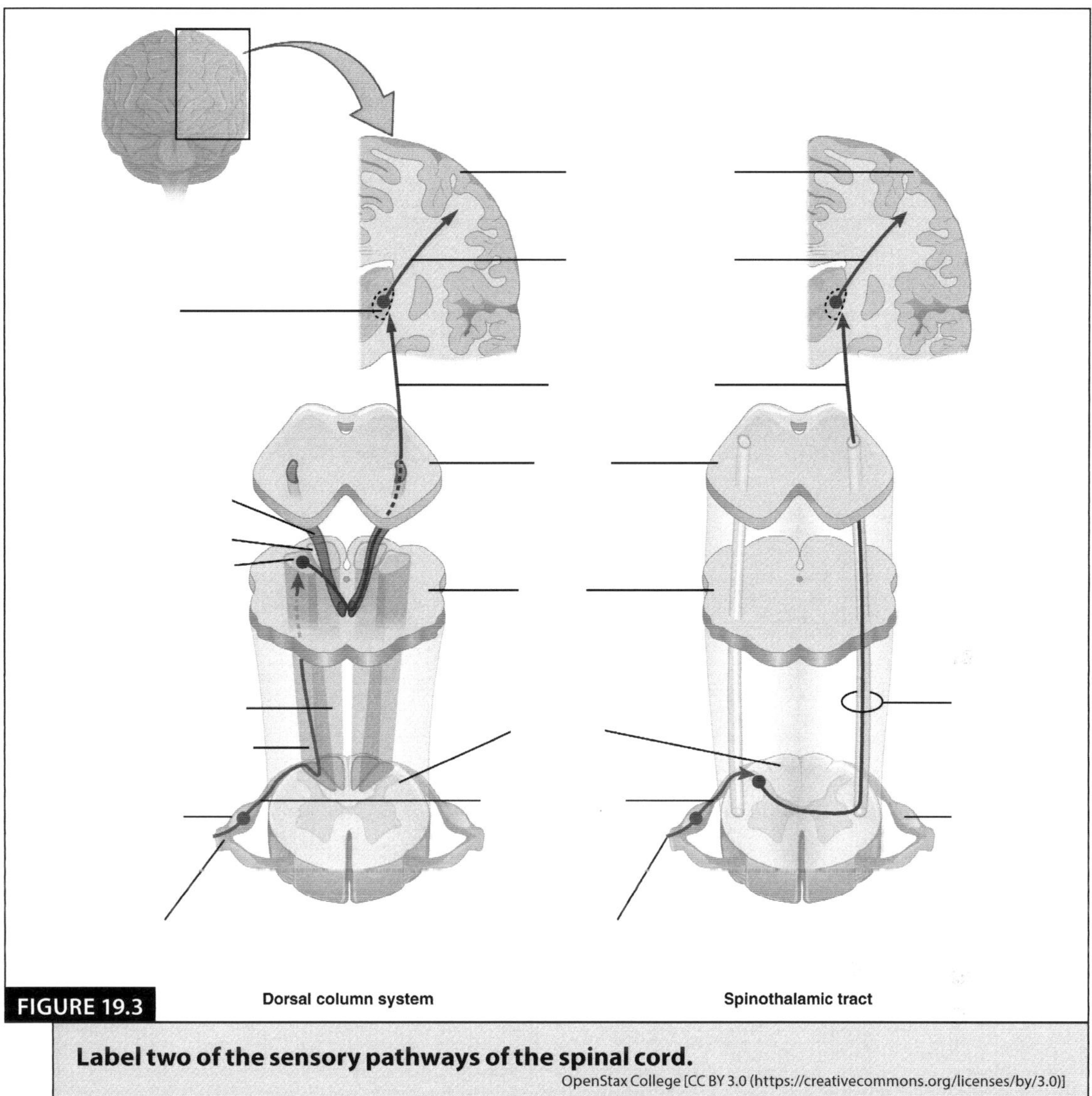


**FIGURE 19.3**  Label two of the sensory pathways of the spinal cord.

OpenStax College [CC BY 3.0 (https://creativecommons.org/licenses/by/3.0)]

2. Using a spinal cord cross section model as well as a brain model in lab, practice tracing the pathway of sensory information in the dorsal column system and the spinothalamic tract.

## ACTIVITY 3: TACTILE SENSITIVITY (TWO-TOUCH DISCRIMINATION DISTANCE)

The mechanoreceptors that are associated with tactile or touch sensations in the skin are not evenly distributed. Some areas of the skin have a higher concentration of receptors than other areas. The skin areas that have the highest concentration of receptors are therefore the areas that have the greatest level of sensitivity and can distinguish between two stimuli at a close distance. Because these more sensitive areas have a greater concentration of receptors, there is more area of the cerebral cortex (primary somatosensory area in the postcentral gyrus) that is devoted to skin areas that have a greater density of tactile receptors. This difference in amount of the primary somatosensory area that is devoted to different regions of the body can be illustrated through an image called the sensory homunculus. Notice on the below illustration that certain parts of the body are more exaggerated then others. Based on the figure below, can you tell which body areas are more sensitive than others?

Based on the figure below, **identify** three areas that have a low density of receptors in the skin. **Put a box** around these areas in the figure below.

One way of testing the sensitivity or the receptor density of different areas of the body is by doing a two-point discrimination test. This test uses an individual's perception of the minimum distance that two stimuli are perceived as two distinct sensations. This distance is referred to as the two-point discrimination distance and indirectly is a measurement of the density of receptors in the skin of that particular body part. The smaller the distance that two stimuli can be perceived by an individual the more receptors are located in that area and the smaller the area that is monitored by each individual sensory receptor. Subsequently, areas that have a greater density of sensory receptors will have more area of the cerebral cortex (primary sensory cortex) devoted to that region.

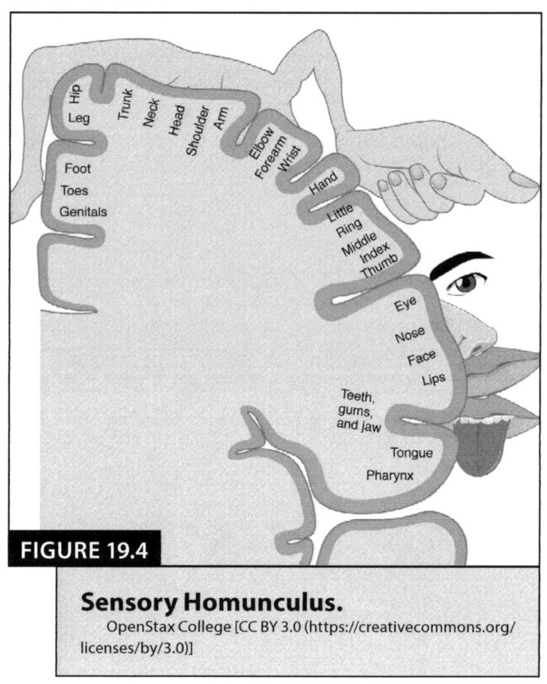


**FIGURE 19.4**

**Sensory Homunculus.**
OpenStax College [CC BY 3.0 (https://creativecommons.org/licenses/by/3.0)]

To perform a two-point discrimination test, an instrument such as a pair of forceps or specialized calipers are used to simultaneously touch an area of skin in two places at the same time, first with the forceps or caliper completely closed and then increasing the distance between the two points in the forceps or the caliper each time before the subject can distinguish two points. The first distance that the subject can distinguish two stimuli as two points is considered the two-point discrimination distance. To estimate the area of the cerebral cortex that is devoted to that requires that the reciprocal of the two-point discrimination distance be used (1/two-point discrimination distance or 1 divided by the two-point discrimination distance). Converting this reciprocal into a percentage (1/two-point discrimination distance × 100 or 1 divided by the two-point distance multiplied by 100) is an estimate of the percentage of the cerebral cortex devoted to that area.

Use the following procedure to perform a two-point discrimination distance test.

1. Get a partner, specialized caliper, forceps, or compass, and a ruler if using a pair of forceps, compass, or caliper without a ruler on it.

2. Ask your partner to close their eyes, and using a forceps or caliper, push the two point together so that the distance between the two points is as small as it gets.

3. Gently but firmly press the instrument on the back of your partner's leg.

4. Ask how many points they feel. If they feel one point, increase the forcep's point or caliper by 2 mm. If they feel two points, stop and record this distance between the two points because that is the two-point discrimination distance.

5. Continue to increase the distance until your partner can perceive two points. Record in the table the smallest distance in which they can perceive two-points. That is the two-discrimination distance.

6. Repeat the following procedure for the forearm, palm, and fingertips.

7. Switch so that your partner can now perform the two-point discrimination test on you.

**Two-point discrimination data table.**

**TABLE 19.2**

| REGION | TWO-POINT DISCRIMINATION DISTANCE | RECIPROCAL (1/TWO-POINT DISCRIMINATION DISTANCE) | % AREA OF THE SENSORY CORTEX |
|---|---|---|---|
| Back of leg | | | |
| Palm | | | |
| Fingertips | | | |
| Forearm | | | |

## ACTIVITY 4: ADAPTATION OF LIGHT PRESSURE

One characteristic of sensory receptors is their ability to adapt to constant stimulation. Adaptation refers to the decrease in the activity of first order neurons in response to a constant stimulus. Different modalities (kind of sensations) differ from each other is based on their ability to adapt to constant stimulation. Some of our sensory receptors such as nociceptors (pain receptors) are slowly adapting, while other sensory receptors such as thermoreceptors (heat or temperature receptors), smell, or light pressure are rapidly adapting. If you have ever stepped outside from a cooler temperature to a warmer temperature environment (or vice versa) but then stopped noticing the temperature after a period of time, you have experienced sensory adaptation. It is only when the stimulus changes or your attention is called to the stimulus that you become consciously aware of the stimulus again. This conscious fading of a stimulus even though the stimulus itself is still present is called adaptation. This process is vital to survival so that the cerebrum can concentrate on the most important task at hand and let the trivial stimuli fade to the background and thus prevent perpetual distraction.

This concept of adaptation also illustrates another very important point; not every stimulus that reaches the cerebrum will elicit a response. With limited resources and time to act, stimuli are ranked in order of importance and integrated to form a complete picture of the external environment. This allows the brain to respond efficiently to only the imperative stimulus or to several at one time.

## ACTIVITY

This activity will test the adaptation of light pressure with the placement of coins.

1.  With a partner, have the subject sit while resting their forearm on the desk. Place a penny on the anterior surface of the forearm.
2.  With a stop watch, measure the length of time that the pressure sensation lasts. _______ secs.
3.  Repeat Steps 1 and 2 with a different area of the forearm. Is there a difference in how long the sensation lasts?
4.  Place 3 more pennies on top of the first one. Does the sensation return and how long does it last?

## ACTIVITY 5: REFERRED PAIN

Though visceral senses are not primarily a part of conscious perception, those sensations sometimes make it to conscious awareness. If a visceral sense is strong enough, it will be perceived. When particularly strong visceral sensations rise to the level of conscious perception, the sensations are often felt in unexpected places. For example, strong visceral sensations of the heart will be felt as pain in the left shoulder and left arm. This irregular pattern of projection of conscious perception of visceral sensations is called **referred pain.** Depending on the organ system affected, the referred pain will project to different areas of the body (see Figure 19.5). The location of referred pain is not random, but a definitive explanation of the mechanism has not been established. The most broadly accepted theory for this phenomenon is that the visceral sensory fibers enter into the same level of the spinal cord as the somatosensory fibers of the referred pain location. By this explanation, the visceral sensory fibers from the mediastinal region, where the heart is located, would enter the spinal cord at the same level as the spinal nerves from the shoulder and arm, so the brain misinterprets the sensations from the mediastinal region as being from the axillary and brachial regions.

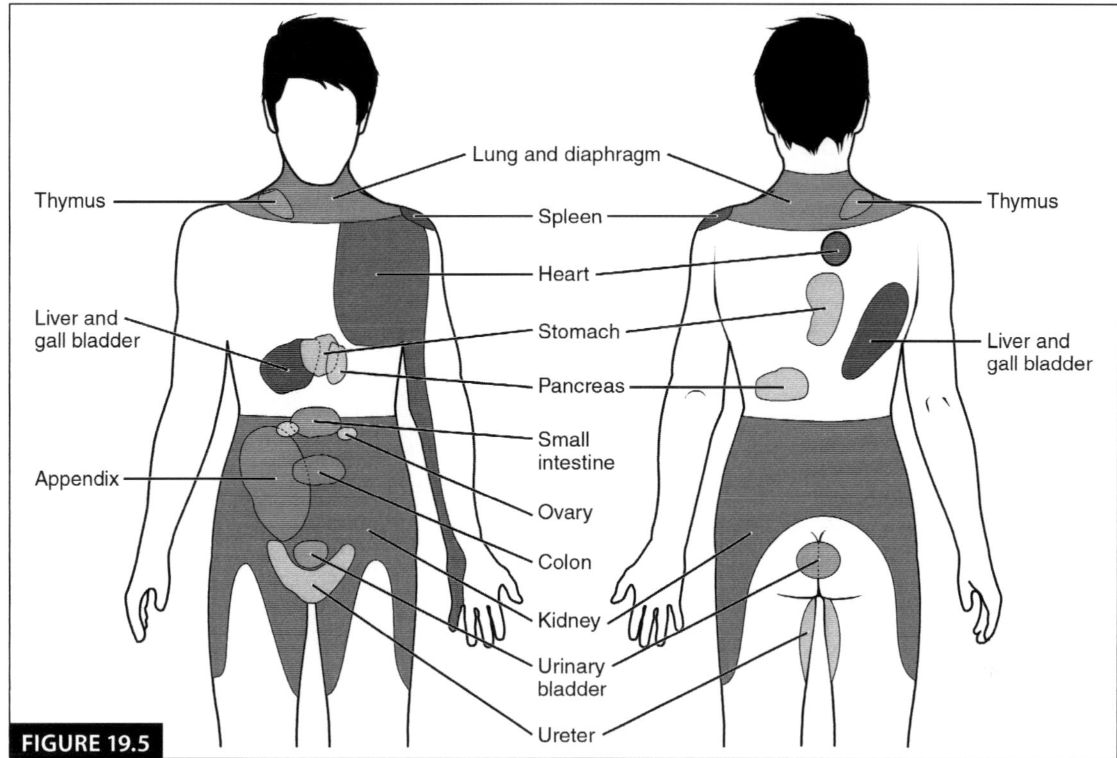


**FIGURE 19.5**

**Conscious perception of visceral sensations map to specific regions of the body, as shown in this chart.** Some sensations are felt locally, whereas others are perceived as affecting areas that are quite distant from the involved organ.

OpenStax College [CC BY 3.0 (https://creativecommons.org/licenses/by/3.0)]

## ACTIVITY

Do the following to demonstrate referred pain. You will need a bowl full of ice water and a timer.

1. Dip your elbow in a bowl full of ice water. Have your partner start the timer.

2. Immediately describe where you perceive the sensation is coming from.

3. After 1 minute, describe the perception of the sensation and where you feel it is coming from.

4. After 2 minutes, describe the perception of the sensation and where you feel it is coming from.

5. Was there an indication that adaptation was taking place?

## REVIEW QUESTIONS

1. Name the general senses that have free nerve endings and those that have encapsulated nerve endings.

2. Describe the correlation between tactile density of a body area and the size of the sensory homunculus as well as the size of the cerebral cortex receiving information from those receptors.

3. What is adaptation? Why do sensory receptors adapt? Name some rapidly adapting sensory receptors. Name some slowly adapting sensory receptors.

4. Define referred pain. Why is it useful to a doctor or nurse to understand the concept of referred pain?

5. Briefly describe for the following organs some areas that pain can be perceived in the following scenarios. Also describe how these perceptions of pain might differ between the genders:

   **a.** Myocardial infarction (heart attack)

   **b.** Kidney stones

   **c.** Appendicitis leading to a ruptured appendix

   **d.** Liver pain

6. Do some research and describe the phenomenon of phantom pain (document your source). What is thought to be the cause of phantom pain?

# 20

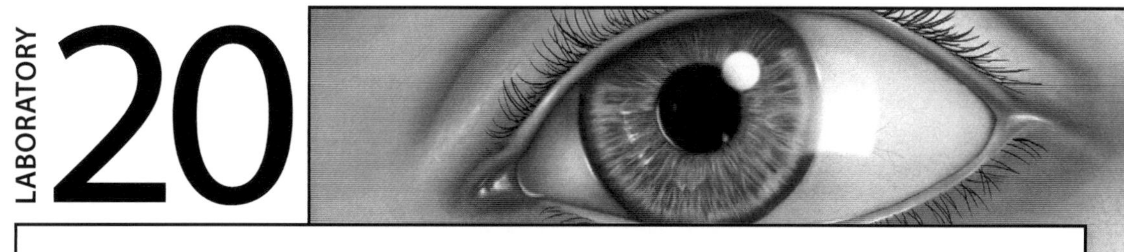

# SPECIAL SENSES
## PRE-LAB

Name: ________________________    Section: __________    Date: _________

## LEARNING OBJECTIVES

- Identify the 6 extrinsic eye muscles.
- Describe 5 of the special senses, their receptors, and their locations.

## INTRODUCTION

Each of the special senses has specialized receptors for helping us taste, hear, see, or smell our surroundings. Any sense that has a specialized organ with receptors sending signals to the brain is one of the special senses *(is there another sense that we can add to this list?)*.

## CHEMORECEPTORS

Like taste, the sense of smell, or **olfaction,** is also responsive to chemical stimuli. The olfactory receptor neurons are located in a small region within the superior nasal cavity. This region is referred to as the **olfactory epithelium** and contains bipolar sensory neurons. Each **olfactory sensory neuron** has dendrites that extend from the apical surface of the epithelium into the mucus lining the cavity. As airborne molecules are inhaled through the nose, they pass over the olfactory epithelial region and dissolve into the mucus. These **odorant molecules** bind to proteins that keep them dissolved in the mucus and help transport them to the olfactory dendrites.

## MECHANORECEPTORS

Hearing, or **audition,** is the transduction of sound waves into a neural signal that is made possible by the structures of the ear. The large, fleshy structure on the lateral aspect of the head is known as the **auricle.** Some sources will also refer to this structure as the pinna, though that term is more appropriate for a structure that can be moved, such as the external ear of a cat. The C-shaped curves of the auricle direct sound waves toward the auditory canal. The canal enters the skull through the external auditory meatus of the temporal bone. At the end of the auditory canal is the **tympanic membrane,** or ear drum, which vibrates after it is struck by sound waves. The auricle, ear canal, and tympanic membrane are often referred to as the **external ear.** The **middle ear** consists of a space spanned by three small bones called the **ossicles.** The three ossicles are the **malleus, incus,** and **stapes** (stape – ees), which are Latin names that roughly translate to hammer, anvil, and stirrup. The malleus is attached to the tympanic membrane and articulates with the incus. The incus, in turn, articulates with the stapes. The stapes is then attached to the **inner ear,** where the sound waves will be transduced into a neural signal. The middle ear is connected to the pharynx through the Eustachian tube, which helps equilibrate air pressure across the tympanic membrane. The tube, which is normally closed, will pop open when the muscles of the pharynx contract during swallowing or yawning. You will find and label the other parts of the ear in lab as well.

Along with audition, the inner ear is responsible for encoding information about **equilibrium,** the sense of balance. A similar mechanoreceptor—a hair cell with stereocilia—senses head position, head movement, and whether our bodies are in motion. These cells are located within the vestibule of the inner ear. Head position is sensed by the **utricle** and **saccule,** whereas head movement is sensed by the **semicircular canals.** The neural signals generated in the **vestibular ganglion** are transmitted through the vestibulocochlear nerve to the brain stem and cerebellum.

## PHOTORECEPTORS

**Vision** is the special sense of sight that is based on the transduction of light stimuli received through the eyes. The eyes are located within either orbit in the skull. The eyelids, with lashes at their leading edges, help to protect the eye from abrasions by blocking particles that may land on the surface of the eye. The inner surface of each lid is a thin membrane known as the **palpebral conjunctiva.** The conjunctiva extends over the white areas of the eye (the sclera), connecting the eyelids to the eyeball. The lacrimal gland, located beneath the lateral edges of the nose, produces tears. Tears produced by this gland flow through the **lacrimal duct** to the medial corner of the eye, where the tears flow over the conjunctiva, washing away foreign particles.

Movement of the eye within the orbit is accomplished by the contraction of six **extra-ocular muscles** that originate from the bones of the orbit and insert into the surface of the eyeball (Figure 20.1). Four of the muscles are arranged at the cardinal points around the eye and are named for those locations. They are the **superior rectus, medial rectus, inferior rectus,** and **lateral rectus.** When each of these muscles contract, the eye moves toward the contracting muscle. For example, when the superior rectus contracts, the eye rotates to look up. The **superior oblique** originates at the posterior orbit, near the origin of the four rectus muscles. However, the tendon of the oblique muscles threads through a pulley-like piece of cartilage known as the **trochlea.** The tendon inserts obliquely into the superior surface of the eye. The angle of the tendon through the trochlea means that contraction of the superior oblique rotates the eye medially. The **inferior oblique** muscle originates from the floor of the orbit and inserts into the infero-lateral surface of the eye. When it contracts, it laterally rotates the eye, in opposition to the superior oblique. Rotation of the eye by the two oblique muscles is necessary because the eye is not perfectly aligned on the sagittal plane. When the eye looks up or down, the eye must also rotate slightly to compensate for the superior rectus pulling at approximately a 20-degree angle, rather than straight up. The same is true for the infe-rior rectus, which is compensated by contraction of the inferior oblique. A seventh muscle in the orbit is the **levator palpebrae superioris,** which is responsible for elevating and retracting the upper eyelid, a movement that usually occurs in concert with elevation of the eye by the superior rectus (not labeled in Figure 20.1).

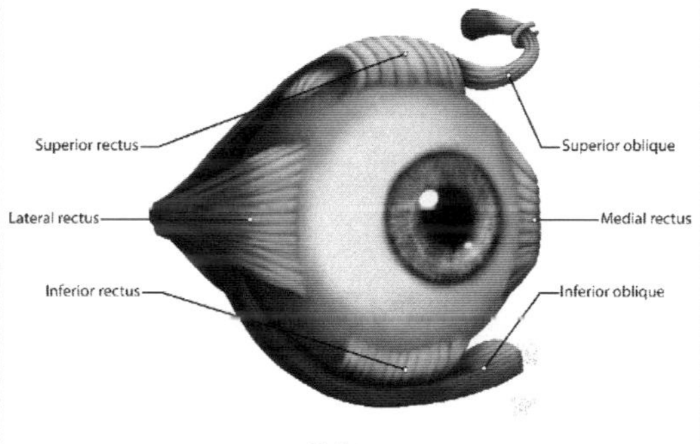

Three cranial nerves innervate the extraocular muscles. The abducens nerve innervates the lateral rectus, which causes abduction of the eye. The superior oblique is innervated by the trochlear nerve. All of the other muscles are innervated by the oculomotor nerve, as is the levator palpebrae superioris. The motor nuclei of these cranial nerves connect to the brain stem, which coordinates eye movements.



**FIGURE 20.1**

**The six extrinsic eye muscles labeled.**
CC BY Brittany Clark. c3bc.

The eye itself is a hollow sphere composed of three layers of tissue. The outermost layer is the **fibrous tunic,** which includes the white **sclera** and clear **cornea.** The transparent cornea covers the anterior tip of the eye and allows light to enter the eye. The middle layer of the eye is the **vascular tunic,** which is mostly composed of the choroid, ciliary body, and iris. The **choroid** is a layer of highly vascularized connective tissue that provides a blood supply to the eyeball. The choroid is posterior to the **ciliary body,** a muscular structure that is attached to the **lens** by **zonule fibers (or suspensory ligaments).** These two structures bend the lens, allowing it to focus light on the back of the eye. Overlaying the ciliary body, and visible in the anterior eye, is the **iris**—the colored part of the eye. The iris is a smooth muscle that opens or closes the **pupil,** which is the hole at the center of the eye that allows light to enter. The iris constricts the pupil in response to bright light and dilates the pupil in response to dim light. The innermost layer of the eye is the **neural tunic,** or **retina,** which contains the nervous tissue responsible for photoreception. The eye is also divided into two cavities: the anterior cavity and the posterior cavity. The anterior cavity is the space between the cornea and lens, including the iris and ciliary body. It is filled with a watery fluid called the **aqueous humor.** The posterior cavity is the space behind the lens that extends to the posterior side of the interior eyeball, where the retina is located. The posterior cavity is filled with a more viscous fluid called the **vitreous humor.** Find all of these anatomical parts on the models in lab this week. In addition, you will be able to dissect a cow eye, where you can appreciate the lens and vitreous humor.

The **retina** is composed of several layers and contains specialized cells for the initial processing of visual stimuli. The photoreceptors (rods and cones) change their membrane potential when stimulated by light energy. The change in membrane potential alters the amount of neurotransmitter that the photoreceptor cells release.

## PRE-LAB ACTIVITY

**Answer the following statements/questions:** Use the reading above as well as your textbook resource (Odigia or Lumen, etc.) to respond and fill in your answers to these statements.

1. Explain the difference between the terms **general senses** and **special senses.**

2. In which region of the body are the entire special senses located?

3. When you hear gustatory or gustation, what do you think of first? What does this term mean?

4. The three layers or tunics that form the wall of the eye are the ________________ (the outermost layer), the ________________ (the middle layer), and the ________________ (the innermost layer).

5. The posterior cavity of the eye is filled with ________________.

6. The two types of photoreceptors of the eye are the ________________ which allow us to see sharp, color images, and the ________________ which allow us to see in dim light.

7. The greatest number of cones are located in an area of the retina called the ________________ which is in the center of a structure called the ________________.

8. A thin membrane that covers the external anterior surface of the eye and the inner surface of the palpebrae is called the ________________.

9. The optic nerves that leave each eye cross to form a structure called the ________________.

10. The ear is divided into three areas, the ________________ ear, the ________________ ear, and the ________________ ear.

11. The three auditory ossicles of the ear are the ________________, the ________________, and the ________________.

12. The middle ear is connected to the nasopharynx by the ________________.

13. A bone of the auditory ossicles called the ________________ covers the oval window of the inner ear.

14. The part of the inner called the ________________ contains the organs of hearing called ________________.

15. The vestibule of the inner ear contains receptors that control ________________.

16. Cranial nerve VIII is called the ________________ nerve.

# 20

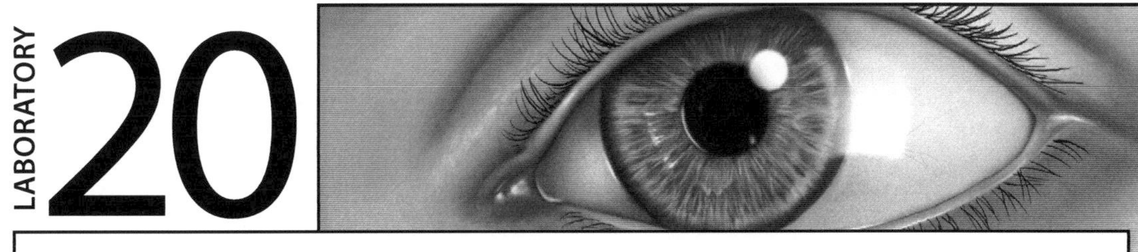

# SPECIAL SENSES
## IN-LAB ACTIVITIES

Name: _________________________  Section: __________  Date: _________

## LEARNING OBJECTIVES

- Identify the anatomy of five of the sensory modalities.
- Explain gustation briefly including the types and locations of receptors.
- Identify the parts of the ear and their functions.
- Identify the parts of the eye and their functions.

## INTRODUCTION

Each of the special senses has specialized receptors for helping us taste, hear, see, or smell our surroundings. Any sense that has a specialized organ with receptors sending signals to the brain is one of the special senses (is there another sense that we can add to this list?). Each of the senses (general or special) is referred to as a sensory modality. Modality refers to the way that information is encoded, which is similar to the idea of transduction. The main sensory modalities can be described on the basis of how each is transduced. The chemical senses are taste and smell and use chemoreceptors. Hearing and balance are sensed by mechanoreceptors. Finally, vision involves the activation of photoreceptors.

Listing all the different sensory modalities, which can number as many as 17, involves separating the five major senses into more specific categories, or submodalities, of the larger sense. An individual sensory modality represents the sensation of a specific type of stimulus. For example, the general sense of touch, which is known as somatosensation, can be separated into light pressure, deep pressure, vibration, itch, pain, temperature, or hair movement.

## GUSTATION

**Gustation** is the special sense associated with the tongue. The surface of the tongue, along with the rest of the oral cavity, is lined by a stratified squamous epithelium. Raised bumps called papillae (singular = papilla) contain the structures for gustatory transduction. These structures, or receptor cells, release neurotransmitters based on the amount of the chemical in the food. Neurotransmitters from the gustatory cells can activate sensory neurons in the facial, glossopharyngeal, and vagus cranial nerves.

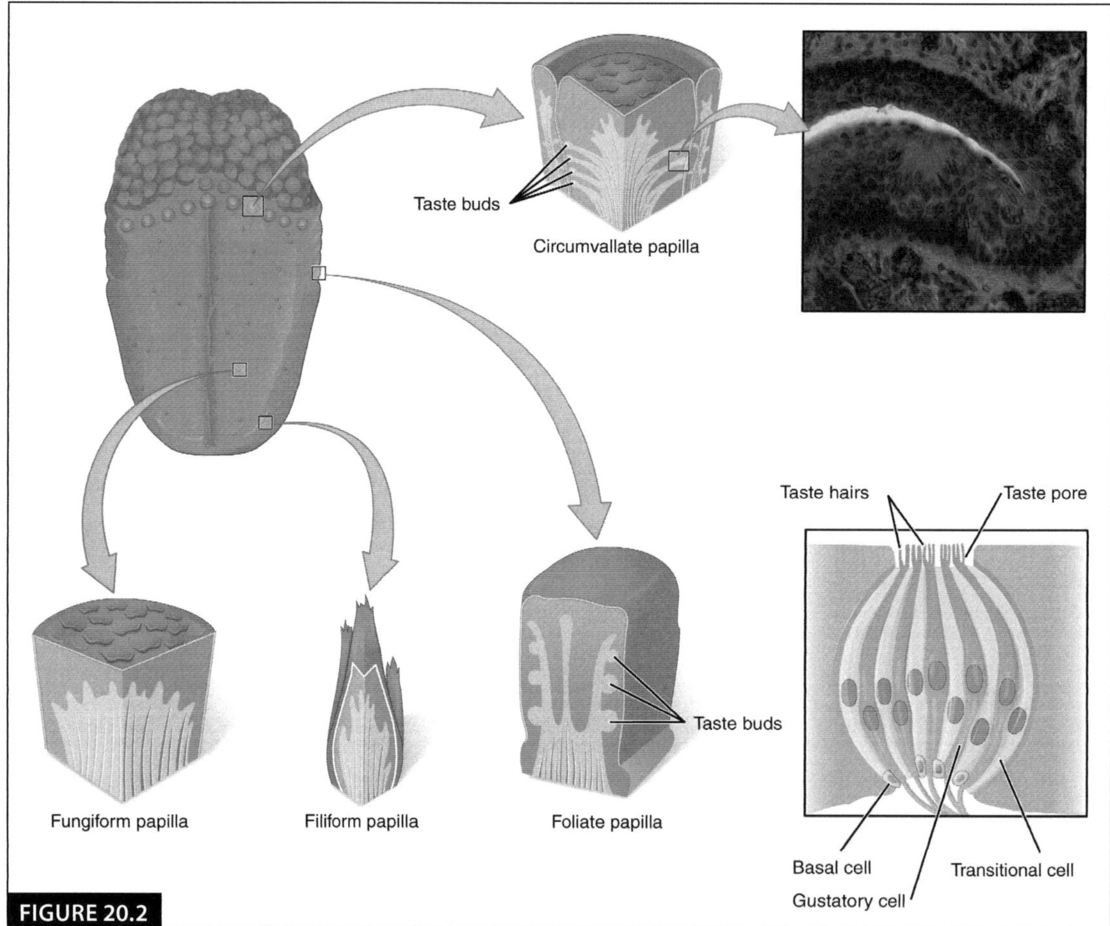


**FIGURE 20.2**

**The tongue is covered with small bumps, called papillae, which contain taste buds that are sensitive to chemicals in ingested food or drink.** Different types of papillae are found in different regions of the tongue (notice the large circumvallate papillae on the back of the tongue, for instance). The taste buds contain specialized gustatory receptor cells that respond to chemical stimuli dissolved in the saliva. These receptor cells activate sensory neurons that are part of the facial and glossopharyngeal nerves. LM × 1600.

OpenStax College [CC BY 3.0 (https://creativecommons.org/licenses/by/3.0)]

## OLFACTION

The other special sense to detect chemical stimuli is the sense of smell or olfaction. Smell integrates with other senses (taste buds and memory) to form the sense of flavor. Olfaction occurs when odorants bind to specific sites on olfactory receptors located in the superior nasal cavity. Tightly packed groups of cells combine signals from these receptors and transmit them to the olfactory bulb, where the sensory input will start to interact with parts of the brain responsible for smell identification, memory, and emotion.

Molecules of odorants passing through the superior nasal concha of the nasal passages dissolve in the mucus that lines the superior portion of the cavity and are detected by olfactory receptors on the dendrites of the olfactory sensory neurons. This may occur by diffusion or by the binding of the odorant to odorant-binding proteins.

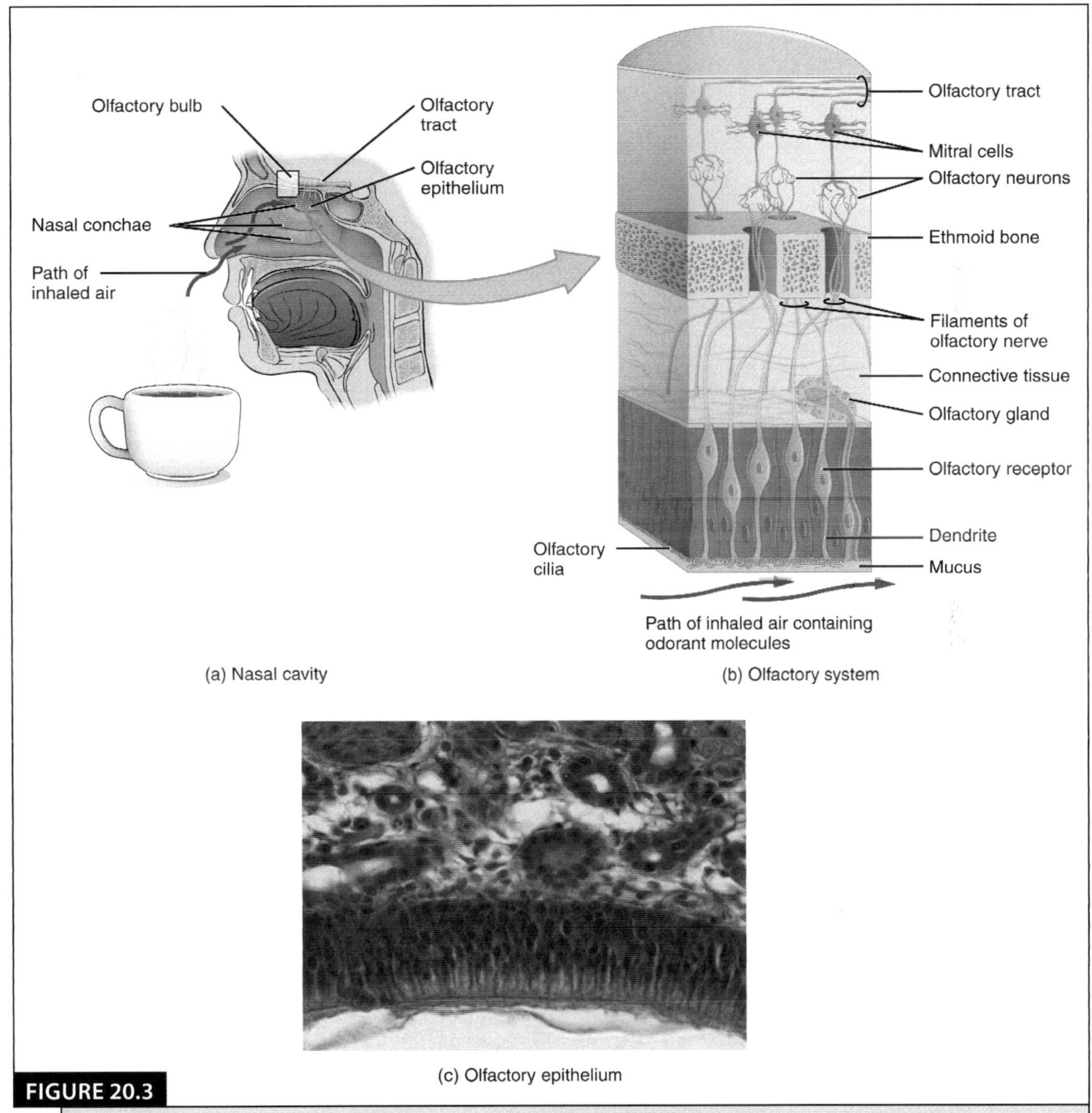


**FIGURE 20.3**

**The olfactory system begins in the peripheral structures of the nasal cavity.** (b) The olfactory receptor neurons are within the olfactory epithelium. Axons of the olfactory receptor neurons project through the cribriform plate of the ethmoid bone and synapse with the neurons of the olfactory bulb (tissue source: simian). LM × 812.

1. Identify the following microscopic structures of the **tongue and nose:**

    a. Taste buds (slide)

        i. Circumvallate papillae

        ii. Fungiform papillae

    b. Olfactory nerve receptors entering through the ethmoid bone/olfactory foramina (model or slide)

## THE EAR—AUDITION AND EQUILIBRIUM

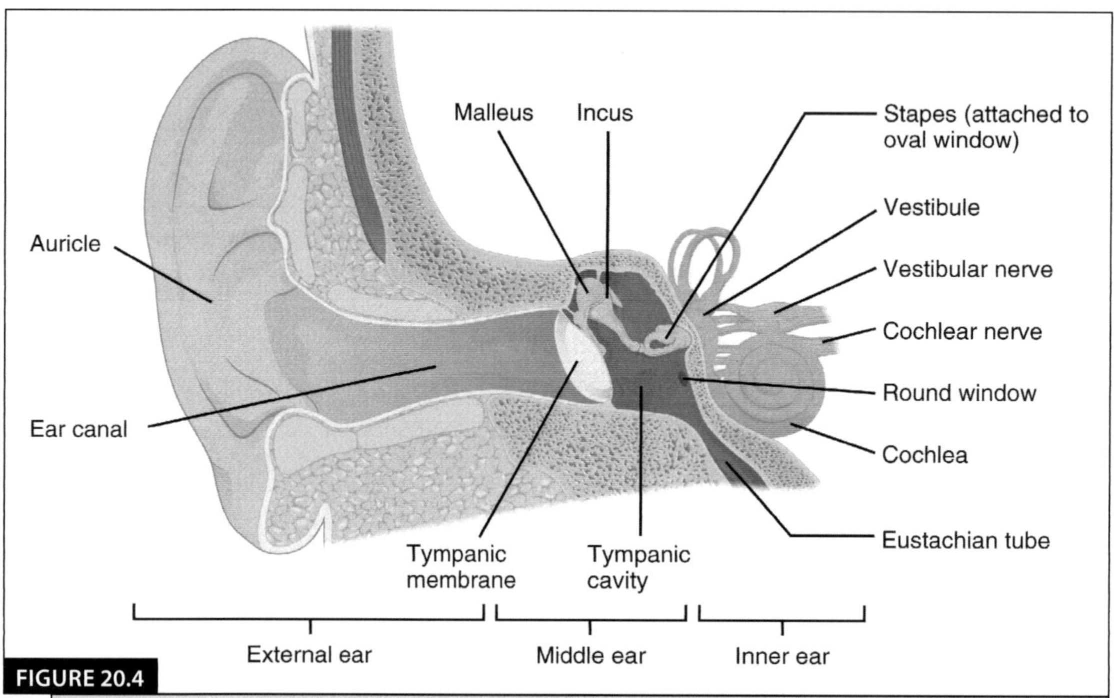


**FIGURE 20.4**

**The external ear contains the auricle, ear canal, and tympanic membrane.** The middle ear contains the ossicles and is connected to the pharynx by the Eustachian tube. The inner ear contains the cochlea and vestibule, which are responsible for audition and equilibrium, respectively. OpenStax College [CC BY 3.0 (https://creativecommons.org/licenses/by/3.0)]

Watch this animation to learn more about the inner ear and to see the cochlea unroll, with the base at the back of the image and the apex at the front. Specific wavelengths of sound cause specific regions of the basilar membrane to vibrate, much like the keys of a piano produce sound at different frequencies. Based on the animation, where do frequencies—from high to low pitches—cause activity in the hair cells within the cochlear duct? (www.openstax.com)

1. Identify the following structures of the **ear:**
   a. External ear
      i. Auricle (pinna)
      ii. External auditory canal
   b. Middle ear
      i. Tympanic membrane
      ii. Auditory ossicles
         1. Malleus
         2. Incus
         3. Stapes
      iii. Oval window
      iv. Auditory tube (Eustachian Tube)
   c. Inner ear
      i. Round window
      ii. Semicircular canals
      iii. Cochlea
      iv. Vestibule
   d. Vestibulocochlear nerve
   e. Internal auditory meatus of the temporal bone

2. Identify the following microscopic structures of the **cochlea:**
   a. Membranous labyrinth (inside osseous labyrinth)
   b. Scala vestibuli (vestibular duct)
   c. Scala media (cochlear duct) (additional physiology here)
   d. Scala tympani (tympanic duct)
   e. Organ of Corti (housed in the Cochlear duct)
      i. Tectorial membrane
      ii. Basilar membrane
      iii. Hair cells
   f. Cochlear nerve

## VISION

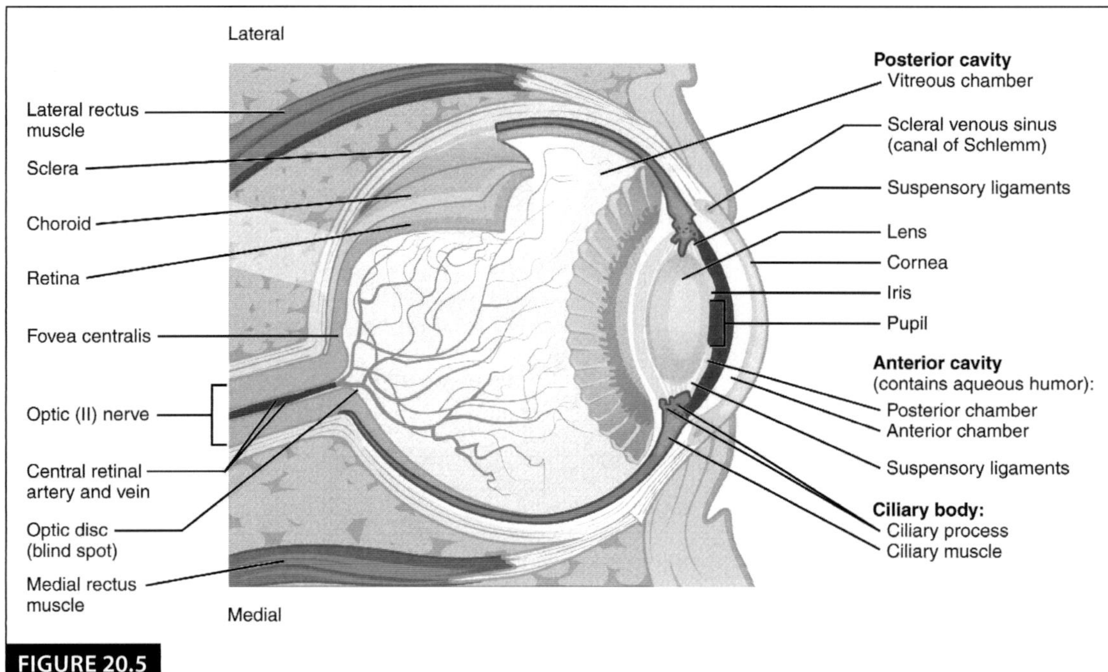


**FIGURE 20.5**

**The sphere of the eye can be divided into anterior and posterior chambers.** The wall of the eye is composed of three layers: the fibrous tunic, vascular tunic, and neural tunic. Within the neural tunic is the retina, with three layers of cells and two synaptic layers in between. The center of the retina has a small indentation known as the fovea.

OpenStax College [CC BY 3.0 (https://creativecommons.org/licenses/by/3.0)]

1. Identify the following layers and structures of the **eyeball** using the **models** in lab or dissection.

   a. Outer fibrous layer (outer tunic)

      i. Cornea

      ii. Sclera

   b. Middle vascular layer (middle tunic)

      i. Choroid coat

      ii. Iris

      iii. Pupil

      iv. Lens

         1. Suspensory ligaments (in the ciliary body)

      v. Aqueous humor in the anterior chamber (secreted from BV in ciliary body)

    **c.** Inner nervous layer (inner tunic)

        **i.** Vitreous body (vitreous humor = fluid)

        **ii.** Retina

            1. Optic disk (produces blind spot)

            2. Macula lutea with central fovea (affected by macular degeneration)

            3. Optic nerve

            4. Optic chiasma

**2.** Identify the following **accessory eye structures**:

    **a.** Superior and inferior palpebrae

    **b.** Conjunctiva

    **c.** Tarsal glands

    **d.** Lacrimal gland

    **e.** Extrinsic muscles (ex. superior rectus muscle)—See Pre-Lab

    **f.** Other muscles that move eyelids

        **i.** Levator palpebrae superioris

    **g.** Orbital bones: frontal bone, zygomatic bone, ethmoid bone, lacrimal bone, maxilla, sphenoid bone (mentioned here, but seen in the bones unit)

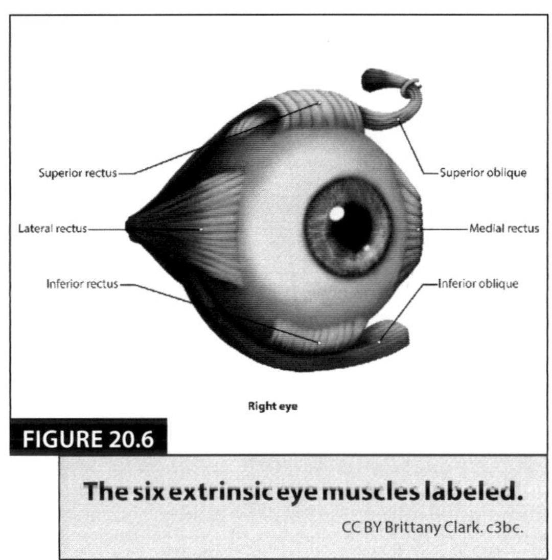


**FIGURE 20.6**

**The six extrinsic eye muscles labeled.**
CC BY Brittany Clark. c3bc.

## DISSECTION OF THE COW EYE

Be sure to wear proper protective equipment—lab coat, gloves, and goggles. Follow directions provided with the eye from your instructor or biological supply house.

## REVIEW

1. List 6 steps of hearing (depending upon how you explain them, there could be 5 steps).

2. List the structures that **light** passes through to produce vision.

3. Do a little research and explain what macular degeneration is and which parts of the eye anatomy are affected.

4. Do a little more research and explain what Meniere's disease is.

5. Why can we not taste foods very well when we have a cold?